Y0-BEA-271

Horizons of Criticism

Horizons of Criticism

AN ASSESSMENT OF RELIGIOUS-LITERARY OPTIONS

by Vernon Ruland, S.J.

CHICAGO
American Library Association
1975

Library of Congress Cataloging in Publication Data

Ruland, Vernon.
Horizons of criticism.

Bibliography: p.
Includes index.
1. Religion and literature. 2. Religious thought. 3. Criticism. I. Title.
PN49.R8 801 75-20162
ISBN 0-8389-0212-X
ISBN 0-8389-0196-4 pbk.

Printed in the United States of America

CONTENTS

PREFACE

I CAN DESCRIBE the genre of this book as a conscious blend of evaluative bibliography and the personal philosophical essay. Its first intent is to introduce readers to the acclaimed landmarks and exciting uncharted frontiers of interdisciplinary religious-literary studies. At the same time it aims to expose specialist literary critics and theologians to a mutually widening comprehension of each others' arcane fiefdoms, often surprisingly parallel in their goals, methods, achievements.

A third purpose behind this book is significantly personal—to put order into my own chaos of insights and reading experiences from the last ten years in a number of disparate specialties. By the effort to articulate and synthesize, no matter how fallibly and provisionally, each of us is privileged to personalize knowledge and thus creatively to extend it.

I recognize this present study is profoundly rooted in my own disturbing complex love-hate relationship with the entire religion and literature field. The labor to analyze and work through these ambivalent feelings suggests a whimsical outline to the book. Parts 1, 2, and 3 are three acts in the dramatization of a serious epistemological quest. As a map for this quest, I have felt driven to construct my own aesthetic and religious metaphysic as a guide to the uneven, scattered religious-literary terrain. Chapters 1, 4, and 10 gather together the fragments of this metaphysic or apologia, centering on the crucial naming of my quest. Perhaps readers will prefer to skim these chapters first to gauge the criteria pervading my choice and assessment of data throughout the book. Also, chapters 3, 9, and 15 provide a quick summary forecast of all my major conclusions.

Part 1 of my odyssey terminates in a distant realm, nominally "religion and literature." But the mood is a very mitigated enthusiasm, dampened by increasing anger at much of the stale crystallization and spiritual monomania exhibited by many explicit religious-literary critics.

Parts 2 and 3 reroute this quest for a comprehensive religious-literary theory and application all the way back to my very starting point. The leading autonomous figures in literary criticism (part 2) and in religious thought (part 3), immersed at their best in unconscious religious-literary transactions, eventually offer the most creative and satisfying fulfillment to the quest. In the end, one learns that it is not so much what literary critics and theologians say, but what both groups consider it unnecessary to say, that proves most fundamental to the religious-literary quest. What counts most is how you conceive your starting point, your implicit assumptions; a quest or problem well stated is half-solved.

Surely the scope of this whole project is open to attack as simultaneously both too large and too small—grandiose, megalomanic, but then again partial and arbitrarily selective. From the beginning I have renounced the poses of both taxative coverage and dispassionate neutrality. I have no doubt omitted materials through unfamiliarity and oversight, but mostly because I expressly judged some materials too commonplace to be exemplary, and others outrageously and pedagogically bad. Clearly, too, the outlines of such a synthesis would snap if stuffed much further. I simply settled on an arbitrary moment to leap to stationary ground from a constantly moving train.

As to the second pose of neutrality, I do not shrink from value judgments about my materials, but try to call attention to such assessments, and to clarify the assumptions behind them which I think too many critics keep subversively tacit. I confess to a chronic writer's dilemma: though sharply aware how much our values color all perceptions, I am still chagrined to find that each step to render my opinions more "truthful," scholarly exacting, and purified actually results in a more colorless impotent prose, hesitant and inhibited.

I acknowledge gratefully the unceasing encouragement of Fr. John O'Malley, S.J., Dr. Anthony Yu, and so many other friends, especially my editor Herbert Bloom. Behind the vision and diversified materials in this book are the many people who have helped shape me intellectually, experientially, spiritually. There are my friends, family, Jesuit and academic colleagues, teachers, gurus, pastoral and psychotherapy clients, cordial librarians, and all my students successively at the Jesuit School of Theology at Chicago, Carleton College, the University of Detroit, and the University of San Francisco. The evolving, challenging needs and interests of my students consistently propel me to wander extensively beyond the speciously clear perimeters of the religious-literary field as I once conceived it in doctoral studies.

In a book committed from the start to so much bibliographical name-dropping, I have tried to streamline my quotations and footnote apparatus to preserve the flow of discussion. Minimal notes are incorporated in parentheses. Quotes are used mostly to sample the pervasive flavor and terminology of a work analyzed; less often they function as handy controversial evidence, and only then is exact source pagination listed. For example, the reference *(Aaron; Tillich 1965, p. 22)* when checked with the Bibliography signifies: confer *passim* the single entry by Aaron; and from the six Tillich entries, examine a significant page from the book published in 1965.

PART 1

RELIGIOUS-LITERARY CRITICISM

1

AN OVERVIEW OF RELIGIOUS-LITERARY CRITICISM

LIKE MANY other cross-disciplinary experiments, the religion and literature field has struggled painfully through stages of rumored illegitimacy, miscegenation, and identity crisis. Literary critics and theologians still maintain their proud separate autonomies and often view the purported religious-literary critic as a callow dilettante, a disinherited embarrassing anomaly. But I do believe this besieged critic's era of touchy self-vindication is ending. Armed combatants must at times be reminded that their enemy has lost interest in fighting, the ground of debate has shifted, enough minor skirmishes remain to delight only those titillated by the stimulus of controversy. Perhaps the present moment in religious-literary criticism is the best time to redefine goals, major issues, and the criteria of achievement.

Since the area of religious-literary criticism has recently been assuming a more and more distinct shape, I propose in this present book to chart and explore its outlines, and to test its strengths. More important, I wish to project deeper possibilities than those already realized. I would like to foresee dead ends, and influence, if possible, the direction of appropriate growth. The aim is not merely to understand, but in Marx's sense, actively to *change* this world. I do not intend simply to map the sprawling terrain of this still somewhat protean area of studies. It needs a creative interpreter and image maker, not just a dictaphonic chronicler.

The term *religion and literature* or *religious-literary* is an umbrella with a tremendously wide span. To lessen prejudicial emphasis and exclusion, I shall apply my category flexibly and broadly, realizing that this decision precludes a tidy manageability. Since a problem correctly articulated is a problem half-solved, I suggest we adopt Dewey's principle of continuity in order to sidestep the apparent religion-literature dualism. We can view *religion* and *literature* not as substantives, but primarily as adjectives, adverbs, dimensions of one integral process of human experiencing. Thus, we focus on a single consciousness, experiencing poetically-religiously, more or less as a pervasive style of being. Figures patently gifted with a combined religious charism and artistic sensitivity come to mind, like Dante, Coleridge, Emerson, Dostoevsky. Perhaps a diagram will clarify the complex analogies involved in this discussion:

(The Experiencing)	(The Symbol)	(Double-take back upon the Symbol)

$$\frac{\text{religious experience of poet-critic}}{\text{literary experience of poet-critic}} = \frac{\text{religion}}{\text{literature}} = \frac{\text{theology}}{\text{literary criticism}}$$

1. First of all, there is a close affinity but not identity between the poet's and his public's shared acts of religious-poetic experiencing. The poet's experience issues in a cultural artifact that partially incorporates but also surpasses the originative experience. The critic's experience of this artifact is only a partial repetition or reenactment of the experience embodied in the work.

2. One's religion and his literary work are both human constructs giving symbolic actualization to aspects of this religious-poetic experiencing. The religious and poetic symbols must not be viewed as any less synergic than the unitary religious-poetic act itself.

3. If we understand religion as a wide functional term delineating the behavior shaped by one's most serious values or philosophy of life, then a few insights developed from the psychologist Gordon Allport will be pertinent. He describes the religious drive as a person's master sentiment, giving comprehensive ultimate shape to all his experiencing, whereas the poetic drive would be a further concrete specification of this same basic dynamism. Thus, the governing entelechy in a poet's and his public's experiencing, in the form of the literary work itself, is the religious drive, given definite poetic specification.

4. At one remove from religion, theology is participatory reflection upon religious experience, as literary criticism is participatory reflection upon literary experience. Theologians and literary critics are expendable, derivative, parasitic by profession. But their task can be a creative one, especially in the act of selective methodological clarification. By the term *participatory* I insist each genuine theologian or critic must be an engaged insider, reenacting sensitively the primary religious-poetic experience itself, before he attempts to understand or assess it.

If my argument is thus far acceptable, then the apparent chasm between religion and literature must be challenged. There is significant dialogue between the two whenever the poet or critic seriously tries to focus upon the hyphen, the dialectical *and* in his own religious-literary experience, or measures his own religious-literary experience against that of others. At this moment, implicitly or consciously, he releases himself from his strictly defined role or discipline and draws upon his wider humanity. Few literary critics, for example, can remain merely literary for long, and judgments that pretend to be solely literary normally become something more. Explicit religious-literary criticism fixes attention intensively on this "becoming something more," this moment of self-transcendence.

So diffusive an interdisciplinary exchange tempts us to two exaggerations. We may recognize such self-transcendence only in the most specific obvious religious examples. Or, on the other hand, we let it vaporize so generously that it begins to appear everywhere with a sort of paranoic regularity. At the first extreme are found critics confining themselves to questions about the authentic Christianity of T. S. Eliot, Auden, Mauriac, Hawthorne. Or they analyze the import of Robert Lowell's deconversion from Roman Catholicism upon his poetry. They detect the Manichean sexual attitudes of Graham Greene's characters, or the manifest parallels between biblical Passion narratives and Billy Budd's martyrdom. Such studies, although maybe productive in their own right, tend to constrict the religious phenomenon to a limited denominational doctrinal framework, deviations from which sometimes assume unwarranted import. These critics are preoccupied with manifest Christ figures and sacramental imagery, a novelist's explicit theological vocabulary, scenes of dialogue on overtly religious topics, the orthodoxy of his obiter dicta. To the average reader, I suppose, the words religion and literature immediately evoke topics and approaches such as these. Here is a recognizable, somewhat limited area of study. We find a critic's tangible set of credentials in divinity and in literature studies; such practitioners are usually not coy about labeling themselves religious-literary. These critics can be easily fitted into the categories chosen by James Thorpe's important Modern Language Association pamphlet *Relations of Literary Study: Essays on Interdisciplinary Contributions* (1967), where literature and religion is given parallel recognition alongside literature and psychology, literature and sociology, literature and music.

At the other extreme from this somewhat literal specificity is the tendency to create a vague mash of literature and all significant being, to employ a sleight-of-hand apologetics so that every great writer emerges on "our side." Religion seeps into the discussion of a literary text whenever life becomes tragic, or time is treated seriously. Sallie TeSelle blames immature, amorphous theological criticism of this type on "the pervasive influence of Tillich's equation of religion with ultimacy—interpreted, diminished, and dissipated by others into whatever is noble, wise, or hopeful (even if ostensibly negative) in creative literature" (1968, p. 614). Even if Tillich himself could apply his criterion of ultimacy to a painting with surprising perceptiveness, the post-Tillichian theological critics are pedestrian sleuths eager to find some vague Christian or religious import within almost every profound impulse in literature. TeSelle concludes her attack with a challenge that these critics clarify their purposes, methods, terms, especially the meaning of *religious*. Theologians ought to remain distinctly and specifically theologians and not presume an expertise in literary criticism. Most significant, TeSelle apparently expects to discover more trustworthy religious-literary critics among those Christians who believe in God as a suprapersonal being, rather than among Liberal Protestant humanists professing an immanent, relational notion of God.

Notice how readily TeSelle's justifiable attack against the sloppy, random performance of some critics combines with an arbitrarily specific dogmatic position on the nature of God and religion. I think three distinct phenomena must be clarified here. First, there is a fallacy that most of us can easily acknowledge: to magnify rumors of the sacred, find a Holy Grail in every goblet, thin out the religious dimension so that it will then be discovered everythere, and consequently nowhere.

Second, theologians with the unquestioned repute of Tillich or Rahner describe God not as *a* suprapersonal being but as the unconditioned ground, height, horizon of all being. Even if one were theologically to dispute such an immanent, relational approach, it has still achieved such nontheological currency in our culture that even the U.S. Supreme Court today recognizes it as an adequate *religious* basis for the conscientious objector. Thus, when the religious-literary critic, with appropriate sophistication, singles out moments of intensified depth or exaltation in a work of literature, he legitimately blurs the deceptively lucid outlines that TeSelle demands for her concept of religion. Some people seem threatened by the menace of arrogant imperialism whenever a theologian or religious-literary critic searches for religious values outside the explicit church sanctuary.

It is a truism that someone's political ideology or characteristic moral style will function more often as his actual religion than do his nominal credal and church positions. We generally agree that explicit religious beliefs issue ideally in attitudes and behavior marked by awe, commitment, moral seriousness, the paradoxical shuddering and ecstasy that Rudolf Otto attributes to the normative religious experience. If I reverse this approach, in the manner of Dewey, Allport, Fromm, Georg Simmel, and many theologians today, I can understand my religion as *whatever* explicit or partially conscious drive, credo, or value system lies at the root of such recognizably religious attitudes and behavior.

Now the religious-literary critic who conceives religion in this complex functional manner cannot settle into a tidy conventional slot alongside literature and psychology or literature and sociology critics. Clearly he would perish if isolated from psychologists, anthropologists, and his other colleagues in the human sciences. But principally by adopting, and at the same time transcending, their multifaceted perspectives, he can attempt to uncover the religious dynamism or value system radically at work in a text. This religious dimension in a piece of literature is not an area localized beside a psychological or historical vein to be mined, nor is it especially an item named once by the sociologist but pasted over with a new theological label. It is a sort of global effulgence, a reverberating quality of experience, an atmosphere and texture in the total meaning of the work. If you cannot tolerate fuzziness and elusive amoebalike aspects of reality, and especially, if you demand Cartesian geometrical clarity, be prepared to discount this dimension out of hand. William James's genuine empiricist would hold paramount the chase for any truth, no matter what the vagueness or risk of error, rather than suspend belief out of a fear of being duped.

My third and final remark occasioned by TeSelle's critique of religious-literary criticism is a corollary to the expansive religious approach I have just described. Granted that a balance must be struck between poles of narrow doctrinal particularity and vacuous universality. The best religious-literary critics, then, might well be found among those who repudiate all particularity, especially the partisan tags of religion and metaphysics. They may reach the limits of their own psychological or archetypal perspective, for example, and push much further than anticipated, addressing themselves intuitively to values too complex and massive to be charted within their express programs of criticism. They would respond with brazen diffidence, of course, to the pontifical announcement that they have been theologians all their lives. But I am convinced that the test for a sound notion of religious-literary criticism lies in comprehensiveness, not in an exacting particularity. My first methodological rule is not to magnify the negligible, concrete, differentiating notes that separate religious-literary critics from other types of critics. I search for a comprehensive religious-literary ideal, achieved implicitly in the best work of our most divergent critics, no matter what their professed origins and ways of access.

THE RELIGIOUS-LITERARY PHENOMENON

Probably the most recognizable form of religious-literary study has originated and persisted most fruitfully in undergraduate humanities courses. In college catalogues there is a widespread recurrence of such course titles as "Faith and Doubt in the Modern Novel," "Modern Drama and the Christian Myth," "Utopian Literature and a Theology of the Future," "Existentialist Themes from Shakespeare to Faulkner," "Dostoevsky: Problems of Revolution and Religious Doubt," "The Catholic Novel: Greene, Waugh, Mauriac," "The American Jewish Novel." Professors offering such classes surely intend to capitalize on the recent popularity of religious topics—an interest generally not doctrinal nor denominational, and often disguised beneath some unique mix of yoga, astrology, and diabolism. College-age students are understandably preoccupied with emotional maturation and moral values, with religious themes and styles. Literature, song lyrics, the cinema and stage offer an especially productive context in which to discover and analyze these perennial concerns. Here at first glance we have literature without tears, without the fussy irrelevances of linguistics and literary history. And we have religion without its demanding, dull scriptural and ecclesiastical baggage.

Yet at best this introductory topical perspective deepens into a rigorous study requiring linguistic competence, experience in aesthetics and literary history, and all the basic theological disciplines. Nathan Scott has presented a utopic blueprint of requirements for a Ph.D. in the area of religion and literature, especially as it has evolved as an explicit field at the University of Chicago (1968). Of course, doctoral dissertations on topics bridging the departments of English and Religious Studies can be arranged at many universities today, notably at Syracuse and Emory. It is difficult to keep track of the innumerable conventions, seminars, and sectional meetings of the Modern Language Association, the American Academy of Religion, and the Society for the Scientific Study of Religion devoted these last few years to papers in religious-literary criticism written by alumni of such programs, and other interested scholars.

One of the obstacles to drawing up a bibliography of characteristic books in religious-literary criticism is the slippery oscillation between the two notions of religion, restrictive and comprehensive, already described. For instance, the critic F. R. Leavis appears prominently in one bibliography of the field but is conspicuously absent from another. A religious critic insofar as he writes almost incessantly in the Arnoldian manner about moral values in literature, Leavis at the same time denounces doctrinal bias in Anglican critics like George Every, the later T. S. Eliot, and other members of a profession he derogatively calls theological gang movements. In effect, he disdains the religious-literary rubric, but in practice defends a wider range of religious consciousness against a meretricious "Christian discrimination" that distorts literary judgments. There is no doubt that Leavis is functionally religious, in the way I have already defined my term. If we attempt a taxative roster of religious critics, then, must we not include Leavis—but if so, then how can any serious established literary critic be justly eliminated? Of course, a manageable bibliography is expected to pick up at least the self-proclaimed religious-literary critic. A further difficulty for the bibliographer is the dispersal of valuable individual articles throughout anthologies of negligible general quality. And often the bewildering counterpoint of themes in single books almost defies a genuine topical classification.

Because of these and other problems, few extensive bibliographies in religious-literary criticism have been attempted. First, there is Nathan Scott's five-part selection of titles, without descriptive comment, in his *New Orpheus* (1964, pp. 420–31). The categories—Problem of a Christian Poetic; Nature of the Christian Vision; Moorings for a Theological Criticism; Belief and Form: The Problem of Correlation; and The "Silence, Exile, and Cunning" of the Modern Imagination—naturally presuppose very arbitrary arrangements. But this fivefold conceptualization itself, following the division of articles in this anthology, seems reduplicative, and more decorative than serviceable. A more ambitious, as yet unpublished "Bibliography of Literature and Religion" by Ernest Griffin (1968) is available from the University of Alberta English Department. Presented alphabetically and nondescriptively are 683 titles. Griffin deliberately omits books about particular authors, and also intends that his list be supplemented by current titles from the *Newsletter of the Conference on Christianity and Literature*. Most instructive is the approximate guide to 21 subjects preceding the 683 numbered titles, which groups series of numbers around each specific rubric. These themes, too, seem almost futile as classifications—e.g., Literature and Vision, Literature and the Human Image, Literature and Modern Existence—especially when entire anthologies are placed capriciously under one vague heading and not under another. But the subject guide serves as a convenient summary of predominant topics and the most flatulent clichés in this field.

Bibliographies by Sallie TeSelle (1966) and by Maralee Frampton (1968) are more selective, but there are two descriptive bibliographies that seem more serviceable. Tom Driver's list (1960a) classifies titles in a somewhat orderly threefold manner: general works explicitly on religion and literature, general books of implicit dialogue and context, and works on specific authors and literary periods. Donald Deffner's list (1965) gives useful paragraph-length synopses of almost 60 titles. In addition to the many books covered in all these bibliographies, we might add more recent paperbacks in the series of critical essays on specific authors, *Contemporary Writers in Christian Perspective*, published by W. W. B. Eerdmans. Also, the frequent reviews and survey articles on religion and literature in the quarterly *Soundings: An Interdisciplinary Journal* (and *The Christian Scholar*, which it superceded in 1968), published by the Society for Religion in Higher Education.

There are a few popular collections of essays that summon together most of the familiar names in religious-literary criticism. In my opinion the two best anthologies are Stanley Hopper's *Spiritual Problems in Contemporary Literature* (1952) and Giles Gunn's *Literature and Religion* (1971). Hopper's few pages of foreword are still accurate today as an assessment of prospects and limitations of studies in this field. He sees the perennial human "limit-situations" of crisis and radical change as the common ground to be pondered by both contemporary poets and theologians. T. S. Eliot and Auden, Marcel and Tillich are Hopper's models of combined aesthetic skill and theological awareness. William Barrett writes about the kinship between the existentialists and such novelists as Mann, Lawrence, and Joyce. The approach to love, choice, death, guilt, anxiety by figures like Sartre and Heidegger is of more interest to the theological critic than is the sterile cerebration of current analytic or academic philosophy. Also included is Denis de Rougemont's famous essay describing the symbolic work of art as a "calculated trap for meditation." According to de Rougemont, the art of literary criticism must combine technical philological skills with an informed metaphysical, ethical, or theological pursuit of the meaning and values embodied. Works of creative literature are ranked according to the intensity and duration of attention to the meaning of life they command. In the romantic view of the artist, a man creates, incarnates, is inspired. These three analogies, roughly parallel to the function of Father, Son, and Holy Spirit, become three models in de

Rougemont's theological criticism of literature, and he somewhat too literally compares excessive or deficient emphases on them with earlier Trinitarian church heresies. In an essay on contemporary poetry, Amos Wilder defines as "protestant" the most hard-won marginal affirmations of poets like Wallace Stevens and Yeats, protesting against narrow orthodoxy, striving toward a fuller recovery of the Christian's deepest religious experience.

The introductory essay by Giles Gunn in the second anthology upholds a principled eclecticism, which attempts to collate the best moments in four types of religious-literary criticism labeled mimetic, expressive, pragmatic, and semantic, following M. H. Abrams's terms for principal theories in the history of criticism. Gunn finds expressive Coleridgean parallels in the tendency of critics like Nathan Scott and William Lynch to move from the individual text to an author's embodied vision, and then to all the influences of the milieu that have enriched it. This anthology gathers vintage chapters from otherwise scattered books; in addition to those pieces mentioned above are chapters exerpted from books by Scott, R. W. B. Lewis, Ong, Auerbach, Heller, Ricoeur, J. Hillis Miller, and others. Nathan Scott discusses poetry and prayer, Miller the immanence of God in concrete poetic realities, Martz the meditative lyric, and Lewis the critic's need to labor through a text's particularity to reach religious generalizations. Heller finds the roots of a dissociation of sensibility in Zwingli's nominalist argument against Calvin's view of the Eucharist as a symbol participating in the reality symbolized. Amos Wilder describes the theologian's perpetual need to repossess his faith, validating it in an experience of life that includes the literary experience. His principal illustration is the Christian doctrine of divine providence, tested against situations in DeVries's *Blood of the Lamb* and Beckett's *All That Fall*, in an attempt to decide whether the implicit life-attitudes here show a sufficiently nuanced "exhaustive faithfulness." My quarrel with Wilder's procedure is that I can distinguish nothing uniquely Christian, or even necessarily monotheistic, in the "providence" phenomenon he claims to identify as specifically Christian. His notion needs more theological precision or, better yet, ought to be liberated from its explicit denominational moorings in Judaeo-Christianity. Interestingly enough, Wilder anticipates the objection that any sound literary critic would probably analyze these authors no differently than he. He thinks a "Christian criticism" correctly employed "will coincide at many points with any grounded humanistic criticism, but, secondly, . . . it can also alert such criticism to the resonances of a profounder anthropology" (p. 46).

Three other recent anthologies have had some currency, the first two edited by Nathan Scott and the third by George Panichas. Scott's *New Orpheus: Essays toward a Christian Poetics* (1964) contains more than twenty essays by such major figures as Eliot, Auden, Marcel, Harvey Cox, Christopher Fry, while his own introductory essay is an outstanding preface to religious-literary criticism. It calls for a criticism that moves outward toward the world or inward toward the poet's subjectivity, beyond formalist obsessions with the "intransitive attention" of an isolated text. Most of the remaining essays function more or less as a casebook on this principal theme, giving source materials or expanded footnotes from which Scott has articulated his own position. To my taste, the dominant Catholic (Anglo and Roman) perspective soon becomes insular, the generalizations on sacraments and the Incarnation lack challenging contact with other viewpoints.

Scott's *Adversity and Grace* (1968), if read as the companion volume to *New Orpheus,* gives disheartening proof that in religious-literary criticism, theory can be magniloquent, actual performance shabby. Much of the applied criticism in this later collection is by Scott's former students, and the achievement is shockingly lightweight. Notice the lengthy portions in essays on F. O'Connor, Malamud, J. F. Powers, for example, devoted to routine plot paraphrase, and how seldom religious reflection in any of the selections rises above the vapid social commentary of commonplace literary critics. Panichas's *Mansions of the Spirit* (1967) gives no more favorable impression than *Adversity* in its quality of applied criticism. The TeSelle article, previously discussed in some detail, was designed mostly as a demolishing book review of *Mansions.* The single outstanding essay in this banal collection, in my opinion, is by Hyatt Waggoner. It is a vigorously reasoned polemic against critics like Irving Howe that accuse Waggoner of a religious doctrinaire bias in his work on Hawthorne, Emerson, Whitman. Waggoner defends his religious beliefs as a consciously affirmed perspective open to new truth and experience, and he rejects a limiting neoorthodox approach that acts simply as another competing ideology. Then with some convincing evidence, Waggoner turns the argument against Howe, convicting this humanist of a reductivist bias. Howe unconsciously presumes his own humanist position is the only authentic one, especially in his frequent use of words like "merely" or "purely" when fixing on the implied psychological aspects of Hawthorne's broadly religious viewpoint.

2

KEY CRITICS AND TEXTS

A RABID taxonomist might successfully collate the names of figures from many of the bibliographies and anthologies introduced in the previous chapter. He could perform a computer check through their contents to discover the frequency of jargon, the works of creative literature preferred for analysis, or the critics and theologians most often cited. In fact, once irrelevant detail is cleared away, there certainly does emerge a small circle of people frequently quoting each other, usually invoking common ancestors and adversaries, and treating many similar themes, often with the same set of unquestioned assumptions.

THE CRITICS

Most probably the critics at the center of this religious-literary stage are Nathan Scott, Amos Wilder, R. W. B. Lewis, J. Hillis Miller, C. S. Lewis, and W. H. Auden. Each seems to have a few characteristic emphases in method, a few limited recurring theses, and some moments of singular accomplishment. Let me try to synthesize in the form of a canon what I think represents the best work of these critics. Scott and Wilder are primarily theologians, R. W. B. Lewis and Miller literary critics with an express religious focus, and C. S. Lewis and Auden belletrists and Christian apologists.

NATHAN SCOTT. Scott is surely the most influential and prolific critic in this field. I see him primarily not as an exacting applied critic, but as a theologian of culture, gifted with a global viewpoint evoking a myriad epochs and styles. I shall divide his best pieces into four categories:

1. A Method of Theological Criticism
   a. "The Modern Experiment in Criticism: A Theological Appraisal" (1964).
   b. "On the Place of *Litterae Humaniores* in the Curriculum of Theological Studies" (1969).

2. A Post-Tillichian Heideggerian Theology of Culture
   a. "The Literary Imagination in a Time of Dearth" (1969).
   b. *The Wild Prayer of Longing: Poetry and the Sacred* (1971).
3. A *Geistesgeschichte* of the Modern Period
   a. "The Name and Nature of Our Period-Style" (1966).
   b. "The 'Conscience' of the New Literature" (1969).
4. The Religious Aspects of Literary Genres
   a. "The Tragic Vision and the Christian Faith" (1966).
   b. "The Bias of Comedy and the Narrow Escape into Faith" (1966).

As I have already noted in an earlier discussion of this first methodological essay from the *New Orpheus,* Scott in his "Modern Experiment" (1964, pp. 141–71) insists the poem is "oriented by the vision, by the belief, by the ultimate concern, of which it is an incarnation," and thus a thorough critique of the poem must be essentially theological. His second essay (1969, pp. 145–68) points up the paradox that critics most disparaging of theology customarily issue the strictest regulations of what religion ought to be. They like to profess a narrow crisis-religion hostile to culture, and when confronting a type of religion partial to the vitalities of culture, declare it a cowardly sellout. This complaint prompts Scott to justify the immanentist aspects of religion, linked first with Bonhoeffer and theologians of radical secularity, and second with anti-Hellenic biblical theologians like Cullmann, who find Jahwe in the center of historical events themselves, not at their horizon as being or a being. I think this departure from Tillich's Hellenic language of being is merely an apparent one, for God is still found, where a theologian of culture like Tillich would most likely expect to find Him, in "all those intellectual and cultural forms" arising from "man's deepest encounter with his world and his own humanity."

The next essay and book, drawing cursorily upon the later ontology of Heidegger, develops this theology of immanence. As "Shepherd of Being," the poet surrenders religiously to the self-disclosing mystery present in each concrete particular thing, exploring his present deprivation, waiting in hope for this revelation. The world, then, must not be treated as mere veil, mirror, metaphor to be stripped away to reach God (1969, pp. 59–88). Scott's *Wild Prayer of Longing* (1971) uncovers in the restless wonder and joy of a poet like Roethke an instinctive fondness for the sacredness of the world in its own reality. This is a phenomenon which Tillich, Heidegger, Teilhard de Chardin, and the mystics of West and East have long prepared us for—a panentheist theology without supranaturalist projections, which locates God at the core of all beings, distinct but inseparable from them.

The two *Geistesgeschichte* articles reveal Scott's more characteristic lecture-style: "It was the best of times, it was the worst of times," with a Miltonic relish for the proper noun and sonorous polysyllable. He conjures up impressionistic scenes of metaphysical isolation, exacerbation of spirit, inner dislocation, at the very heart of which only a religious miracle could explain a man still able to affirm his humanity with "the courage of despair" (1966, pp. 1–24). The latter essay (1969, pp. 25–58) associates tendencies in Robbe-Grillet's *roman objectif*, Beckett and the theater of the absurd, the American black humor novel, Godard's films, Cage's music, with a Heideggerian reverence for the primal realities. In this art there is amazement at the simple facticity of things, their ragged angles and surfaces, without the impatience of Yeats or Joyce to resolve and subdue these ambiguities by personalizing them in some type of myth. Scott labels this current style antiteleological, a tendency he aptly discovers in the early Christian Antiochan theologians' resistance to the allegorical Platonizing trends of Alexandria. Of the two final essays I have selected, the quintessence can be expressed briefly. Comedy in its highest religious implications is symbolized by a humorous Charlie Chaplin tramp, managing to remain human amid the rituals of a money culture—man laughable as imperfect man, gloriously earthbound and finite. Overachievement, overseriousness, and rebellion against human boundaries are the basic idolatry (1966, pp. 77–118). In the experience of tragic literature, on the other hand, a Christian's basically joyous vision of life can include a tragic dimension, but only provisionally. For in the liturgy, especially, he reenacts Christ's bitter Good Friday desolation and waits in hope for the Second Coming. Because God is present, no tragedy seems ultimate; yet because God in Jesus Christ is experienced as hidden and suffering, the tragic is genuinely possible (1966, pp. 119–44).

AMOS WILDER. The best access to the work of Amos Wilder is *The Language of the Gospel: Early Christian Rhetoric* (1964). On steadiest ground as a rare combination of biblical exegete and literary critic, he examines how the Gospel message and various media of utterance mutually condition each other. The literary form of gospel, acts, epistle, apocalypse, anecdote, dialogue, and genealogy, for instance, cannot be reduced into our present categories of history, poetry, biography, oratory. He sifts out New Testament liturgical passages, rhythms of extempore utterance, aphorisms, and prophetic oracles. These distinctive narrative and dialogue forms both give specific shape to the historical revelation, and also influence the speech and writing habits of early Christians. Later essays, such as the "Biblical Epos and Modern Narrative" (1969, pp. 41–77) and "The Symbolics of the New Testament" (1969, pp. 99–122), add little to this thesis, except to acclaim Old Testament narratives, thus subscribing to Auerbach's tendentious position on the uniqueness of biblical narrative styles, which I shall discuss later. Wilder thinks the Bible yields criteria of "holism" and "total humanism" against which contemporary novels can be tested. In his other books, Wilder turns his attention from biblical prophets to unorthodox contemporary poets, since he is convinced that church theologians have lost the authentic prophetic strain, and in their discursive intellectualist mode of expression, they impoverish the full emotive, imaginative reality of what God continues to reveal. Always flirting with Docetism, comfortable with Christ's divinity but not His humanity, theologians need recurrent corrective baptism in the secular, the human, and the artistic.

"Religious Dimensions in Modern Literature" (1958, pp. 12–37) is Wilder's finest essay on the rationale of a religious-literary criticism. Just as lay prophets shape new versions of the old religious myths of Paradise, Flood, Sodom, Cain, so there must arise critics with religious sensibility to help interpret them adequately. He suggests a list of the more obvious writers who cannot be properly understood without the theologian's expertise, including Swedenborg's influence on Blake and the Jameses, Gallic Catholicism and Jansenism on Bernanos and Mauriac, Higher Biblical Criticism on Lessing, Puritanism on Emerson and Dickinson. The plea that theologians should read modern literature to encounter secular prophecy and new styles of transcendence pervades this and almost every other Wilder essay, too, especially the two I have already mentioned in the Hopper and Gunn anthologies. Wilder's applied criticism is meager and casually illustrative of whatever religious theme or methodological principle he develops. In skimming *Modern Poetry and the Christian Tradition* (1952a), for example, one can find some perceptive interpretations of passages from Stevens, G. M. Hopkins, and other poets, selected to show how poetry must be read on its own terms, without forcing it into preconceived theological patterns.

R. W. B. LEWIS. The clearest statements thus far of R. W. B. Lewis's theory of religious literary criticism occur in *Trials of the Word.* Paradoxically he denies from the beginning any kinship between this volume and the field of religion and literature. Moreover, if he should occasionally advert to the religious dimension in a work, he insists this shall not occur from an explicitly Christian viewpoint. Here again is the literary critic impatient of restrictive loyalties, anxious to spot religious overtones outside a strict doctrinal perimeter. Lewis leaves no doubt about this focus. What attracts him in literature is "the tug of the transcendent," "the fertile tug-of-war between the transcendent and the concrete." His tendency is mostly "to focus upon those phases of a work of literature in which what have to be called religious considerations are overtly or secretly paramount" (1965, p. viii). He is enticed by the way a religious consciousness breaks into expression in the very midst of the secular and ordinary.

I can think of almost no one more sensitive than Lewis to the anomaly that sometimes the least apparently religious moments are actually the most religious, or conversely, as Kierkegaard puts it, even the truth can become a lie on the lips of some people. Lewis wants to perceive the *functionally* religious phenomenon, as I have previously defined it, no matter how this aspect is named or disguised or denied. And he uses the very word *religious* with perceptive reluctance because it is often applied so facilely to efforts unworthy of the name. His best essay in this collection, "Hold on Hard to the Huckleberry Bushes" (pp. 97–111), develops Emerson's remark about the tendency of pious people to soar immediately into theological generalities without digging into hard particulars. In reviewing a book by Randall Stewart, Lewis contrasts the specific Christian stance and Stewart's eagerness to baptize Hawthorne or excommunicate Thoreau, with Lewis's own quest for religious values "stained with restless ambiguity." The unique religious scepticism in Hawthorne and Henry James, for instance, cannot be grasped accurately without following the actual evolution of persistent themes and images in each work, and from one novel to the next.

In Lewis's applied criticism, I suppose *The Poetry of Hart Crane* (1967) remains his major attempt to embody these demanding ideals. Crane is proclaimed controversially "the religious poet par excellence in his generation." Like Rilke or Wallace Stevens, Crane asks modern man to recover a religious consciousness that reveres the transcendence pervading actual everyday situations. Lewis reads the first half of *The Bridge* as an expression of the death of God, the loss of old modes of transcendence. The second half celebrates the advent of the poet or Nietzschean Superman, a mastersinger who will lead man to new styles of the sacred. In other words, Lewis finds in Crane a panentheism and all the Heideggerian exaltation of the poet as mystical bard that Scott's *Wild Prayer of Longing* later discovers in the poet Roethke. Unlike Scott, Lewis does not need to invoke the sanction of Heidegger's inflated teutonisms, for he perceives more immediate parallels in American transcendentalism. Emerson, too, attacked the weary supranaturalism and knee-drill of the churches, affirmed his belief in an immanent "oversoul," and canonized the poet as oracle. In this book Lewis provides many close readings of Crane's poetry, usually ranging from one poem to another so that he can synthesize recurring themes, constantly talking about Crane's total "vision." But I think Lewis often overleaps his huckleberry bushes to snatch at hints of the sacred too eagerly, noting the patent religious term but missing the functionally religious pseudonym. "Fortunate Fall" (pp. 106f.), "divine grace" (pp. 126f.), sin and redemption are threadbare unexamined theological clichés in Lewis's vocabulary. In some of the Crane lines most exciting for Lewis, I hear the poet singing about nothing whatsoever distinct from the human phenomenon itself, or my ear suggests to me that Crane has merely lapsed into a bit of stock romantic religious diction.

The American Adam (1955) and *The Picaresque Saint* (1959) are two of the most deservedly popular books in religious-literary criticism. The first unravels the dialectical conflict implicit in a myth dominating our national literature roughly from 1820 to 1860. The voice of "Irony" (Hawthorne-Melville-the senior James-Bushnell-Brownson) mediated a struggle between the voice of "Memory" (Calvinist orthodoxy) and of "Hope" (Emerson-Thoreau-Whitman-Parker). There was a new collective experience of self-reliant innocence and emancipation from a degenerate European past, yet at the same time a sense of tragic guilt. Was the new Adam innocent, then, or sinful; or had he perhaps evolved beyond Edenic innocence by the rite de passage of a "fortunate fall"? The chapters on Hawthorne and Melville are central to Lewis's theme, with supplementary essays on critics and historians of this period, earlier novelists, and twentieth-century descendents of the warring parties. Unquestionably the whole book is a brilliant study in the history of ideas, a lively dramaturgic version of Matthieson's *American Renaissance* (1941) thesis on "the possibilities of democracy," affirmed in Emerson-Thoreau-Whitman, controverted in Hawthorne-Melville. As happens so often in concise architechtonic treatises, a neat exfoliation of the American Adam theme overstrains the actual implications of the data. Because of its obvious Adamic affinities, *Billy Budd* inappropriately becomes a more important novel than *Moby Dick*, and *The Marble Faun* more than *The Scarlet Letter*. Lewis's "Party of Memory" needs a study of the majestic Edwards and the Puritans in their prime. Instead, he presents Calvinist thought in its most absurd distortions, weak antiquarian straw men too easily brushed aside in the dialectic.

The Picaresque Saint examines the heterodox outsider heroes in novels by Camus, Faulkner, Greene, Malraux, Moravia, and Silone. In contrast to Joyce and Mann, and their perspective on life as a venture in artistic myth making, this generation of writers with deeper immediacy explore the tragic destiny of figures who try simply to be human. Their representative story deals with the episodic dangerous odyssey of a criminal stranger, a roguish saint. The roguishness is precisely what makes these characters such empathic, sinful human beings, their dedication not so much "to a supernatural god as to what yet remains of the sacred in the ravaged human community." The sacred, then, will be apprehended usually in political and social terms. Sainthood itself means participating in the sufferings of mankind "as a way of touching and of submitting to what is most *real* in the world today." Recognize Lewis's confident touch here in conceptualizing the religious function of human values—basically the same theological position of his Hart Crane book. The criticism in this book is generally of high quality, though most of these novelists present such overt religious dialogue and symbolism that Lewis's discovery of sacrality seems hardly surprising.

More impressive than the applied criticism in *The Picaresque Saint,* in my opinion, are two pieces from *Trials of the Word,* "The Wings of the Dove" (1965, pp. 120–28) and "Hawthorne and James: The Matter of the Heart" (pp. 77–96). I think it is a more demanding test of Lewis's functional religious criterion to apply it successfully to that least obviously religious of novelists, Henry James. Milly's smile in chapter 11 of *The Wings of the Dove* marks the "closest approach possible in James to a religious experience." Inanimate surfaces take on sacramental overtones. The revered marital relationship and the "sanctity of the human heart" prove to be something that can be blasphemed.

J. HILLIS MILLER. The achievements of Miller and Lewis in religious-literary criticism bear a few clear resemblances. They both define themselves essentially as literary critics pursuing a religious orientation only in the widest sense, mostly because an adequate interpretation of their material forces them to become theologians *manqué*—and then, only with a sort of disciplined hesitation, disclaiming too close an association with the religious-literary clique. Miller's essay, "Literature and Religion" (1967) is as pithy and challenging a manifesto as Lewis's "Hold on Hard to the Huckleberry Bushes," demanding no less painstaking a textual explication before the critic rushes to themes and archetypes. With Lewis's *Picaresque Saint* I would compare Miller's *Disappearance of God: Five Nineteenth-Century Writers* on DeQuincey, Browning, E. Brontë, Arnold, and Hopkins; and *Poets of Reality: Six Twentieth-Century Writers* (1965) on Conrad, Yeats, Eliot, Thomas, Stevens, and W. C. Williams. Both critics attempt to reconstruct imaginatively the separate world views of successive parallel figures, and constantly focus on newly devised styles of transcendence. The counterpart of Lewis's intensive study of Hart Crane is Miller's *Thomas Hardy* (1970).

In my opinion Miller, especially in the quality and solidity of his applied criticism, outdistances Lewis at every stage of the comparison.

Miller's exemplary critic is one living fully the tension between dispassionate objectivity and engagement, taking on the nature of whatever poet he interprets, but also measuring this new perspective against the critic's own personal beliefs. To feign an objective or neutral position toward the religious theme in a work is simply to trivialize it. Miller's "Literature and Religion" essay gives some incisive illustrations of both the distortion of texts to support the critic's own ideology, and also an exaggerated detachment. A problem of more personal concern to Miller in this essay is how to preserve the appropriate tension between a poem's integrity and its place in the author's entire corpus, or more widely, in the spiritual history of the whole milieu. *The Disappearance of God* copes admirably with this dialectic, by drawing separate sets of three concentric circles for each of five writers. For example, there is one circle for a specific novel, then the novelist's corpus, then all the writings of an epoch. Miller then proceeds "with a constant narrowing and expansion of the focus of attention," on the principle that "in literature the organism creates the environment as much as it is created by it" (1963, p. viii). He decides that in these five men their "theological experience is most important and determines everything else." They all seem to be straining for a hidden spiritual force in nature, as did the earlier romantics, but now more desperately, no longer in a poetry of religious presence but of allusion and absence. In *Wuthering Heights,* for example, the chapel of Gimmerton Slough is without a pastor, a detail I think Miller milks disproportionately. Yet shattering all the institutional barriers, Heathcliff and Cathy, by violent strain and longing, achieve supernatural communion with each other and the immanent God of the heath. Browning finally discovers in each individual man an incarnation of God, an image of His explosive eternity in man's driving motion within time. The quintessence of Hopkins is a blind violence of will toward a God absent this side of one's own death. Miller's later *Poets of Reality* we might view as a study of third-generation romantics searching for transcendence, closer in their religious stance to Wordsworth than to Browning, no longer obsessed with the "romantic dichotomy of subject and object." These writers are "poets not of absense but of proximity," perceiving the sacred as inseparable from things and people. Each writer begins with an experience of nihilism, but then Yeats recovers an infinite richness in the finite, Eliot learns that the Incarnation is an ongoing present reality, and Stevens can assert: "We seek / Nothing beyond reality, Within it, / Everything . . . ." We are confronted again by the panentheism of

Lewis's *Picaresque Saint, The Poetry of Hart Crane,* and also Scott's *Wild Prayer of Longing.*

Miller's chastened, straightforward prose makes pleasurable reading, and his explications of individual novels and poems are usually no less satisfying. Without discussion of his longer books on Dickens and other Victorians, I want to commend a few sample criticisms of specific authors, especially his sensitive "Franz Kafka and the Metaphysics of Alienation" (1957, pp. 281–305) and *Thomas Hardy.* Although I must admit all sketches on Kafka are beginning to sound the same to me, Miller generates some excitement as he closely follows Kafka's evolution in the fiction and notebooks from alienation, to liberation through the act of writing, to his final "terrifying discovery that the space of literature is identical with the place of exile where he first began." This is concisely written in the evocative, imaginative style of Bachelard, Richard, and other French-Swiss phenomenological critics. Incidentally, their influence is especially evident in Miller's habitual fascination with myths of space.

In his preface to the Hardy book, Miller explicitly locates Hardy within the context of his theme and method embodied in *Disappearance of God* and *Poets of Reality.* Anxious to lay hold of the "underlying structures" in Hardy's corpus, he solves this problem again largely in terms of spatial symbols. In Hardy there is a detachment of consciousness in the narrative voice, an emotional void in his characters, a "distance of oneself from oneself" that drives each character to seek another person to fill this emptiness. And the "Immanent Will," Hardy's cruel, awesome image of the sacred, is the basis of all desire, yet always projected elsewhere, unconscious, in reserve, keeping its distance. The function of Hardy's creative act of writing is to "close the distance between the Immanent Will and its mediate signs." His novel *Tess of the D'Urbervilles,* for example, attempts to give meaning to her otherwise mute agony. Within the covers of a book, in a cycle of timeless recurrences, her life is maintained in being, and "art is therefore a victory of consciousness over suffering."

C. S. LEWIS. Dating from his early conversion from atheism to Christianity, C. S. Lewis retained a zealous, twice-born suspicion of all apparent ploys to accommodate Christianity. This would include Liberal Protestantism, Tillich, and John A. T. Robinson, and implicitly, I am sure, the sort of panentheism now expounded by Miller, R. W. B. Lewis, and Nathan Scott. Progress in faith comes precisely from not skipping or slurring over those repellent doctrines that do not fit in with current theories. Easy doctrines simply sanction what has already been known; perplexing ones demand reconsideration and the chance for new knowledge. God must remain an actual outside presence that loves and makes demands on me, not just a gaseous life-force almost indistinguishable from my own whims. Christ is God, not just an ideal man; theology must center on God creating, less on man searching and symbolizing.

Lewis is above all else the religious "apologist" in the strict meaning of this term: one who emphasizes the defensibility, reasonableness, consistency of the religious factor in its relationships with other values and types of experience. You might predict, then, that Lewis as theological critic will appear to be a pushy doctrinaire sort of figure. On the contrary, he has produced a criticism with broad humanist sympathies, and a theory of criticism that slaps down theologians who presume to trespass within its boundaries. This is a subtle apologist, calculating that books on botany and astronomy, for example, written by intelligent Christians are more likely to convert non-Christians than are books on Christianity. "Its Christianity would have to be latent, not explicit: and of course its science perfectly honest. Science twisted in the interest of apologetics would be sin and folly" (1970, p. 93).

Four essays in *An Experiment in Criticism* (1961) give a succinct presentation of Lewis's theory. I must read the poem in its actuality, enact the ritual and submit to the pattern, enter into the total "primary literary experience" of the work. Only after this can I reflect theologically on my own experience, never presuming to grasp the poem in a quick paraphrase. The best critic is the textual and historical explicator helping me to analyze and articulate my experience of the work, not the evaluator eager to purify the reader's taste. Every critic has an implicit scheme of values behind his critical judgments, the credentials for which ought to be challenged on their own ground by moral theologians, philosophers, and psychologists. An excellent illustration of this point occurs in *A Preface to Paradise Lost* (1942, pp. 130f.), in which Lewis demonstrates that he and F. R. Leavis recognize the same qualities in Milton's epic verse, yet one critic loves and another hates the same object. They differ not about Milton's poetry but about the nature of man and human joy itself, and are thus beyond the realm of a criticism that is merely literary. The critic does not have to believe or approve of the world view or logos of a specific poem. A Christian immerses himself in a work by Lucretius, for example, hoping to see with other eyes, experience with another imagination, achieve an enlargement of being. His "Shelley, Dryden, and Mr. Eliot" (1969b, pp. 187–208) is a virtuoso case study of the correlation between a critic's implicit beliefs and his critical evaluations. Whereas Eliot favors Dryden and abominates Shelley, Lewis concedes Shelley's deficiencies but amasses evidence to rank him higher than Dryden, mostly in rebuttal to Eliot's questionable criteria. Some other fine essays on method are the piece "On Criticism" (1967, pp. 43–58), in which Lewis sifts out the theological presuppositions in assorted attacks against him by colleagues; also "Psycho-Analysis and Literary Criticism" (1969b, pp. 286–300) and "The Anthropological Approach" (1969b, pp. 301–11) against excessive Freudian and archetypal positions.

At its most unfortunate moments, there is a careless, kittenish, Chestertonian quality about Lewis's oral style that I actively dislike. It suggests the complacent, chatty amateur, feeling superficially at home in too many specialties, with a clumsy professorial choice of the dated slang phrase or quaint metaphor. My difficulty could be caused by the indiscipline of the British informal essay style itself. But perhaps my feelings give a clue to the cultural or personality factors that may deprive Lewis of the serious hearing he legitimately deserves from fellow theologians and literary critics.

As a practical critic, Lewis exemplifies admirably what his theoretical essays demand. He analyzes a person's sense of duty and work within an intimate closed circle, for example, and elaborately expands this theme to include most of Kipling's works. Kipling is an agnostic about ultimates, but the immediate values of the "Inner Ring" demand the public servant's almost unquestioning loyalty, no matter how dehumanizing and dishonest. In "A Note on Jane Austen" (1969b, pp. 175–86) Lewis begins by lining up passages from four of her novels, scenes where the character is being "undeceived." This leads to the discovery of a few serious unyielding moral standards at the core of this undeception, which account for the characteristic ironic world of the novels. Lewis's two most significant works of applied criticism are *The Allegory of Love* (1936) and *A Preface to Paradise Lost* (1942). The first is a long historical study of courtly love themes and images, designed to give contemporary readers an experience of the world of the late medieval allegorical love poem, especially *Troilus* and *Fairie Queene,* resourcefully explicated. The *Preface* is too whimsical at times, but the essay "Milton and Augustine" (pp. 65–71) provides a useful documented comparison between these two figures on their theory of Original Sin. And "The Theology of *Paradise Lost*" is a tour de force response to a list of alleged Miltonic heresies charged by Saurat. Lewis distinguishes between popular Christian commonplaces Saurat misunderstands as heresies, those on the list actually heretical but not in Milton, those specifically in Milton's *De Doctrina Christiana* but not in *Paradise Lost,* and those possibly in *Paradise Lost.*

W. H. AUDEN. I rank Auden a weak sixth alongside the previous five important figures, principally because his record as literary critic seems spotty, elusive, quite difficult to substantiate. It is instructive that in a foreword to *The Dyer's Hand* (1962) he denounces any sort of systematic literary criticism, observing with an affected diffidence that his own random lectures, reviews, and introductions consist of padded, oversimplified insights. Consistent with his preference for the notebooks of any critic rather than the developed treatises, Auden has published his own lectures and reviews as a set of dehydrated outlines, jottings, and undeveloped hunches. This is his habitual style of critical utterance, a truly oracular body of aphorisms, always glib and sometimes profound. They are usually ceremonious pronouncements, often including brief incisive explications of a specific passage—much like Wittgenstein's or Kafka's notebooks, apt for quotation, provoking further critical reflection in the reader. Recall, for instance, how neatly Auden distills his set of three themes upon which so much poetry has been written: "This was sacred but now it is profane. Alas, or thank goodness! This is sacred but ought it to be? This is sacred but is that so important?" (p. 59). Or his typically careless, tempting remark about apparent Christian overtones in two passages from Ibsen's *Brand*, that the willful asceticism is Nietzschean rather than Kierkegaardian (pp. 444–45). Precise definition and the exhaustive scrutiny of texts are not Auden's forte, but something of his wit, imagination, and candor, has become a significant catalyst in the best religious-literary discussions.

I have some forthright suggestions for a judicious editing and interpretation of Auden's criticism. First, in his theoretical pronouncements, try to minimize the silly inflated dichotomies between a pre-Christian and Christian ethos, a tragic hero and a religious martyr, poets and scientists, Henry Adams's hackneyed "Virgin and the Dynamo," the Prospero-poet and Ariel-poet, classical versus romantic styles. Most of his palatial bromides about the present era are merely an unreflective replay of the Hulme-Eliot repetitive strictures against Rousseau, Whitman, the Humanists, and their self-deifying optimism.

Second, follow some intelligent synopsis of his scattered evolving work as critic, such as George Bahlke's essay "Auden's Literary Criticism" (1970, pp. 61–84). Bahlke sweeps all the random fragments chiefly under one generalization: Auden's resourceful application of Kierkegaard's aesthetic-ethical-religious categories to divergent periods and styles of literature.

The third step is to focus mainly on Auden's applied criticism, at its most accomplished in *The Enchafèd Flood* (1951), an archetypal analysis of sea and desert symbols in romantic literature. Besides an extended religious allegorical explication of *Moby Dick,* Auden introduces a variety of questing heroes—presented in Kierkegaardian roles as an aesthetic Odysseus and Oedipus, an ethical Socrates, a religious positive Don Quixote and negative Ahab. In the later collection *Dyer's Hand,* too, there is an essay on "D. H. Lawrence" (pp. 277–95), with carefully chosen lines from both fiction and poetry to prove Lawrence's characteristic flaws and strengths. Lawrence's credo of the artist as religious apostle is given a somewhat sympathetic exposition—Auden is perplexed that Lawrence should succeed because of, not despite, a religious position which Auden fundamentally rejects. In this same volume is "The Guilty Vicarage" (pp. 146–58), Auden's widely anthologized humorous treatment of various detective story fashions, a genre he concludes that at best does not gratify violent fantasies. He conjectures that readers usually dissociate themselves from both crime and murderer, and thus use the detective myth as an Edenic escape from feelings of sin and guilt.

MAJOR TEXTS

The previous six figures stand at the center of religious-literary studies, but we must still account for a few more critics of slightly less magnitude. At the present moment I am interested in a canon of standard works, rather than the corpus of each specific critic. Two group of titles, each set arranged alphabetically, are listed below. The first set contains ten books of special importance. The final twenty-five "Further Representative Titles" include some of the most widely disseminated religious-literary materials, of the broadest variation in quality.

MIMESIS: THE REPRESENTATION OF REALITY IN WESTERN LITERATURE. Erich Auerbach's *Mimesis* is a superior primer of practical criticism. Auerbach takes a series of random texts from antiquity to the present and, concentrating usually on a minute analysis of the text itself, expands this circle of significance until it reaches out to encompass the whole work, the author's vision, the trends of an era. His best use of texts "as test cases for my ideas" is his frequently lauded explication of a short descriptive paragraph from *Madame Bovary* (1957, pp. 425–34). Here in an exacting, selective, psychological arrangement of concrete sensations in Emma's consciousness, Flaubert lets things themselves speak, manifesting an explosive tenseness in the otherwise viscous, sluggish flow of life characteristic of this bourgeois era.

My only misgivings about Auerbach center on his controversial thesis about the Judaeo-Christian contributions to realism. Neoclassicist periods in literature inhibited realistic representation by their fixed rule of styles, whereas the Middle Ages, Renaissance, and late nineteenth century favored the presentation of everyday realistic detail, somehow patterned after "the story of Christ, with its mixture of everyday reality and the highest and most sublime tragedy." Robert Scholes and Robert Kellogg (1966b, pp. 5f.) accurately discredit Auerbach's uncritical reliance on nineteenth-century standards of realistic plotting that close him off to more experimental narrative styles in Woolf, Joyce, and Proust.

Such a doctrinaire position on the biblical derivation of realism, most clearly enunciated in the essay on "Odysseus' Scar" (pp. 1–19), strikes me as outrageous. Unlike a Homeric episode from book 19 of the *Odyssey*, the biblical Abraham-Isaac narrative allegedly shows a superior historicity, blending the everyday and sublime and nearly all the perfections of the narrator's art. My own reading experience simply cannot corroborate Auerbach's argument, even if I were to accept his naive criteria of realistic narrative. His *Dante: Poet of the Secular World* (1961) stresses Dante's concern for the language and bearing of individual concrete characters, "something the Greek tragedy scorned." Dante's graphic apportionment of separate tortures or blessings seems to give weight to the individual destiny of each person. Besides its serviceable Auerbach bibliography, *Literary Language and Its Public in Late Latin Antiquity and in the Middle Ages* (1965, pp. 391–406) provides an introductory essay in which Auerbach expounds the historicist method of criticism, based on Vico's hermeneutics, that he employed earlier in *Mimesis*. His explorations into the ancient notion of three levels of style was actually a historical category he took provisionally from the classical era itself. In addressing this question to a series of specific texts in later periods, Auerbach brought to consciousness the purpose that had already been operative, "to disclose something of the influence of Christianity on the development of literary expression" (p. 20). In the *Mimesis* book, Auerbach mentions formulating his argument "only as I went along, playing as it were with my texts, and for long stretches of my way I have been guided only by the texts themselves" (1957, pp. 490–91). Especially when guided by the texts themselves, he does indeed show unquestioned mastery at explication, and I do recognize that despite the doubtful validity of his simplistic "Christian" thesis, it still functions as a useful organizing insight.

POETRY AND THE SACRED. Vincent Buckley has written a superb book, with discriminating analyses of poems ranging from the Elizabethans to Roethke, marked by a deep familiarity with Eliade and other current religious thinkers (1968). After one of the most rigorous and documented discussions of the religious phenomenon I have found in any religious-literary critic, Buckley shows how to find hierophanies in the psychological, social, and many other areas of life. In the poetic act itself, man sets aside and heightens experiences or places or memories to a point where they reveal, become numinous. The sacred is not a separable category of experience within the poem—Spenser and Wyatt are more religious in celebrating love than when trying to appear religiously devout; Donne in his consciously holy moments is often cheaply histrionic.

By no means theological degenerates, Blake, Wordsworth, Whitman, Yeats, and Lawrence are trying to remythologize God in terms of the self and cosmos. Yet Hopkins, the later Eliot and Auden, and the early Lowell are trying to redefine a specific doctrinal tradition in terms of worship and sinfulness. Both lines of these poets view poetry as sacred speech, and the first group is not necessarily less religious than the second. Roethke's poetry remains the exemplar of this post-Wordsworthian celebratory mode for Buckley, as for both Miller and Scott. A strange blind spot in Buckley's comprehensive perspective is the curious express exclusion of Arnold, Shelley, and especially Tennyson's *In Memoriam* from his discussion of "religious" poetry. In another excellent book, *Poetry and Morality: Studies on the Criticism of Matthew Arnold, T. S. Eliot, and F. R. Leavis* (1959), Buckley traces the force and meaning of the word "moral" in all these critics, each somehow finding "the moral value co-extensive with the artistic value of any work." In an appendix, "Criticism and Theological Standards" (pp. 214–26), Buckley dispassionately analyzes the weaknesses of Leavis's Anglican adversaries—Bethell, Every, and Jarrett-Kerr. They habitually digress to recite what they think the definitively orthodox Christian doctrine on an issue, and fault the poet's misunderstanding of it. They withhold affectivity in responding to the work, "using theology as an intellectual interest and not as the guarantee of inward sensitive life." Emphasizing less the Christian and more the human dimension, Buckley in his own practical criticism gives sanction to his statement, worthy of C. S. Lewis's model apologist: "the more it declares its own Christian nature the less good a Christian criticism will do."

LITERATURE AND RELIGION: A STUDY IN CONFLICT. For Charles Glicksberg, great poets and critics must have sensibilities tainted with doubt, fully open to the ambiguity and absurdity of life (1960). And neither myth, ideology, nor dogma must be invoked to flee what is ugly and demonic. This is the philosophy of Camus's Sisyphus, refusing the Kierkegaardian leap of faith, content to remain human no matter how painful and illogical the burden. Unlike TeSelle and stricter Barthians, Glicksberg thinks that insofar as a writer grapples honestly with these hazards and paradoxes, in the very moment of his atheism and negation he is essentially religious. Even the creative Christian personality must be somewhat heretical, essentially freed from dogma and institutional forms, tolerant of no censor or other intermediary between his vision and the reality perceived. G. M. Hopkins, for instance, handicapped by the scrupulously rigid manner in which he understood his Catholic beliefs and his responsibilities as a Jesuit, remained a truly great poet because as a man he expressed the harrowing tensions of his personal religious experience. But the later Eliot suffered artistic loss by identifying himself with orthodoxy in his intellect and will but not in his full human sensibility. He strained unsuccessfully to translate into abstract formula and dogma the ineffably concrete experience. Glicksberg is especially alert to the modern writer's desperate compensatory resort to myth and political ideology as surrogates for an abandoned God, alternatives in which the writer often only half-believes. Glicksberg in his applied criticism seldom does intensive textual analysis, but his illustrations show that he grasps the specific dilemma accurately. In his later *Tragic Vision in Twentieth-Century Literature* (1963), he roams through Dostoevsky, Kafka, Camus, O'Neill, cautioning against the tendency to absolutize the absurd in human experience, as does Beckett, a position that makes genuine tragedy impossible. A really tragic vision must never be closed to the possibility of self-transcendence.

STUDIES IN LITERATURE AND BELIEF. An initial essay on "The Literary Margins of Belief" (1954, pp. 1–16) is Martin Jarrett-Kerr's rebuttal to F. R. Leavis's disparagement of Anglican Christian discrimination critics. Leavis himself continues to employ artistic criteria of maturity, health, seriousness, and responsibility, which ironically bear an unrecognized "distant theological resonance." Jarrett-Kerr's "Calderon and the Imperialism of Belief" (pp. 38–63) bases Calderon's dramatic weaknesses on his voluntaristic faith, with little room for sympathy and doubt, holding the trump cards of immortality and bliss, so that his victims never confront the genuine tragic destinies of Faust and Macbeth. A similar point is made in "Pilgrims and Explorers" (pp. 155–87) when discussing the aggressive Catholicism of Greene and Mauriac versus the open Catholic humanism of Manzoni. Artistically, creative scepticism seems to function best, whereas "on both sides, the rejectors and the enthusiastic acceptors, one feels that the terrible agony of belief (or disbelief) has passed them by." Jarrett-Kerr is a belletrist in the C. S. Lewis vein, an adequate practical critic capable of lucid theoretical responses to characteristic religious-literary problems. "The Lie-Detectors" in *The Secular Promise* (1964, pp. 148–78), describing the artist as antenna and seismologist of subterranean currents in his society, defends sociological critics like Lukács and explicit religious critics. Another brief piece of applied criticism is *William Faulkner* (1970), a competent essay on Faulkner's corpus which fortunately shuns any attempt to claim him as a crypto-Christian, but wastes time trying to classify his work in traditional genres of farce, comedy, and tragedy. To distil Faulkner's major themes, Jarrett-Kerr centers wise attention on those ubiquitous Faulknerian words "implacable" and "outrage."

SACRED AND PROFANE BEAUTY: THE HOLY IN ART. Drawing from an encyclopedic knowledge in the history of religions, Gerardus van der Leeuw approaches each of the fine arts as an original primitive synthesis of art and religion. This unity has been broken in history by a gradual secularization of the artist; but finally, in recent times, there has occurred a tentative, ambiguous phase of rapprochement again with religion. Such a tidy dialectic seems more philosophical than verifiably chronological, and sometimes van der Leeuw's Hegelian method blends the philosophical and historical aspects without precision. Although a synthesis-analysis-synthesis rhythm proves too mechanical after the treatment of a few arts, it at least helps to organize a tremendous sweep of rich detail, from the early art of New Guinea through medieval France to modern Holland. This is a flabby book, crying out for the scissors of an austere editorship. But it is also an extraordinarily evocative work, daring in its speculation and suggestive of so many fertile parallels between the aesthetic and religious experience. Like the numinous phenomenon, beauty enchants but disturbs, and it marks a consummatory phase of human knowledge and affectivity that resembles religious ecstasy. Van der Leeuw can be especially eloquent about what he calls "eschatological art," in which the word and music dissolve into silence, the image melts into the background, the building is lost in the stretches of landscape, the human symbol transcends itself. "Climb up upon this height and you will see how the paths of beauty and holiness approach each other, growing distant, until finally, in the far distance, they can no longer be told apart" (1963b, p. 337). It is usually style and form, rather than content, that attract his attention, and his illustrations of sacrality are often drawn from art dry, stylized, least apparently devout. I find both labored and stimulating a concluding theological essay on "The Image of God" (pp. 304–28), with its awkward gymnastic yet courageous attempt to harmonize the dour Calvinist view of man van der Leeuw professes with his own felt liberal Christian humanist perspective on man's artistic creativity.

THE POETRY OF MEDITATION: A STUDY IN ENGLISH RELIGIOUS LITERATURE OF THE SEVENTEENTH CENTURY. Louis Martz studies correspondences between the metaphysical poets and ascetical writers of the same era (1954). There are similarities between a certain rhetorical style, a sequence of ideas and moods in the reflective lyric; and the type of prayer commended by numerous current meditation manuals, consisting of an opening dramatic biblical image, followed by reflection and a final colloquy. Martz gives some intriguing explications of individual poems, but he presses the thesis itself immoderately. There are indeed close parallels between these styles of prayer and poetry, but Martz is too oversensitive to the possibility of direct horizontal influences from the manuals upon the metaphysical poets. In any epoch I would suspect that both prayer and poetry as human utterance can only assume a limited range of archetypal shapes and styles anyway. By the time Martz has extended his notion of conventional meditation to envelope Rilke, Blake, and Dickinson, we are left with only a few rhetorical devices such as apostrophe, dramatic everyday diction, interior debate—the characteristics of almost any type of informal prayer, philosophical lyric, or what C. S. Peirce calls "musement." The bankruptcy of this overdriven position occurs in *The Poem of the Mind,* where Whitman, W. C. Williams, and Stevens are also conscripted into this tradition. Here Martz finally gets behind his stock ascetical conventions, dissolves his earlier facile dichotomy between sacred and profane, and learns that the qualities of common human discourse have all this time been his relevant topic. In Stevens he decides that "meditation becomes attentive thinking about concrete things with the aim of developing an understanding of how good it is to be alive" (1969, p. 218).

THE BARBARIAN WITHIN AND OTHER FUGITIVE ESSAYS AND STUDIES. Walter Ong's collection of essays (1962) centers on a few distinct themes of importance, reiterated with scant new development in later collections, *The Presence of the Word* (1967b) and *In the Human Grain* (1967a). The emergence of Anglo-American textual New Criticism from a history-oriented Old Criticism accompanied the shift in recent academic life from Graeco-Latin classics to modern vernacular literatures. No longer swept along into the tradition of Roman oratory and rhetoric, recent formalist critics leaned instead on the newly developed social sciences. The convergence of academic disciplines today, resisting the trend to overspecialize, presages an era when interdisciplinary styles of literary criticism will replace this narrow formalism. Theology and poetry are less disparate than anticipated, for they both use the rhetoric of paradox and ambiguity to express what is too massive or fragile for ordinary discourse.

In another essay, Ong argues that since an emphasis on sight experience is Hellenic, but an emphasis on aural-oral is Hebraic, our Christian tradition, which historically originated in both contexts, must now transcend its present visual linear bias to cope with a new McLuhanesque sensorium. There is a contrived apocalyptic urgency in such manifestos with which I confess myself unsympathetic. Perhaps Ong's most effective essay in *The Barbarian Within* is "The Jinnee in the Well Wrought Urn." Poems demand more of the formalist critic than a precise antiseptic analysis of the work simply as object. Each poem, emanating from the poet's self, and participating in the quality of self-possession properly attributed only to persons, invites a committed personal response. I find Ong's global dicta usually insightful, but often overworked, squeezed dry, insulated from the concrete illuminating example.

LOVE IN THE WESTERN WORLD. In a deluge of books, Denis de Rougemont has managed to get an unbelievable mileage out of his single theme, the Christian concept of adult agape love versus the Manichean courtly love tradition of passionate eros love at first sight. The Tristan-Iseult and Don Juan myths are his eros archetypes, which he exhaustively traces into spheres of modern literature, mysticism, the art of war, marital morals, and the contemporary worship of woman as sex goddess (1956). This is a theme of major import, I must admit, and often de Rougemont develops it perceptively. But especially in the essays of *Love Declared* (1963b), when he continues to detect Don Juan and Tristan prototypes in the lives of Kierkegaard and Gide, in *Doctor Zhivago, Lolita,* and other new guises, de Rougemont's pursuit declines into stubborn monomanic distortion of his texts. He reduces books to what he perversely describes as "their mythic diagram," or "archetypal resumé," what their authors *would* write "had they accepted my hypothesis and adopted the angle of vision I propose." It is both characteristic and swaggering of de Rougemont in *The Christian Opportunity* to view the transaction between religion and literature as unilateral. Theologians have no need of poets, but theologians themselves are needed for "spiritual guidance . . . of the literary tendencies of the age" (1963a, p. 71). They render an important service to the writer and his public by clarifying the implicit theology embodied in every literary work, whether the author recognizes this or not, a theology less of subject matter than of form and style.

LITERATURE AND THE CHRISTIAN LIFE. This book (1966) is Sallie TeSelle's survey of different approaches to religious-literary criticism, an expansion especially of the polemic I described before in her article, "What Is 'Religion' in Literature?" (1968). She insists there can be no honest bridge-building except between two definite autonomous entities, literature rather than amorphous aesthetics or culture, and Christian life rather than vague religion or inhibitory doctrine. Tillich, Scott, and Wilder are censured for "religious amiability" and "theological imperialism" in their anxiety to make reality crypto-religious. They are inferior to critics like George Steiner, Heller, and Auerbach, who view a text first in its integrity and then as an expression of values, both of its author and epoch. By amiability and imperialism, TeSelle means the apologist's temptation to bless the most alienated artistic vision as an invitation to the dramatic leap of faith. She also has in mind the Arnoldian tendency to reduce the scope of great art to a fiefdom of didactic ethics. Such a critic does not read literature as literature; instead "He sucks up the secular into the sacred, so that there is no such thing as an atheist, an autonomous culture, or a really secular secularity."

TeSelle is unrelenting and shrill in her bias against the Tillich camp. Yet this critique can act as a bracing corrective against those who carelessly dilute the hard specifics of a particular poem or an historical revelation by using the soggy abstract language of archetypes or general metaphysics. Her own position derives from the theologians of radical secularity, and especially from the sectarianism of Barth. She censures purported Christian theologians who underplay the "distinctive note of Christianity," and employ "philosophical categories to the exclusion of biblical ones." Despite so partisan and fundamentalist a stance, she will not be pinned down to the support of critics like Cleanth Brooks or Randall Stewart, who she thinks reduce Christian life to a few arid, specific doctrines. In the final section of this book TeSelle at last presents her own approach to literature: the Christian should read literature as an education in wonder and openness to new aspects of human life. This seems to me a banal, evangelistic, disappointingly vulnerable alternative to the many positions she anathematizes.

THE FIGURE OF BEATRICE: A STUDY IN DANTE. This work by Charles Williams (1943) is a sympathetic and knowledgeable approach to Dante, the complement to de Rougemont's near-repudiation of the courtly love tradition as a Christian heresy. Where de Rougemont sees dualism and sexual distortions, Williams takes a more panentheist interpretation and magnifies the ideal, platonic aspects. He observes Dante's encounter with Beatrice in *The New Life,* progressing to a more intellectualized relationship with her in *The Banquet* and *The Divine Comedy,* and constructs from these elements the profound theology of love Dante implies. Beatrice, Virgil, and the city of Florence are images of divine love, of poetry and human learning, of the community. The fact of God's Incarnation makes it possible for man to discover and participate in the divine reality immanent within these icons. Williams expands the symbol of Beatrice into a paradigm of man's movement toward God through the "Way of Affirmation," or through communion and intimacy, alert to the presence of Christ even in everyday romantic love for a girl. This "Way" cannot be followed exclusively, but needs dialectical balance with the "Way of Rejection," the *Via Negativa* of the mystics, seeking God as transcendent "Other," attempting to empty oneself of images and loves. A succinct presentation of this same thesis occurs in a later essay by Williams on "The Theology of Romantic Love" (1950, pp. 62–81). I am convinced these affirmation-rejection, immanent-transcendent correlatives offer a more productive inroad into the mystery of human love than the eros-agape dialectic.

FURTHER REPRESENTATIVE TITLES

SHAKESPEAREAN TRAGEDY, ITS ART AND ITS CHRISTIAN PREMISES. Is the world view of mainstream Christianity perhaps a more useful approach to Shakespeare's fundamental premises than, say, the Hegelian perspective of A. C. Bradley? Roy Battenhouse at first seems alert to tendentious Christian readings of Shakespeare (1969, pp. 133f.). Yet he himself fixates on Augustine and the Manicheans in his own interpretations, tracking down the most strained biblical analogues, such as the pearl Othello has lost and the New Testament pearl of great price, or Othello murdering with the Judas kiss of death. He reduces complex plays to moral sermons: *Romeo* shrinks to the stature of a homily against the sin of suicide, *Hamlet* against the idolatry of love for one's father.

IMAGES OF ETERNITY: STUDIES IN THE POETRY OF RELIGIOUS VISION FROM WORDSWORTH TO T. S. ELIOT. James Benziger's book (1964) is yet another defense of the romantics as religious visionaries. Sacral categories of "presence" and "the infinite" in Wordsworth, like "eternity" for Keats, should be read as "derivatives of the whole Western religious tradition," truer to each poet's own imaginative experiences than were the dead tokens of traditional Christianity. T. S. Eliot emerges as messiah, the normative religious poet through whose perspective we can better understand the romantic poem as religious presage and dissent.

A MIRROR OF THE MINISTRY IN MODERN NOVELS. Although marred by a trivial homiletic perspective often blind to the literary qualities of a work, this Horton Davies study (1959) presents a variety of satirical or sympathetic portraits of ministers and priests in fiction. Alongside Bernanos, Greene, Frederic, and Alan Paton, are unfortunately such negligible satellites as James Street and Hartzell Spence. Davies's representative story eulogizes the minister who, as evangelist, confessor, or community leader, remains true to himself in the moment of rejection by society or his own narrow religious tradition. I was curious to uncover the dubious criteria for Davies's assessment that within his selected novels, the role of the Catholic priest was dramatized more successfully than that of the Protestant minister. The priest's distinctive functions and dress supposedly remove him more from trite plot situations centering on the moralism of respectability. Divine grace is more emphatically symbolized in the confessional than in the vaguer tasks of community leadership. Celibacy frees him for a greater variety of mobile, picaresque activities. Davies seems especially competent in explicating passages that highlight the conflict between tact and truth, expediency and Christian fidelity.

FOUR SPIRITUAL CRISES IN MID-CENTURY AMERICAN FICTION. Robert Detweiler selects Styron's *Set This House on Fire,* Updike's *Rabbit Run,* Roth's *Letting Go,* and Salinger's *Franny and Zooey.* He begins with a short plot synopsis of each book, then connects Tillich's "courage to be" with the first work, Reinhold Niebuhr's indictment of "Cultural Protestantism" with the second, Buber's personalism with the third, Zen Buddhism with Franny's self-liberation in the fourth. Each of these four theological positions evolves as the specific novel is explicated, with illustrations from character and event. Detweiler sees these particular novels "presenting individuals in dilemmas that are first characteristically human and then open to theological definition" (1964). Each portrays a religious consciousness that has discarded the traditional religious forms. Detweiler succeeds by letting the literary work itself elicit an appropriate theological stance, which the critic then proceeds eclectically to explain and correlate; he fails in too neat a reduction of a rich novel to one limited illustrative theological approach. Though not incapable of sound interpretation, he too often ludicrously transposes plot paraphrases into the ceremonious jargon of some theologian. If we play the game by Tillich's rules, for example, does Cas in *Set This House on Fire* finally accept acceptance and thereby affirm being, consciously or not?

THE NOVELIST AND THE PASSION STORY. Frederick Dillstone believes the best contempory enactments of Christ's death ought to be indirect, paradoxical accounts of contemporary life redeemed through suffering, rather than historical novels like *Ben Hur.* He selects Kazantzakis's *Greek Passion,* Melville's *Billy Budd,* Mauriac's *Lamb,* and Faulkner's *Fable.* Although unfortunately abstaining from literary assessments of his material, Dillistone speculates on the appropriate christological similarities and conflicts embodied in four different cultural traditions behind the novels. He supports a portrait of Christ that combines Grünewald's human decay and turmoil with Fra Angelico's divine dispassionate serenity. The book's outline is shrewd, but once grasped, its fulfillment becomes too predictable (1960).

THE SENSE OF HISTORY IN GREEK AND SHAKESPEAREAN DRAMA. In this book by Tom Driver, apparent divergences in style and theme between particular Greek and Shakespearean dramas are traced to two distinct ways of conceiving historical time, the Greek and Judaeo-Christian. Greek dramas usually begin near the end of an action and then recapitulate preceding events, whereas Shakespeare prefers the sequential chronicle. Or in Shakespeare the future is usually open to the truly novel, whereas the Greeks see it as closed or insignificant. Although Driver is often sensitive to the nuances of continuity and discontinuity between these two styles, and competent in his analysis of individual plays, I think his thesis on the religious origins of such complex phenomena is much too grandiose, and basically unverifiable.

First, I believe his selection of evidence provides too convenient a heightening of differences. I would expand the comparison between the entire Shakespearean corpus and a wider range of Greek dramas. Second, I challenge value judgments that ground Shakespeare's artistic superiority so emphatically on his linear concept of time. Third, no one can prove that such a notion of temporality derives from Christian faith specifically and not simply from man's sheer evolution in consciousness and interiority. Fourth, Driver consciously depends on Auerbach's preference for Hebraic rather than Hellenic narrative styles (1960b, pp. 45f.), which I have already criticized. The exaggerated dichotomy between Hebraic and Hellenic concepts of time has been repudiated by a number of biblical critics (e.g., Barr, 1961). Fifth, I would like to see this purported biblical linear time complemented dialectically by the cyclical time of Judaeo-Christian liturgical reenactment, which is no less biblical.

Most important, it seems arbitrarily inconsistent that Christianity could legitimately assimilate Hebraic categories, yet prove unable, in an appropriately disciplined development of doctrine, to assimilate Hellenic, European, American, or Far Eastern categories of experience. More recently Driver has published a clear, simplified lecture on religious-literary criticism, "The Latent Image: Literary Sources of Theological Understanding" (1968). Again he questions how traditional Christian belief in "the self-revelation of God as a *story*" can be squared with the stress in recent fiction on nontemporal form and immediacy, which presumably disregards man's growth in time. This entire temporality dilemma seems specious to me, with a trumped-up urgency. New literary styles become censoriously suspect, simply because of this constricted theological stance on time and human experience.

RELIGIOUS TRENDS IN ENGLISH POETRY. This is Hoxie Fairchild's prodigious six-volume survey, author by author, of poetic responses to the philosophic, scientific, or widely conceived religious problems of their epochs, from the eighteenth century to 1965 (1939–68). Fairchild is fearlessly outspoken, quite insightful in his general commentary though never resting too long on any particular text, and he cites his biographers and critics well. He thinks Browning a prophet of vigorous inactivity, for example, who appealed to both Victorian liberals and conservatives through a ringing challenge to be up and doing, but without disturbing the constitutional order. He judges Keats's concept of negative capability a "factitious defense-mechanism," and his idealistic letters to Fanny no more than poorly sublimated sexual releases. Fairchild scolds most of the romantics for their sentimentality and especially their arrogant creation of ersatz deities. Quite simply, the Christian believes God creates man, the "true" romantic says man creates God or *is* God. In his preface to the first volume, he flaunts his Anglo-Catholic bias candidly, cautioning his readers against its excesses. But then Fairchild reveals the secret that drove him to amass six architectonic volumes: a loud repellent hubris begging to be toppled. "I have read the work of 118 poets either completely or so nearly completely that I can hardly have missed in them anything of value for my subject" (1939, p. ix).

PROBLEMATIC REBEL: AN IMAGE OF MODERN MAN. Maurice Friedman scans Melville, Dostoevsky, Kafka, and Camus to compose a portrait of modern man, discussed in vapid incantatory existentialist clichés such as bad faith, self-fragmentation, alienation, authentic existence, the risk of absurdity, the problematic of guilt. An expert on Buber, whom he cites sparingly and judiciously in the book, Friedman knows his way through Kierkegaard and Freud, and his religious interpretations of Kafka's *Castle* and Dostoevsky's *Possessed* are especially thorough and creditable. But he plays up the shadow side of Melville and Dostoevsky simply to square them with his theme, largely derivative of Camus's *Rebel*. The authentic rebel both contends with and accepts the world, stands his own ground yet meets whatever comes, trusting that meaning can emerge from "wrestling with the absurd." Friedman gives a slippery definition to his key term "image of man": neither an ideal nor a mere description but the tension between these two. When he refers to contemporary man repeatedly as a combined Prometheus and Job, accordingly, I pick up an indecisive muddle of descriptive and normative judgments (1963).

PERSPECTIVE ON MAN: LITERATURE AND THE CHRISTIAN TRADITION. This book by Roland Mushat Frye is a loose, uneven assembly containing a few significant individual pieces, such as "Protestantism and Literary Study" (1961, pp. 171–80) on surprising humanist emphases in the early reformers, and a passable discussion of Bultmann as implicit literary critic in "Myth and Symbol" (pp. 33–56). Frye's concept of Christian faith is generous and broad enough to acknowledge religious revelation in Graeco-Roman literature and elsewhere. The rest of this book treats the literary work somewhat crudely as "the most faithful mirror of human existence which man can create," and skims over surfaces of recognized old and recent classics to glean themes of death, guilt, pilgrimage, and man's nobility.

MAN IN MODERN FICTION: SOME MINORITY OPINIONS ON CONTEMPORARY AMERICAN WRITING. In Edmund Fuller's book (1958), we have a strident complaint against Mailer, Jones, Kerouac, Tennessee Williams, Nelson Algren, and their sniveling compassion for sin and subversion, their clinical anatomical detail, and deformed bias against the "great Western, Judaeo-Christian view of man." Fuller ingenuously measures a work's greatness by the largeness and fullness of its vision of man as loving, choosing, worshipping. Instinctively he finds himself in the religious-literary ghetto because he thinks any criticism that analyzes texts and refrains from the theological assessment of beliefs is shallow. His touchstones are the Bible, Tolstoy, Dostoevsky, Romain Rolland, and the early Joyce, sources he edits into pale Sunday school classics, in an uptight petulant McCarthy era restaging of the old realism-naturalism debate from the late nineteenth century.

A CHRISTIAN CRITIQUE OF AMERICAN CULTURE: AN ESSAY IN PRACTICAL THEOLOGY. Julian Hartt supports a solid theology of culture that is not merely the apologist's prelude weaning an audience gradually to more heady doctrine, nor the old uncritical "Social Gospel" affirmation of an entire culture. If we distinguish the prevailing styles in any culture from the recessive, dissident, and prophetic forms, then each creative work of literature must be apprehended as a symbol of that culture only in this complex sense. This important point in the sociology of knowledge, Hartt's discussions of politics and mass culture, and his definition of the term religious in the chapter, "Is Civilization Itself a Religious Enterprise?" (1967, pp. 49–61) are helpful essays delineating the implied methodology in his earlier *Lost Image of Man* (1963). As applied criticism, this latter book is an undistinguished set of variations on the theme of sanctity in Greene and Eliot, and of declining erotic beauty in Durrell and Lawrence.

UNFINISHED MAN AND THE IMAGINATION: TOWARD AN ONTOLOGY AND A RHETORIC OF REVELATION. The topic is stimulating, but Ray Hart's voice is frequently solipsistic, almost unaware that theologians have been pursuing this same discussion for twenty years. His style, too, is labored, opaque, vatic, cute, with a dreadfully eccentric terminology. Yet an isolated voice can at times happen upon unique slants or not get caught in the unexamined context in which the discussion has customarily been framed. In one brilliant allusion he suddenly produces Vico's imaginative universal, Spinoza's singular essence, Hegel's concrete universal, and Dilthey's essential of an actuality, all linked to the intentionality of a work of art. Hart asks what man's creative imagination adds to the specific revelatory act of the spirit guiding the human prophet. This question prompts him to explore modes of human poetic disclosure and find analogies there for the sacred "imaginative existential" at work in Scripture. This book (1968) attempts to assemble a new fundamental theology that breaks with a strict neoorthodox approach to God's Revelation as an extrinsic vertical summons.

THE DISINHERITED MIND: ESSAYS IN MODERN GERMAN THOUGHT AND LITERATURE. From Erich Heller's collection I have already discussed "The Hazard of Modern Poetry" (1957, pp. 257–96) excerpted in the Gunn anthology. Perhaps the best piece is "Rilke and Nietzsche, with a Discourse on Thought, Belief, and Poetry" (pp. 121–77), which drives a final nail into the lid of Eliot's infamous utterance about poets feeling but not thinking: "Rilke *as a poet* is interested 'in the thought itself,' and Nietzsche *as a thinker* also expresses 'the emotional equivalent of thought'. . . ." Rilke's Angel and Orpheus symbols had a function very similar to Nietzsche's Superman and his myth of eternal recurrence. Both men resisted their epoch's dichotomy between thought and feeling, and both tried to wrest the utmost immanent spirituality from a life ceasing to be religious in its traditional forms. Other essays here and in Heller's later collection *The Artist's Journey into the Interior* (1965), though sometimes evocative, are most typically pedantic and digressive, a set of baggy generalities without the support of thorough literary analysis.

THE FAILURE OF THEOLOGY IN MODERN LITERATURE. By "failure" in this sensationalist title (1963), John Killinger means that today's theology has not made the impact on our literature that it achieved in the era of Dante and Milton. Ridiculing those preachers who think godliness in literature must imply aesthetic merit, Killinger still generates a number of thin, lengthy plot summaries to show how the moderns fail artistically because they are too concerned with God's absence, rather than with His Incarnation and Resurrection. He believes a Christian critic's principal task is to decide on the presence or absence of "the historical content of the Christian faith" in a specific text. But how shall we decide this? O'Neill's *Lazarus Laughed* is Gnostic because it lacks "the sense of an objective atonement." In spiritual quality few novels excel those of the devout Charles Williams. And "literature that reflects only the loss of God is not Christian literature, any more than a pamphlet on anarchy is pro-government." It is startling to learn that Killinger believes a reflective Christian can intuit when a work of literature has been written "in the Holy Spirit." James Street's *The High Calling*, for example, "gives me such a feeling. I cannot put my finger precisely on the thing that evokes this feeling." The really pertinent failure of theology, I think, lies in Killinger's own deficient purpose, criteria, theological method, and literary sensitivity.

THE TRAGIC VISION: VARIATIONS ON A THEME IN LITERARY INTERPRETATION. Some insightful readings of Gide, Lawrence, Mann, Kafka, Conrad, Dostoevsky, and others scarcely redeem a book written in so periphrastic and dense a style that there often seems less here than meets the eye. Murray Krieger's final chapter, "Recent Criticism, 'Thematics,' and the Existential Dilemma" (1960, pp. 228–68) summarizes and updates his earlier *New Apologists for Poetry* (1956). The main thesis is that contemporary literature at its greatest is I. A. Richards's poetry of inclusion, a literature of paradox and irony. For reality in its dramatic availability is ambiguous, dualistic, "full of extremity," and the poet always draws upon his implicit religious belief insofar as he introduces some sort of thematic order into this material. The dialectic between one's personal vision and this "Manichean face of reality" is the source of real tension and tragic profundity. I have discussed this proposition before in Glicksberg's book, and it has become a commonplace. Man must immerse himself in Camus's full experience of the absurd, Keats's negative capability, and not panic into the cop-out of Kierkegaard's leap of faith, or what Sidney Hook has called a new failure of nerve, the security blanket of dogma. I am annoyed with Krieger's obsessive repetition of the term "Manichean" with the daring shock-value of its heretical connotations, as though he were toying with a naughty word.

CHRIST AND APOLLO: THE DIMENSIONS OF THE LITERARY IMAGINATION. According to William Lynch's book (1960), "Christ" symbolizes the finite, limited, and real, whereas "Apollo" is the escapist dream, man's superhuman leap into the infinite. First there is Lynch the Christian theologian of culture, second the antiromantic social critic, and third the explicator of literature. As theologian he offers numerous fragmentary insights on Christ's authentic humanity, man's temporality and contingency, reality as an icon of God—all more or less in a difficult wedding of Reinhold Niebuhr and Catholic humanism. But Lynch in his second role merely rehashes the Hulme-Eliot-New Critic quarrel against the romantics, whom he generally excommunicates from his surprisingly restricted Christian purview. Finally as practical critic, Lynch is too eager to read angelism-Cartesianism-conceptualism-Manicheism-Gnosticism or some other doctrinal heresy into a Greene or Camus text. He has an unfortunate taste for the second-class illustration, such as the pedestrian quotes from Odets, Thornton Wilder, or Maxwell Anderson, but his readings of Dostoevsky and the Greek classics are impressive. His later *Christ and Prometheus: A New Image of the Secular* (1970), rejecting the exaggerated tensions of dialectical theology and the rotten world of alleged Manicheans like Graham Greene and the early Eliot, suggests new humanistic myths to de-escalate the heightened secular-sacred dichotomy.

LITTERATURE DU XXE SIECLE ET CHRISTIANISME. Popular apologetics is Charles Moeller's genre; lengthy plot synopses and quotes from modern literature are his decorative medium. Each of four volumes (1962–) centers on a particular theme. Volume 1, for example, follows the topic of God's silence through the works of Camus, Gide, Huxley, Weil, Graham and Julian Greene, and Bernanos—their corpus, notebooks and letters, and the evaluations of their work by various critics. The style is devotional and gently homiletic, with initial worries about each writer's orthodoxy that get quieted eventually by confident assertions of his anonymous Christianity. A characteristic Moeller passage occurs in his book *Man and Salvation in Literature,* where he first drops a few bland theological remarks on salvation, and then illustrates these by describing lovers hearing various sounds at their window in a scene from the film *Hiroshima mon amour.* Moeller continues: "A personal happiness that was not open to this window at Hiroshima would be sterile. We are together for better or worse. We are bound to the earth. It is the place of our incarnation, and salvation can only be justice and love on this earth" (1970, p. 185).

PSEUDONYMS OF CHRIST IN THE MODERN NOVEL: MOTIFS AND METHODS. Edwin Moseley takes soundings beneath the historical Christ and finds an archetype common to all religions: the spring-god messiah, a scapegoat figure that triumphs through his suffering. Thus freed from a particular dogmatic framework, Moseley is able to trace in this work (1962) interesting variations on a single pattern in a group of novels as divergent as *Crime and Punishment, Great Gatsby,* and *Passage to India.* He is generally alert as a literary critic, conscious of the relativity of influences at work in any critic's literary judgments. He thinks Whitehead and Sartre, for example, and man's increased religious awareness unconsciously affect the best critics today. His explication of *Lord Jim* deserves a few comments, because it exemplifies the hurried sacralization that mars too much of religious-literary criticism. Moseley thinks "the second half of the book is a kind of New Testament, in which the protagonist is no longer man, but a god who assumes the shape of man to show him by a life of sacrifice the way to redemption." Jim seems at first glance a scapegoat Christ; his adversary Brown is Satan. But this interpretation sidesteps Conrad's deep irony, for the portrait of Jim is mirrored through the consciousness of Stein, Marlowe, and many other ambiguous filters. Jim might also be a phony redeemer, again enacting a role that is self-destructive and romanticized, even far more so than in his earlier life.

THE PROPHETIC VOICE IN MODERN FICTION. William Mueller's book (1959) matches a different biblical theme with each novel chosen for explication—vocation in *Portrait of an Artist*, sin in *The Fall*, suffering in *Sound and the Fury*, love in *Heart of the Matter*, the Remnant in *Handful of Blackberries*. We are invited to watch modern prophets chart a redemptive road through the sickness of their own civilization, but unfortunately they are not allowed to speak in their own authentic language. The biblical labels themselves are the most superficial platitudes, applied so unimaginatively that the reader sits in bored expectancy at what the critic will discover—e.g., is Rocco a true member of the Remnant, is the excommunicated Dedalus actually beyond God's help, have the stripes of Dilsey healed the Compsons, her chastisement made them whole? These questions trivialize the work of art. Mueller ought to ask what deeper insight Kafka and Greene, for example, bring back to Mueller's hitherto unexamined biblical category, and not simply who in the novel is saved or damned according to that category.

SYMBOLISM AND THE CHRISTIAN IMAGINATION. These essays by Herbert Musurillo move through Patristic literature from Hermas and New Testament imagery, into Jerome, Basil, Augustine, to the high Middle Ages (1962). I think the best chapters are "The Growth of Early Christian Poetry" and "The Symbolism of Martyrdom and Asceticism" (pp. 45–66), the latter an introduction to the confessional genre, and the stock light-dark and love imagery in later mystical writings. Musurillo also highlights the conflict between Christian apologists and pagan humanists, and analyzes the Christian humanist's concern to express his imagination in a specifically Christian way. The approach in this book is lucid, casual, and perhaps too elementary. Yet so few theologians or literary critics today have experienced anything deeper than an introductory skimming of the early Christian Fathers, that "elementary" might prove adequate enough.

POETRY AND DOGMA: THE TRANSFIGURATION OF EUCHARISTIC SYMBOLS IN SEVENTEENTH CENTURY ENGLISH POETRY. Malcolm Ross's book is another variation on T. S. Eliot's dreary dissociation of sensibility lament, with that grand medieval synthesis shattered into fragments at the time of the Reformation. And man's post-Renaissance imagination is condemned to strain for bloodless abstractions or else hunt nostalgically for lost sacramental symbols. The culprits are Calvin's iconoclasm and Luther's passive Eucharist. After the Reformation, things are no longer seen as iconic and linked with the sacred, but as mere metaphors of the divine. A number of points must be scored against Ross's controversial thesis. Faith in the Incarnation and the Real Presence, not belief in a particular denominational theory of transubstantiation, ought to be the crucial determinant to form whatever might be specifically Christian in a Christian humanist imagination. Also, the doctrinal passages cited from poets seem scarcely probative, especially in the light of Ross's slavish enthusiasm for Eliot's own *Four Quartets* as the exemplar of Eliot's theory calling for a unified sensibility. What incautious arrogance, too, to boast that "the Christian is able or should be able to use the new symbols provided him by physics, anthropology, psychology. The non-Christian is used by these symbols" (1954, p. 245). We are told that Eliot and Auden use such symbols and are Christian; Yeats, Blake, and Lawrence are instead used, and so are not Christian. This complex link between their nominal beliefs, their operative implicit faith, and the debatable artistic value of their poetry cannot be demonstrated with such brazen facility.

THE MIND OF THE MAKER. In the spirit of the psychological axiom that what *A* says about *B* reveals as much about *A* as about *B*, Dorothy Sayers reads traditional Christian credal statements to discover what the human believer also affirms about the structure of his own mind. All theology implies an anthropology, as most theologians living after Feuerbach have insisted. "Idea, Energy, Power" (1956, pp. 45–56) is an essay on the Trinitarian structure of man's own creative imagination. Augustine's *De Trinitate* treatise, for example, forced him to piece together a complex human psychology to find paradigms for his Trinitarian God-language. "Free Will and Miracle" (pp. 69–88) suggests that a remarkable analogue for the mystery of God's sovereignty and man's freedom occurs in the way an author refuses to tamper with the autonomy of his own characters in the fictive universe emanating from his creative subconscious mind. There are moments when a reader can sense the novelist has contrived an event or personality change that seems implausible when the situation or character is viewed from the inside, as it unravels intrinsically. From a later essay collection, "Charles Williams: A Poet's Critic (1963, pp. 69–90) is a defense of Williams's Dante scholarship, and of other Anglican literary critics. The remainder of Sayers's two books of essays seem persistently mediocre in comparison with these three fine essays.

THE GOSPEL ACCORDING TO PEANUTS. For a few years Robert Short's brief work (1965) became one of the most familiar introductions to religious-literary criticism—"Good Grief!" in the words of Charlie Brown. Short presents a cloying evangelical "stand up and be counted for Jesus" sermon, illustrated by strings of biblical quotes and Charles Schulz's *Peanuts* cartoon snippets. These cartoons are cute modern parables, their ethical message too obvious and fragile to withstand clumsy elucidation by dumping out the stalest, most ponderous religious-literary clichés. The dog Snoopy in this comic strip, for example, becomes a "little Christ," the "hound of heaven," an archetypal stereotype that immediately prompts Short to cite biblical Servant passages from Isaiah and John's Gospel. When we observe Snoopy cherishing a Van Gogh in his doghouse, Short tracks down Van Gogh's remark about artists having to lead a dog's life. There are banal desultory comments on the nature of comedy and the Christian's role as apologist. I find the cartoons delightful in their own right, but the gloss by Short is paradoxically humorless, a reductio ad absurdum of the religious-literary critic's silliest pretensions.

NATURAL RELIGION IN AMERICAN LITERATURE. If we sketch two streams in the American tradition, the Hawthorne-James-Faulkner emphasis on man's contingency and sin, and the Emerson-Whitman-Steinbeck assertion of man's perfectibility, it is clear that the first, more traditional Christian "supernatural" strain has received more attention in recent years. Arnold Smithline tries to compensate for this imbalance by developing the "natural" type from Cotton Mather in 1720, Locke and Shaftesbury, Paine and Jefferson, deism-transcendentalism-naturalism-modern primitivism. This is instructive history of ideas criticism, gathering material from creative literature and other sources to exemplify themes of individual freedom, the novelty of experience, the attempts to redefine the relations between man, nature, and God (1966).

MODERN LITERATURE AND THE CHRISTIAN FAITH. Martin Turnell's book (1961) is a brief anecdotal, somewhat preachy discussion of what constitutes a "truly Christian" work of literature, and the effect of changes in belief on the style and themes of various writers. Turnell concludes that in the best literature these beliefs must be lived intuitively, not willfully imposed on one's aesthetic experience. His *Poetry and Crisis* (1938) idealizes Chaucer, Dante, Villon, and other writers from the Ages of Faith, and associates many recent artistic ills with the Reformation and modern secularization. The argument in both these books I find untenable and naively sectarian, but Turnell's brief explications are sometimes of incidental merit.

3

THEMES AND FALLACIES IN RELIGIOUS-LITERARY CRITICISM

AT THIS POINT I can summarize what seem the most animated and productive themes in the religious-literary criticism thus far analyzed.

First theme: The poem and the poet's experience, as expressions of a corporate sensibility universal to man or specific to a particular epoch.

Wilder approaches his poets as heterodox prophets, a contemporary imaginative locus of the revealing spirit. Jarrett-Kerr compares them to seismographs alert to the hidden religious tremors in their civilization. Scott, Auerbach, and the average religious-literary critic simply rely on their own taste to select appropriate novels, films, and other human symbols to frame philosophical generalizations on the typical styles and concerns of an entire era. Questions about the complex juxtaposition of dissident, recessive, and more widely endorsed styles in a specific period are treated briefly by Julian Hartt and J. Hillis Miller. Arthur Lovejoy and other scholars in the controversial domain of the history of ideas must always confront the complaint that third-rate pop literature, textbooks, box-office successes, and opinion polls are more valid criteria of a corporate sensibility than are poems by anti-social, alienated freaks. This is the major issue troubling the sociological critic, of course. But it must especially preoccupy the sensitive archetypal critic, unwilling to oscillate back and forth sloppily between the consciousness of a single man and the conjectured consciousness of a nation, or an era, or the human race.

I have mentioned in reviewing Maurice Friedman's book that he seemed unable or unwilling to decide whether his composite "Problematic Rebel" actually does, or rather ought to, represent a man living in the twentieth century. Many *Geistesgeschichte* sketches of the present epoch try to describe a new artistic or theological style. But they often forget Marx's concern not merely to report but create actively and normatively an intended style. We are aware of the manner in which *Time* and other news reportage nurture or torpedo fashions of New Theology and subcult fads simply by articulating them. However, to create means to be responsible, to exert oneself and take risks, perhaps to make mistakes.

The average religious-literary critic seems almost comfortably insulated from these concerns. He talks about the "Image of Man," "Nineteenth-Century Man," the "Christian Artist," the "American Experience," a "Catholic Sensibility," "Black Consciousness," the "Jewish Novel"—often distancing himself from the complex untidy pluralism disguised under this intemperate fondness for capital letters. We are reluctant captives to his intuitive leaps from a Roethke stanza to Roethke's vision, and then to the critic's own world view, perhaps followed by the American mind, the human condition, and even the deep purposes of a revealing God. There is need here for an exacting textual exploration, for epistemological sophistication, for a bracing purification of language by analytic philosophers, but especially for modesty. Metaphysical and religious generalities are important tools for the best critic, but they should be hard-won, tested, grounded in the particularity of R. W. B. Lewis's "Huckleberry Bushes."

Second theme: Beyond the positivism of the Anglo-American New Criticism and Christian neoorthodoxy: the relative autonomy of the poem, the relative specificity of God's revealing Word.

It is instructive to recall that one factor prompting recent formalist critics' conscientious focus on the "Well Wrought Urn" itself was their wariness of flighty, intuitive, dilettante types of criticism such as I have just described. The historical and impressionistic types of critic habitually wander irresponsibly away from the text in front of them, much in the style of current biographical and anecdotal program notes written by connoisseurs of classical music. There was also a second factor influencing their formalism. The neoorthodox Christianity of Barth, the Niebuhrs, and others is best understood as a prophetic reaction to the vague nationalistic cultural religion of the romantic era—a popularized Theodore Parker or Schleiermacher, Liberal Protestantism and "Civic Religion." At times this romantic viewpoint seemed as satisfied with the import in a poem or political inaugural as in the biblical Word that cuts vertically and passes judgment on man's culture. Thus, the slogan of both neoorthodoxy and the so-called Anglo-American New Criticism was a rigorous positivism: man must stop this cultural accommodation and metaphysics, leave social criticism to appropriate specialists, concentrate on the scientific exegesis of a text, whether it be the Bible or the poem itself (*see* Norman Cary, *Christian Criticism in the Twentieth-Century*, 1968, pp. 43–59).

Most theoretical work in the field of religious-literary criticism has strained to establish a separate peace within this wary, inhibitory regime of textual fundamentalism. Some critics have been more able than others to reconcile a somewhat strict doctrinal or biblical religious orientation with their instinctive literary sensibility. Writers from a strict Protestant Fundamentalist tradition, for example, often concentrate on patent religious themes, presuming the "Good" cannot be present anywhere without his hidden courtesan "Beauty." Those with a biblical orientation like Battenhouse spontaneously search for literal scriptural correspondences in Shakespeare, and Mueller feels the most appropriate Christian approach to literature involves matching a particular biblical theme to a modern literary text. W. H. Auden, Glicksberg, and Friedman have squared their critical insights with existentialist humanism and the Kierkegaardian crisis-thought congenial to early Barth and conservative Judaism. I have already mentioned the discomfort of TeSelle and C. S. Lewis over elusive comprehensive theories of religion, and their demand that an authentic interdisciplinary transaction can occur only between the specialist theologian representing a specific historical religion, and the professionally validated critic.

Yet other critics have experienced far less pressure from this entire dilemma. Buckley shows how a touch of Eliade and religious phenomenology can widen an otherwise confining Christian perspective, and provide a theological criterion more serviceable for reading literature drawn from a variety of religious perspectives. Moseley in a few deft steps gets behind the biblical Jesus to the more universal archetype of scapegoat or Frazer's dying king, and has little difficulty calling this a Christian myth-criticism, though its name and specificity could be challenged. Van der Leeuw submerges his restrictive neo-Calvinist anthropology beneath a tolerant history of religions perspective. "Natural Religion" is the rubric which gives Smithline access to Emerson, Whitman, and R. W. B. Lewis's "Party of Hope," rejected as heretics by Original Sin-oriented religious critics. R. W. B. Lewis and J. Hillis Miller, in the tradition of Tillich and Eliade, adopt a flexible, comprehensive approach to man's religion as functional, often expressly unnamed or denied. Lynch, Ong, Scott, and others in the Anglican and Catholic traditions have generally been able to draw upon a conciliatory via media Christian humanism, that disdains to approach the Bible as the exclusive locus of revelation. Lynch expounds the Greek myths as reverently as he would Gospel parables; Charles Williams and Auerbach treat the text of Dante almost as a sacred oracle; Wilder unhesitantly places Eliot and Stevens in the biblical company of Amos and Jeremiah.

Most religious-literary critics have eventually discarded mere defensive strategies against exaggerated formalist critics' attacks on them and have mounted a bold offensive. First, we can observe that outstanding formalists like Tate, Cleanth Brooks, Eliot, Leavis have often in their best applied criticism actually transcended the strict perimeters demanded by their own theory, especially as codified by their disciples. Moreover, they have evolved later theoretical positions that in many ways soften their occasional distorted polemics about pure poetry and the almost absolute autonomy of a text. Second, we might uncover the basically religious premises implicit in the agrarian and antiromantic roots of the Anglo-American movement itself. "Poetry and belief" has always proved a favorite topic to this group, especially I. A. Richards, Eliot, and Brooks. There is the disturbing clash between a critic's humanist faith, for example, and his intent to explicate with relative objectivity a text by Dante, pervaded by the author's commitment to Catholic doctrine. Heller, Jarrett-Kerr, and C. S. Lewis, among others, have continued this discussion very much in the context of Eliot's formulation of the dilemma. A critic's radical suspension of disbelief means tolerant openness to other positions, readiness to explore new hypothetical world views from the inside. One should accept experientially the poet's sincere faith orientation, rather than merely emphasize a strictly intellectualist avowal or repudiation of his beliefs stated in propositional form. Jarrett-Kerr, Glicksberg, Buckley, Turnell, and Krieger demonstrate that beliefs must be experienced creatively and lived to be artistically viable. C. S. Lewis most cleverly separates the roles of critic and unconscious theologian in both Leavis and Eliot; Waggoner exposes an unrecognized theology in the confidently neutral critic Irving Howe. The Christian, the agnostic, or the anti-theist who writes literary criticism is already committed to or against something or someone. Even alleged neutrality is itself a position, maintained with delicate balance between two polarities carefully understood and resisted. In the constant implicit dialogue between formalist, Freudian, sociological, archetypal, and religious-literary critics, the latter have at the very least made one important contribution. They have emphasized the pervasiveness of one's own values and unconscious theological premises within each act of literary judgment.

Third theme: Romantic literature as a religious phenomenon—anti-Christian, para-Christian, or anonymous Christian?

This third problem is a typical illustration of more specific religious-literary preoccupations. Part of the unrecognized theological heritage from the Anglo-American New Critics has been Hulme's early diatribe against the hubris of romanticism. This he ridiculed as "spilt religion," releasing man from his sinful finitude, and propelling him into the circumambient gases. T. S. Eliot and especially his American followers sustained this battle, connecting with it their penchant for assembling canons of writers in the authentic tradition, from which Lawrence, Whitman, Shelley, and most of the popular romantic poets were expelled for their immaturity or lack of philosophical seriousness. In the emerging field of religious-literary criticism, W. H. Auden, Turnell, Lynch, Fairchild, and the early R. W. B. Lewis and Scott seem to have gone through the same ritualistic antiromantic motions, in almost unreflective atavism. They justified their rejection of the romantics by various rationalizations sanctioned especially by the crisis theology fashionable from the thirties through the fifties. The romantics, obviously cut adrift from the biblical and Christian doctrinal mainstream, idolatrous in their optimistic humanism, were simply shallow "Cultural Christians" or Unitarians or pantheists. They were Lewis's naive "Party of Hope," without some corrective irony from the tradition of Kierkegaard and Reinhold Niebuhr. But most truthfully, these romantics were simply not the neoclassicists that Hulme and T. S. Eliot themselves were—that was their essential deficiency.

The weathervanes to mark a change in opinion on the romantics, quite long overdue, are books commending Whitman, Lawrence, Wordsworth, and contemporary humanist poets like Stevens and Roethke. It is fascinating to study the rapid shift of ground in Scott and R. W. B. Lewis, supported by books from Miller, Martz, Buckley, and others, within a few years of each other. Has there been a mere romantic literary revival, a cyclical switch in reading fashions; or has a change in theological positions occasioned a widening of sensibilities; or have both phenomena mutually influenced each other? The German idealists and their immanent divine spirit, which neoorthodox sectarians excommunicated, is now reclaimed through the mediation of Heidegger, modern American transcendentalists, the mystics of West and East. New fashions of Christian theology through the sixties have no doubt proved influential: the theology of radical secularity, of wonder and celebration and hope, of process thought and experience, of a newly affirmed immanence and panentheism or panenchristism. Few religious-literary critics trapped in this reversal, however, seem ready to admit their previously mistaken dogmatic bias about the nature of religion, the scope of Christian criticism, and their own inherited positivist fixations.

FALLACIES

What, then, are the characteristic fallacies to which religious-literary critics are most vulnerable? Before this century of pluralism, it used to be witty to observe that truth is one, but error multiple and thus uncategorizable. In the extended descriptive bibliographies of chapter 2, I have pointed again and again to the numberless excesses. We have impassioned witch hunting, proselytism, partisanship, the resolute or unconscious distortions of a poem, an insensitivity to the primary resident aesthetic values in a text, a penchant for grand unverified generalizations. More subtle sources of error have been suggested in the varying weak, simplistic, or totally unaware ways critics have wrestled with the three principal themes just delineated. But it is almost impossible to map out the labyrinths of pious ineptitude and downright fraud that continue to undermine the religious-literary terrain.

I suppose the most endemic religious-literary fallacy is what might be called spiritual monomania, an uptight, overconfident, obsessive singleness of vision. The more devout and serene, the more dangerous it is. This leads a Fundamentalist like Beatrice Batson to fatuous errors of artistic judgment, ranking alongside novels by Faulkner and Hemingway works by Hannah Whitall Smith, George MacDonald, and Philip Doddridge. I have mentioned Davies's susceptibility to James Street and Hartzell Spence. Even though Killinger admits the artistic crudity of Street's *The High Calling*, he still thinks of it as written "in the Holy Spirit," with "a kind of doctrinally informed sweetness" (1963). Aloysius Norton and Joan Nourse, in their anthology *A Christian Approach to Western Literature* (1961), are convinced that the Christian critical tradition, as exemplified by Chesterton, Ronald Knox, Christopher Dawson, E. I. Watkin "is in many ways a saner and more constructive one than any other known today."

Not only does this fallacy blind a critic to the literary merit of books with showy religious wrappings, but it tempts him to filter the primary literary experience through his partisan vision and vocabulary. One meets too many Christ figures, biblical symbols of garden-desert-mountain, crib-cross-pietá, sacramental water and bread. Partings are mystical dark nights, homecomings are redemptions. Friedman paraphrases Dostoevsky and Kafka into existentialist patois, Mueller into stale biblical clichés, Moeller into the sentimental argot of devotional literature, Detweiler into the conceptual jargon of Tillich, Buber, or Reinhold Niebuhr. There is usually, too, a willful moralistic drive that often suffocates the fragile aesthetic sense in this type of critic. Battenhouse, for example, misses very much of *Romeo* by concentrating on the suicides, Fuller fixates on the sexual hanky-panky in Kerouac and James Jones. Tom Driver and Robert Fitch have published a heated, enlightening exchange on Fitch's moralistic bias, unalert to a writer's use of imagery, mood, and the discipline of his craft (Fitch, 1957). This fussy censorious mentality is often joined to a sort of nervous religiosity, not actually confident of its own identity and credentials. At its most extreme, such a religion seems extrinsic, resolutely willed, fearful of itself and ready to project this fear onto scapegoats. In a less destructive form, this type of religious impulse goads a critic fretfully until he uncovers something special to distinguish Christianity or authentic religious experience from its counterfeits. Auerbach, Wilder, and Driver feel compelled to isolate some vital difference in the Judaeo-Christian style of historical narrative. Ross and Fuller must discover a dissociated sensibility or some deficiency in a person's "wholeness of vision" to account for the predetermined artistic failure of the non-Christian poet.

A REFORMULATED QUEST

In the foregoing I have synthesized and interpreted what appear to me the major figures, books, and representative topics in the field of religious-literary criticism. The tenor of my critique, I think, has been cautiously enthusiastic, dampened by mounting disaffection and impatience. The client may at first seem magnificently sound, but as the diagnosis continues there appear symptoms of an enveloping atrophy and anemia. Perhaps the transaction between religion and literature has begun to die at the very instant it completes its exciting initial phase as a fluid tentative pioneer venture. Once it crystallizes into a recognizable field, with its dignitaries and protocols, its bureaucracies, degree programs, journals, and national conventions, the field risks all the dangers of what Max Weber called a routinization of the charism. Today the religious-literary set often seem to be talking only to themselves, in a confining atmosphere of intellectual incest, too dilettantish and donnish and churchy.

I have already suggested that the best religious-literary critics might well be those who most stubbornly repudiate this partisan tag and clique, thus managing to get excluded from any of the familiar explicit bibliographies. Their dissent and solitary integrity might yet preserve the vigorous experimentation of earlier preinstitutional religion and literature exchanges. In the next two parts of this book, my intent is to step beyond the perimeters of an express religious-literary criticism I have sketched before as an arbitrary framework to clarify outlines of this field. First, in chapters 4 through 9 I shall attempt to smoke out the crypto-religious critics among the most vital literary figures of both the New and Old Criticism. Then in chapters 10 through 15, I shall hunt for the outstanding crypto-literary critics, aestheticians, philosophers of culture in recent controversial varieties of religious thought. It is by no means easy to locate this dialogic middle ground, where religious thought holds itself open to the literary experience, and differing stances of literary criticism reach down toward the *Tao* or furthermost dimension of a poem. But this unthematized religious-literary criticism will now prove, I hope, more productive and diversified than the limited field explored in the previous chapters. I am convinced there is rich new blood in the implicit religious thought among these literary critics, and in the implicit literary and aesthetic focus among these theologians and philosophers.

PART 2

RELIGIOUS ASPECTS OF LITERARY CRITICISM

4

THE LITERARY SYMBOL: AN INCLUSIVE THEORY

I SHALL introduce part 2 by clarifying my own position on the nature of literature and the act of literary criticism. Gaetano Salvemini once cautioned his own historian colleagues that no one can write strict documentaries, sterilized of troublesome passions and value judgments. Impartiality is a dream and honesty a duty. A person can try only to be intellectually candid, aware and wary of his biases, prepared to warn readers of the dangers into which his partial views may lead them. One of my insistent themes thus far has been the implicit valuing endemic to every act of literary criticism. It would be inconsistent of me to feign impartiality, ranging serenely above a battlefield where so many literary theories presume exclusive mastery, even ignoring a rival's existence.

The four presuppositions I listed at the opening of chapter 1 about the unitary act of religious-poetic experience attempted to preserve in fragile suspension the paradox of continuity and discontinuity. I defined a literary work as the symbolic actualization of a poetic experience. As a symbol—according to one fanciful etymology, "sym-bol," pressing together, folding meaning in upon itself—it has an existence of its own. It is a hypothetical universe, permeated and shaped into a fictive whole by its own formal dynamism. I do not want to reduce the symbolic reality of *Brothers Karamazov,* for example, to the genetic ingredients from which it originated in the creative mind—the psychological, cultural, religious vectors influencing Dostoevsky. Nor shall I reduce the novel simply to the myriad possible ways actively receptive readers have perceived and interpreted it by placing this novel in divergent contexts of discourse. I insist on separating the originative experience (*A*) in Dostoevsky himself, first from the embodied objective experience (*B*) virtually operative in *Brothers Karamazov,* and both of these from what informed, appreciative critics actually experience (*C*) in reading this novel.

Now this strategy may seem fastidious and needlessly complicated, but it takes account of a few crucial epistemological problems encountered in all serious aesthetic criticism. First, there is a phenomenon one can verify in his own artistic creativity and in the notebooks of any genuine artist: one does not usually begin with a clearly perceived experience, and then engage in a painful wrestling with technique until the finished artifact encapsulates the exact initial experience. On the contrary, the artist's originative experience evolves, clarifies, and transforms itself in the very process of laboring toward expression. The very actualization process is creative, drawing upon the most unforeseen subconscious impulses and materials. Dostoevsky himself can be said to have written in *Brothers Karamazov* better than he knew and planned, and his own conscious reading of the final draft is not necessarily more accurate and profound an interpretation than that given by any other critic.

Another phenomenon is closely related to this first example. In the art of music, for example, there is the creative productivity of the composer, the creative empathy of the interpretative performer, and the creative attention of the critical listener. These are three distinct, separable modes of creativity. The three sometimes combine in a single person, yet one charism often exists in isolation from the others. Thus again, the most perceptive experience of a poem (*C*) may either approximate or diverge widely from the poet's originative experience (*A*). Just as critics of novels most often are notoriously unable to write them, so novelists can be mindless critics.

The motive for this epistemological caution is escape from a set of traps familiar to most contemporary critics. The intentional fallacy reduces the objective cognitive intentionality of *Brothers Karamazov* (*B*) to Dostoevsky's conscious experience of the novel (*A*). The affective fallacy reduces this objective intentionality (*B*) to the critic's experience of the novel (*C*). However, an exaggerated compensation against these two pitfalls leads to yet a third fallacy, to which few formalist critics have given sufficient attention. I shall call this the *autotelic fallacy*.

In this autotelic fallacy, the literary work is cut adrift from the consciousness of both author and critic, between whom the work is not a medium of communication but simply a third entity. We are asked to surround the text of *Brothers Karamazov* with a nimbus of autonomy, first insulating it from the currents of political nihilism, Russian Orthodox piety, the disturbed personal life of Dostoevsky, and then also bracketing it away from our own interpretation, stained by all the personal and cultural determinants of our own times. Completely enwrapped within its own narcissistic universe, the literary symbol becomes sacral, solipsistic, resisting all attempts at interpretation. It simply *is*. The literary critic victimized by this fallacy must pretend to be a mere neutral dissector of texts, straining to cleanse himself antiseptically of value judgments—a position I believe both impracticable and dull. For his values, affectivity, and vision will be atrophied, or else operative unconsciously and therefore disastrously.

Most of these damaging exaggerations can be avoided by a fundamental shift in paradigms. The autotelist world view presumes a space filled with innumerable self-contained monads, each governed by independent formal specifications, separate worlds occasionally colliding and interpenetrating, but communicating only in the most opaque, obscure language. Such a model is pluralistic, emphasizing a strict subject-object dichtomy, and the crucial values of autonomy, integrity, clarity, discontinuity. I think the paradigm that must replace this is the universe of Dewey, Whitehead, and other process philosophers, an evolving dynamic flux without sharp breaks and fixed separated entities. Here an organism shapes its context and in turn is shaped by it. There is an ongoing, mutually conditioning transaction between the novelist experiencing, the novel experienced, and the critic experiencing. A work of literature still possesses its own organic formal identity; however, it cannot be reduced to the experience it generates or is generated by. The literary text of *Brothers Karamazov* has the status, then, of only a relative autonomy—better, a correlative or *relational* autonomy.

My initial statement in chapter 1 dramatized this paradox of relational autonomy, sidestepping the traps of intentionality, affectivity, and autotelism. I asserted with an attempt at precision that the experiential continuum of poet-poem-critic was a close affinity but not identity, that the poem partially incorporates but also surpasses the originative experience, that the critic's experience is only a partial repetition or reenactment of the experience embodied in the work. Moreover, I rejected the desirability, even the possibility of critical neutrality. The authentic critic must first participate or become an engaged insider, and only then reflect and clarify methodologically. Kierkegaard calls this first phase *repetition,* fully translating a text or creating a new context so that the work will be experienced appropriately. The model critic, then, balances an attitude of subjective empathy with one of quasi-objective understanding and assessment. These are not opposed. Whitehead calls this a combination of the moment of romance with the moment of precision. Similarly, the psychotherapist expects both engagement and disengagement, participation and observation in apprehending a client's recounted experience. As therapist, my observant-ego enlists the client's observant-ego to interpret what both of our participant-egos experience together in therapy.

Accordingly, an important phase of the critical transaction involves a confrontation of values, ideologies, sets of priorities, religions in the wide inclusive sense of my definition. This religion is a master sentiment at the root of Dostoevsky's creative act, and it permeates *Brothers Karamazov* as a structural dynamic. As genuinely participatory, the best critic opens himself wide to this dynamic, hoping to experience with another imagination, enlarge his own vision, realize how it feels to live in a universe pervaded by this religious drive. As systematically reflective, the critic then tries to articulate this experience so that he can measure his own personal values over against the values sensitively perceived, and assess how they mutually thwart or enrich each other.

I believe the literary symbol is polysemous, or laden with many potential meanings dependent on the context of critical interpretation. Vectors of meaning move within the literary work in two different directions. Insofar as the work is an aesthetic symbol it has a private meaning that turns in upon itself centripetally. Insofar as the work is more than purely aesthetic, marked by a religious dynamic, and employing words that already possess connotations wrested from other universes of discourse, its meaning extends back toward the author's consciousness and outwards toward the world centrifugally or referentially. I have called this latter movement the literary symbol's self-transcendence, which evokes a corresponding movement of self-transcendence in the critic. I see no reason for any a priori restrictions against the critic's pursuit of these centrifugal vectors moving from the heart of the text to its borders, there to confront the psychologist, the anthropologist, and the theologian of culture. He is welcome to employ any style of literary criticism and any body of knowledge relevant to the elucidation of this particular text, just so long as he can handle these proficiently, and can recognize what he is doing and why. I prefer a disciplined pluralism of critical method, dictated by the emphases and obscurities of each specific text, not a rigid systematic exploitation of a single approach.

You will observe significant parallels between the inclusive theory of criticism I am advocating and the comprehensive functional approach to the religious phenomenon I sketched in chapter 1. In fact, the restrictive autotelist literary theory I now reject corresponds closely with what I called a doctrinaire constrictive stance toward religion as specifically Christian or some other sharply outlined historical revelation. My thesis obviously is that interdisciplinary transactions are sidetracked irrelevantly or torpedoed when either party or both adhere to the restrictive literary or theological stance, but they are facilitated when either or both adopt the inclusive approach. In fact, the two inclusive positions merge serviceably into a single comprehensive religious-literary theory. I have defined as functionally religious whatever explicit or partially conscious drive, credo, or value system can be conjectured to lie behind attitudes and behavior marked by awe, commitment, moral seriousness, or simultaneous withdrawal and ecstatic communion. In a similar pragmatic reversal, I declare any style of criticism functionally valid as literary criticism insofar as it enhances understanding and appreciation of the text. And any literary criticism becomes a functionally valid religious-literary criticism insofar as it centers on the phenomena of awe, commitment, and moral seriousness.

A few of the most easily recognizable ingredients in the position I have expounded thus far are concepts introduced in the famous essays by W. K. Wimsatt and Monroe Beardsley on "The Intentional Fallacy" (1946) and "The Affective Fallacy" (1949). They attempt to deflect the critic's attention back to the work itself, away from the author and its genesis, its historical relevance and context in the literary tradition, its effect on readers. Although profiting from their warnings, I still conceive the problem less narrowly than they, and within a different paradigm. David Daiches caustically detects in Wimsatt and Beardsley the opposite ontological fallacy, which I have called autotelic. He faults them for the seductive tidiness of their theories, their excessive ingenuity of explication, the technical jargon, aesthetic puritanism, and the reductionist positivism forcing every work of literature into some straightjacket of paradox or complex inner coherence. Daiches argues that the best poetry is not the most poetical poetry, employing aspects of language that differentiate the poet's use from other types of use. Similarly, critics are not to be defined and ranked exclusively by those qualities that distinguish them from other beings. The literary work, he believes, can be elucidated in whatever way leads to increased communicative impact on the reader. It can be interpreted variously as a piece of rhetoric, a fable, a document in the mental history of its author, a reflection of the cultural climate, a unique insight into some facet of human experience (1956).

Notice in this discussion how the unconscious borrowing of formulas and paradigms from a specific tradition of criticism predetermines one's present critical options. For instance, I was predisposed initially to separate literary criticisms into those intrinsic and extrinsic to the text, until I recognized my instinctive dependence on the neat schematization presented by formalist critics Wellek and Warren in their widely influential *Theory of Literature* (1949). Alongside their own favored

"Intrinsic Approach," they list under "The Extrinsic Approach to the Study of Literature," topics such as literature and biography, literature and psychology, literature and society. E. D. Hirsch in his remarkable *Validity in Interpretation* brands such a division specious. For even the most autotelist criticism must be extrinsic to textual meanings and standards endorsed by the author, insofar as it directs attention to criteria derived from the discipline of rhetoric, the arts, or a particular literary tradition selected and created by the critic himself. "Objectivity in criticism as elsewhere depends less on the approach or criteria a critic uses than on his assumptions and biases that deflect his judgments" (1967, p. 157). Hirsch dislikes critical monism, or the lazy application of the same privileged approach and criterion to all texts. The essential task of any interpretation is to establish the appropriate intrinsic genre of a text, so that I have a valid general horizon within which to define limits and standards of meaning. His chapter on "Critical Freedom and Interpretative Constraint" (pp. 155–63) is a superior vindication of opting for any critical style "based on a broad generic idea." As an adjunct to valid interpretation, Hirsch prefers what he describes as a "judicial criticism," which means a critic's right "to search for generalities, to plump for a favored system of values, and to ignore local [textual] values when these do not suit his purposes" (p. 162).

There is one important dimension in my theory of literary criticism that might get overlooked in this dense abstract discussion. The authentic critic must be measured less by the soundness of his theoretical pronouncements, more by the quality of his applied criticism. I prefer qualified practice and theory combined, but have learned that even an interpretation grounded on a simplistic or faulty theory can still be intuitively sound and therefore of value. In my opinion, the eventual test of applied criticism must be how skillfully a single text can be elucidated in microcosm, and only then after this first step, correlated resourcefully with the macrocosm of the author's corpus, the literary genre, era, and total human situation. I support entirely F. R. Leavis's conviction that a critic must guard against "abstracting improperly from what is in front of him and against any premature or irrelevant generalizing—of it or from it. His first concern is to enter into possession of the given poem . . . in its concrete fullness, and his constant concern is never to lose his completeness of possession, but rather to increase it" (1953a, p. 213).

As a practicing critic, then, my primary focus is upon what C. S. Lewis calls the core or logos or Tao of a literary work. It is difficult to describe this religious dynamic, but Tao seems preferable to logos because it connotes a total path or way of life, a felt and lived set of values, and not merely an intelligibility to be plundered by the mind. D. H. Lawrence has perceptively named this center the metaphysic of a work. Although art is "pure passionate experience," it is utterly dependent on the artist's philosophy. "The metaphysic or philosophy may not be anywhere very accurately stated and may be quite unconscious, in the artist, yet it is a metaphysic that governs men at the time, and is by all men more or less comprehended, and lived. Men live and see according to some gradually developing and gradually withering vision," a dynamic idea unfolded in one's life and art (1922, pp. vii–xv). Helen Gardner characterizes this same search more formalistically as the "discovery of a work's center, the source of its life in all its parts, and a response to its total movement" (1959, p. 23). From a more comprehensive perspective, Stephen Spender says he looks for the Jamesian "Figure in the Carpet," an "experience of life," the "moral—or in my wide use of the word—the political life" of the literary symbol (1936, pp. 15–20).

The center of moral, political, or religious life, the vision or metaphysic in a work of literature—this is the object of the quest, no matter what a specific critic's method or rationale. From now on, I shall name it the functional *religious dynamic* or *metaphysic,* and invite readers to play the language game by my arbitrary set of rules, simply to call attention to the same reality, given such different names in this discussion by other critics. To hunt out this metaphysic, the attributes of subtlety and rigor and sensitivity are requisite. I have previously cited the approach adopted by J. Hillis Miller and R. W. B. Lewis, who try not to pounce upon the patent religious language in a text but labor to reconstruct the functional religious pseudonym, patiently following the actual evolution of persistent themes and images from page to page, and from one work to another in a single author. Stephen Spender has exemplified his efforts to recover a work's vision or "panorama of a great extent of life—perhaps of all life—surrounding a central idea or image" (1954). The focusing point of vision is often to be found in a single image, phrase, or sentence which the critic apprehends intuitively and then is able to extend as a unifying insight throughout the entire work and then far beyond it. I have already mentioned Auerbach's mastery of this technique in his famous explication of a short *Bovary* passage in widening circles of meaning. Spender's own examples strike me as accurate and instructive, though perhaps too tame. He sums up Lawrence in the image of two people in love, implying that the world might be saved if this love could be duplicated. In Proust's *Remembrance of Things Past* it is a little cake, the madeleine, the fragile center of a vision that believes time can be redeemed in the perception of a single moment. Or the words "In the destructive element immerse" for *Lord Jim*, "These fragments have I shored against my ruin" for *Waste Land*, or the single word "and" in *Finnegans Wake*.

Although his topic is literary biography and the emphasis psychoanalytical, Mark Schorer (1965) gives an engaging case study of his vigorous search for Sinclair Lewis's metaphysic. The chart of Lewis's mind is to be detected in the recurrence of certain situations, themes, images, and definite character types that seem to haunt him. This eventually gives Schorer a unifying attitude, "a general shape, or form, or rhythm," habitual "tensions or preoccupations or behavior patterns" at the heart of Lewis's experience. The prototypical situation in the novels is a character's attempt to escape from restrictions upon his freedom—from institutions, injustice, hypocrisy. These become metaphors which Schorer reads back to interpret Lewis's quarrel with his environment, then his quarrel with his own self, and the frenetic, impossible attempts to escape the restrictions of his self through an illusory freedom. Schorer stops at this relationship between Lewis's corpus and the vision that molded—and simultaneously was molded by—his own experience. It would be easy to program this discussion one step further into a *Geistesgeschichte* on freedom-restriction patterns in the American twenties and thirties, or into a study of comparative imprisonment-liberation archetypes.

Sheldon Sacks in the shrewd relentless methodology of his *Fiction and the Shape of Belief* (1966) searches out Henry Fielding's "ethical commitments, intuitive or conscious" that lie behind every artistic choice in his novels. The question Sacks addresses to *Tom Jones*, for example, is "What must this novelist have believed to have evaluated characters, acts, and thoughts in such a manner in such a work?" The critic should be cautious not to convert explicit local ethical statements in the book directly back into Fielding's governing ethical predilections. But he looks for the indirect formal signals of evaluation by which Fielding indicates how a reader should respond to a character's actions. John Hospers, too, believes that most literary works imply ethical-religious propositions about the human situation, sometimes prominently as in an Ibsen problem play, but most often indirectly, offering an hypothesis not for logical but experiential verification. Again, explicit faith statements in the text can often be expressly bypassed, but not the belief cues in an author like Dreiser, for example. Dreiser's metaphysic can be reconstructed by "observing carefully which passages contain the greatest passion and intensity, which themes are most often reiterated, how the plot is made to evolve, which characters are treated with the greatest sympathy . . . ." (1968).

With this statement of my own inclusive theory of literature, closed off to no significant impulse in the text itself or in its relationship to all virtual contexts, I propose now to make the theory a touchstone of proficiency among contemporary critics. This is my principal question: what factors in a critic's practice and theory enhance or diminish his embodiment of this ideal blueprint I have sketched? In other words, what are the religious implications of his literary criticism, or how close does he come to the religious dynamic in a literary work?

The multiplicity of modern critical voices and competing schools is staggering. And there are confusing disparities in the ways differing critics are grouped in various anthologies and literary histories, not to mention the slippery strategies and groping self-definition by which an individual critic today initiates a new movement explicitly, only to disclaim any allegiance and labels tomorrow. Yet however hazardous and presumptuous the effort to schematize these many unallied soliloquies into implicit conversations, I am convinced that mediation of this kind should always be attempted.

I intend to group all the familiar contemporary critical styles into four concentric circles of ever widening scope beyond the literary text itself. My construction of labels for these approaches is resolutely arbitrary, and I hope the terms are cacophonous and eccentric enough to resist being borrowed. The four classifications are not to be transposed into the literal-allegorical-tropological-anagogical typology of Dante's famous letter to Can Grande della Scala, nor into Abrams's mimetic-expressive-pragmatic-semantic labels, nor any other familiar schemata. I simply wish to plow into new ground, imposing fresh categories on the critical theories and performances I actually confront empirically, with minimal regard for more traditional labels, admittedly inadequate approximations anyway. For example, the rubric *New Criticism* names two differing movements in America and in France, as a label it has a confused shifting temporal relativity, and some of its most celebrated advocates dissociate themselves from the explicit name. With no pretense at exact classification, my neologisms try to introduce a resourceful overview and illusion of order into the evolving, diverging tendencies within a single movement or even within the career of one literary critic. The least I wish is that these groupings be taken as comprehensive identifications of the highly idiosyncratic figures conveniently tucked under them.

I have divided these critical trends into the following four categories, each of which I shall define and illustrate in the next four chapters. The *autotelist* surface occurs at the outside rim of concentric circles around the literary text, an area farthest isolated from the implicit religious values emphasized in my own inclusive theory of criticism, and nearest to the resident aesthetic values. Deeper successively is the circle of *humanist semiotic* criticism, next the *ortho-cultural,* and closest to the metaphysic or religious dynamic of the work, a circle of *psycho-mythic* criticism. I am somewhat trapped by the limitations of this spatial metaphor I have selected, because one could also argue for a reverse sequence, mapping the autotelist layer closest to the formalistic heart of the text, and the psycho-mythic most inclusively open to the space outside the perimeter. It is perhaps significant that the Latin word *altus* means both depth and height. However, the paradox highlighted in this circle diagram is definitely intended: Each authentic attempt to transcend the literary text itself leads to a deeper penetration into its innermost reality.

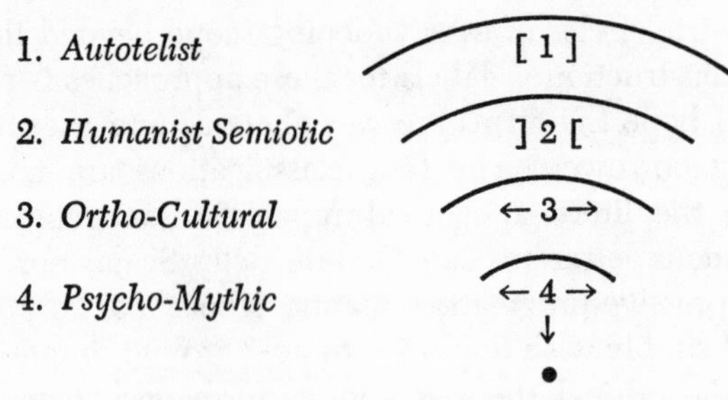

5

AUTOTELIST CRITICISM

One of T. S. Eliot's most quoted aphorisms is that "the 'greatness' of literature cannot be determined solely by literary standards; though we must remember that whether it is literature or not can be determined only by literary standards" (1936, p. 92). The autotelist critic emphasizes exclusively the final half of this statement, a focus on qualities that set the literary symbol and its appreciation apart from other objects and other human situations. This tendency is exactly what prompts single-minded aestheticians like Roger Fry and Clive Bell to analyze a painting of the Crucifixion without once mentioning the figure of Christ except as a central mass of color. Such a purist stance invites remorseless satire. Theodore Spencer's parody "How to Criticize a Poem" (1969) slyly adopts a mock pedantic tone to explicate the metrical proverb "Thirty Days Hath September," noting the ingenious ways initial capital letters of the months, the harsh "pt" sound in September, and the suspenseful alteration of chronological sequence affect the reader's "proto-response," a term he coins ponderously, as well as the phrase "fundamental dynamic." The feeling generated by the final line of the first stanza is sadness and excruciating frustration that society will not permit February one day more or less. The vices Spencer ridicules are fastidiousness, unrestrained cerebration, and the claustrophobic atmosphere surrounding a single small text. A more tragic illustration of this determined narrowing of focus occurs in Paul Goodman's *Structure of Literature* (1954), where Goodman's usual political and psychological viewpoint is displaced almost entirely by formal analysis, perhaps in constrained deference to the neo-Aristotelian criticism then in vogue at the University of Chicago. He defends this close textual method as a "prerequisite for the nonformal analysis, whether genetic or final, historical, social, or psychological," which are "not among the topics of this book; nevertheless they will often come into the discussion indirectly . . . ." In an exhaustive explication of Milton's sonnet "On His Blindness," Goodman maps the rhetorical buildup from man's initial self-justification to divine "satisfaction" and therefore divine justification (pp. 192–210). He becomes preoccupied with the mere logic of the quarrel, the techniques of meter and diction, not in the deeper religious feelings. Another book of Goodman's, *Kafka's Prayer* (1947), written in a studied professorial Freudian style, gives more express emphasis to what he calls the "religious thought" in Kafka's fiction, the "metapsychology in which the events are organized" (pp. 6, 65).

At its best, this type of criticism can be idealized in definite arrested instants of skillful explication. And the work to be explicated should be a compacted lyric poem, perhaps the furthest that language can be refined to approach the pure aesthetic moment more available in the other fine arts. I think the most successful examples are Cleanth Brooks's interpretation of Donne and Herrick philosophical lyrics (1947), and Wimsatt's use of Blake poems to illustrate the explanatory, descriptive, and explicatory phases of his own critical method (1968). Best of all is the astonishingly concise analysis of a Dylan Thomas lyric by the person whose name has been most closely identified with the explication process, William Empson (1968). These conscious virtuoso pieces almost defy modeling into a habitual style of criticism.

What is the philosophical and aesthetic basis for this austere formalism? Suggested sources are as various as the maze of attitudes from which the contemporary imagination arises (Kennick; Ellmann and Feidelson). Apparently Wimsatt, Brooks, and other more formalist types among the Anglo-American rhetorical critics have been influenced by Jacques Maritain's *Art and Scholasticism* (1943), stressing the separate ontology of each poem, linking poetic creativity, not only with the other fine arts, but also in the medieval manner with carpentry, rhetoric, and grammar. In an even more pronounced way the neo-Aristotelian "Chicago School" would claim similar parentage. Croce's aesthetic has surely generated an influence. Bergson must not be discounted, especially through the later Maritain's *Creative Intuition in Art and Poetry* (1953), and through T. E. Hulme, Bergson's impassioned British apologist. But the source most congenial to modern formalism, in my opinion, is the outstanding work in semiotics by neo-Kantians like Cassirer and especially Susanne Langer.

SUSANNE LANGER

Langer's autotelist theory is not easy to paraphrase. Her anthology *Reflections on Art* (1958) is a source book of basic materials entering into her personal theory. *Philosophy in a New Key* (1957) and *Feeling and Form* (1953) are Langer's principal works, highlighting her crucial distinction between the presentational symbol of art and the representational symbol of prose discourse. Drawn from Cassirer, this distinction is both more sharply conceived and sensitively applied than the similar emotive-referential dichotomy of I. A. Richards. Artistic form is essentially *semblance* or illusion, Schiller's *schein,* constituted by feeling that has been abstracted from worldly purposes and utility, now given self-sufficiency and otherness. The artist creates logically expressive forms. That is, he heightens direct aesthetic qualities in his original material to express a semblance of imagined objective feelings distinct from his own actual feelings. In sculpture he gives us only virtual kinetic volume, in painting virtual scene, in architecture virtual domain, in music virtual time, in literature virtual experience or events.

My inner life, for example, has definite formal properties similar to those of music: motion and rest, tension and release, proportion and fulfilment, sudden change. These are the vital forms of sentience. Since music and human feeling have a similar logical form, the composer can construct a highly articulated sensuous object to give me a tonal analogue of the feeling, life, motion, and emotion of my inner life. An art work cannot be true or false in a philosophical sense, for it asserts nothing; the artist can only be censured for not sufficiently transforming or abstracting the virtual forms from his original material. He fails in a proper semblance, in what James called *rendering* or creating an impression of felt life. Most important, Langer insists that literature, like the other fine arts, aims not to communicate or persuade, but to create only the semblance of experience: "the seriousness, strain and progress, the sense of growing knowledge, growing clearness, conviction and acceptance—the whole experience of philosophical thinking" (1953, p. 219). For example, she judges Goldsmith's "Deserted Village" a failure, not because of its content or didactic style, but only because the philosophy was not authentically integrated into the poetic gestalt.

Langer's aesthetic for me has always seemed a cogent approach to music especially, and even to a Chinese lyric poem, but it risks trivializing the problem play, the philosophical novel, epic, and most literature of apparent massive content. The theory needs to be supplemented by wider critical alternatives. Yet I have already shown how critics like Buckley, Jarrett-Kerr, and Glicksberg, for example, use Langer's canon of adequate semblance resourcefully. It is surprising to chance upon a warning issued by as confirmed a formalist as Wimsatt (1967) against misleading analyses that arise from associating literature too closely with the other fine arts. He fears the more a poem is forced to approximate painting or music, the less truly verbal it becomes.

Instead, a poem should be perceived as hyper-verbal in comparison with other types of discourse.

RUSSIAN FORMALISTS

The school of criticism giving most fervent obeisance to the autotelist ideal has been the so-called Russian formalist group, especially their work during the 1920s (Erlich, 1955; Lemon, 1965; Wellek and Warren, 1949; Wellek, 1970, pp. 275–303). There exists an English translation of four essays by the representative formalists V. Schklovsky, B. Tomashevsky, and B. Eichenbaum, including a thorough historical introduction to the movement. One of Schklovsky's pieces is fortunately a work of applied criticism, "Sterne's Tristram Shandy: Stylistic Commentary," illustrative of an heroic attention to the linguistic minutiae of the text (1965). The keynote of Russian formalism could be summed up in Roman Jakobson's motto: the subject of literary scholarship is "not literature in its totality, but literariness, i.e., that which makes of a given work a work of literature" (Erlich, 1955, p. 146).

In this movement, flourishing from 1914 until its suppression by the dogmatic political critics of the Stalinist era, I can spot at least four characteristics almost duplicated in Anglo-American rhetorical criticism. Schklovsky and Zhirmunsky denounce what they describe as the fallacy of separable content, the effort to tear ideas out of a poem and to discuss them psychologically or politically. This is no different from Cleanth Brooks's "Heresy of Paraphrase" (1947). Second, there is an ongoing battle against earlier ideological extratextual critics like Belinsky, much like the sparring by T. S. Eliot and others against Arnold and the New Humanists, and especially against impressionistic and historical academic criticism. Third, the Russian critics, in concentrating on the autonomous literary symbol, differentiate between the connotative density of poetry and the denotative clarity of scientific discourse—a replica of Langer's presentational-representational dialectic, and I. A. Richards's dichotomy between the scientific and emotive use of language (1926, pp. 267–74). Fourth, by their theory of "creative de-formation" or "deliberately impeded form," the Russian formalists recognize the ways a poet must transpose his material into symbolic form, wrenching a word from its prosaic context of stock responses, and trans-forming it by investing new rhythm and texture into it. This theme recalls Langer's symbolic transformation, and especially T. E. Hulme's plea for a new imagist poetry in his description of the poet's creative "discovery and disentanglement," straining for new freshness of form and impression. "Prose is in fact the museum where the dead metaphors of the poets are preserved," Hulme asserts in "Bergson's Theory of Art" (1936, pp. 141–70). "It is only by a certain tension of mind that he is able to force the mechanism of expression out of the way in which it tends to go and into the way he wants."

Finally, it is significant that Tynjanov, other formalists, and at last even Schklovsky retracted their strict autotelism of the 1920s, bullied by the tough Marxist historical-sociological critics in their ascendency. The formalists now confessed in the pressure of controversy that they could indeed perceive not only immanent laws at work in a text, but also transcendent relationships with extratextual concerns. Accordingly, they decided the present was an appropriate time to concentrate on the latter. This rapid conversion resembles an allegedly similar change among some American formalists during the anti-Communist fifties, when they exhibited a more patent religious and political consciousness than they permitted themselves during the isolationist thirties. But I shall discuss this dubious metamorphosis in the humanist semiotic group later. Russian formalism had an important impact in Poland and notably in Czechoslovakia, where Jakobson left the Moscow Linguistic Circle to join the Prague Linguistic Circle. Most important, it is from this Prague Circle that René Wellek emigrated to America, where at Yale his own autotelist tendencies have marked his work as prolific historian and bibliographer of recent movements in literary criticism. His books, I believe, have created an impression beyond factual evidence of the strength and pervasiveness of autotelism in American criticism.

Wellek admits the influential *Theory of Literature,* of which he is co-author, is "at least in part, a deliberate attempt to bring together the insights I had acquired as a junior member of the [Prague] Circle with my new knowledge of American criticism" (1949, p. 276). Although his personal theory is sometimes difficult to separate from a particular theory he may at the moment be chronicling, Wellek reluctantly permits interdisciplinary studies of the literary text, but only if literary criticism itself remains strictly literary and does not slide into philosophy or theology (1963, pp. 282–95). Convinced that most *Geistesgeschichte* efforts are fantastic card palaces, he endorses the Kantian and neo-Aristotelian stress on the autonomy of literature (1963, pp. 316–43; 1970, pp. 122–42).

At times a fretful arbiter of formalist orthodoxy, Wellek extols Wimsatt and Cleanth Brooks of the Yale group because they have kept "a sharp distinction between aesthetics and theology" (1963, p. 328), but anathematizes Tate's criticism after his conversion to Roman Catholicism, when the man of faith "destroyed the critic in Tate" (1970, p. 273). I especially reprove Wellek for his partisan reluctance to support the submerged religious impulse struggling for expression in Eliot's literary criticism: "Eliot is a much more satisfactory critic when he forgets about sincerity, the mare's nest of 'belief' and the whole question of the antecedents of the work of art in the mind of the poet, and turns his attention resolutely to the work of art itself as a describable object, as a symbolic world which is amenable to analysis and judgment" (1956, p. 418). Yet it is precisely because Eliot and many of his colleagues disappoint Wellek's arbitrary formalist criteria that we shall treat these critics under the humanist semiotic category of the next chapter, and not as marginal or apostate autotelists.

6

HUMANIST SEMIOTIC CRITICISM

My reason for devising the elaborate *humanist semiotic* label is my previously stated complaint about the confusions generated by the term "New Criticism." I am pointing here to a prominent critical tendency with the following characteristics. First, the literary work is essentially a *semiotic* unit of discourse, with an emphatic but relational autonomy. It is organically interrelated with the wider human *tradition* of literature, and with the functionally religious experience of both the poet and his public. Second, the critic must draw upon all his own resources as a human being, and upon semantics, the social sciences, and all available specialized knowledge to gain full understanding of the text itself. Then he must analyze his experience and articulate it. In its textual focus this movement is not autotelist but inclusively semiotic or linguistic. It is *humanist* in its concern to reconstruct an ideal cultural tradition as the appropriate context to appreciate the text as a human symbol.

Two major schools can be distinguished. The first is Anglo-American, centered originally around the religious-cultural rationale and charism of T. S. Eliot, and the explicatory techniques of I. A. Richards and William Empson. I call it *rhetorical* in the sense of a classical Aristotelian and Quintilian tradition of rhetoric, with its emphasis on the verbal texture and dynamics in a literary work. This first school includes two recognizable subgroups—F. R. Leavis and his small Cambridge circle; and the Southern agrarians Cleanth Brooks, Allen Tate, R. P. Warren, with a handful of associated critics such as J. C. Ransom, R. P. Blackmur, Yvor Winters, and Eliseo Vivas, whose articles have frequently appeared in agrarian magazines and anthologies. Here, too, I would include the bantling adversaries against this latter group, R. S. Crane, Elder Olsen, Wayne Booth, and other neo-Aristotelian "Chicago Critics," most of whose productions seem scarcely distinguishable from the movement itself except that they often read like dreary interlinear translations of the *Poetics* (Crane, 1952 and 1953).

The second school is the French structuralist or phenomenologist group, influenced by the phenomenological themes and methods of Merleau-Ponty, Heidegger, Sartre, and especially during the last decade, Claude Levi-Strauss. It includes Sartre himself, and figures like Gaston Bachelard, Georges Poulet, Roland Barthes, Albert Beguin, Maurice Blanchot, Jean-Pierre Richard, Lucien Goldmann, Michel Foucault, and others. Reacting against a previous generation of biographical and historical criticism, both Anglo-American rhetoricians and French phenomenologists favor the explication de texte method traditional to French secondary school education, with intensive quotation and commentary to reveal the total internal biology of a work.

RHETORICAL CRITICISM

Raconteurs delight to tell of the weary autotelist who, finally recognizing the constraints imposed on his method as too spartan and unexciting, capitulated and became an opportunist convert to flabby voluble religious-literary criticism. I admit some careers among the Anglo-American rhetoricians can be so interpreted, as though premature senility had loosened their tongues and made them moral sages, released from an earlier inhibitory textual positivism. Yet the empirical data of this movement's brief history can be construed more than one way. What before seemed isolated random deviations from an autotelist fixity suddenly, in a quick retrospective gestalt shift, now look like the authentic hidden dynamic. T. S. Eliot and Cleanth Brooks, for example, can be seen drifting randomly closer to a religious emphasis; on the other hand, stimulated by the corrective pressures of controversy, they may simply have clarified tendencies present from the beginning. I take the latter interpretation.

My intent here is not to regurgitate the by now familiar history of the Anglo-American group's origins, conquests, and vicissitudes (Stallman, 1949 and 1950; Day, 1966). But I intend to throw into relief the crypto-religious strain that was actually pervasive from the start. A number of books have noticed this ethical, visionary undercurrent within the entire movement. I have already cited Wellek's distress over Eliot's religious digressions, and the exposure by Buckley of the covert theology operative in Leavis's very act of denouncing so-called Christian discrimination theologians. Kathleen Nott ridicules most of these critics for their "literary neo-Scholasticism," the fuss about Original Sin and religious orthodoxy, and especially the dogmatic antiromanticism of Eliot, Hulme, and others. Ostensibly antiromantic, the content of their criticism does stress an austere classicist approach to taste and the good life, but their style and imagery have the power of a deeply felt messianic romantic sensibility.

A survey of rhetorical criticism in back issues of *Scrutiny, Explicator,* and the *Kenyon* and *Sewanee* reviews will detect the surprising recurrence of such ethical and religious topics as the problem of poetic meaning, poetry and belief, the loss of tradition, the opposition between art and science. Southern agrarian critics usually presume a myth of the pre-Civil War Southern past, after which arose all the Northern industrial vices. Socialism, big capitalism, positivism, and the bland egalitarianism of public education are only a few of the major contemporary religious heresies. In this myth there is a modern hell, a fall from grace because men have abused their fatal knowledge of technology. And there is salvation in the literate humanized life, preserved in a more deeply religious past (R. Foster, 1962; Bradbury, 1965; Karanikas, 1966; Stewart, 1965). Geoffrey Hartman suggests that the code words of rhetorical criticism are "unity, complexity, maturity, coherence," expressing a quiet nostalgia for "the ordered life; and a secret recoil from aggressive ideologies, substitute religions, and dogmatic concepts of order" (1970, p. 365).

T. S. ELIOT. At the center of T. S. Eliot's literary criticism is a myth very similar to the agrarian utopia of the Southern fugitive group. The sublime medieval synthesis of culture and religion, at its final apotheosis in an Anglo-Catholic paradise of the seventeenth century, fragmented into a dispersion of thought and feeling. In the United States, of course, the wilderness and frontier displace ruined abbeys as more indigenous metaphors for this dialectic between the machine and an idealized past. Eliot's manifesto to recover this forsaken ideal can be drawn from *Christianity and Culture* (1949), and especially the important essay of 1917, "Tradition and the Individual Talent" (1932). An authentic poet in the creative act must surrender his individualism, listen to the organic past at work in his blood, and strain to give it present expression. The poet and his poem cannot be valued alone. "You must set him, for contrast and comparison, among the dead. I mean this as a principle of aesthetic, not merely historical, criticism" (1932, p. 5). Even this early, Eliot is asserting the need for valuing and comparing, reaching beyond a rigid autotelism to embrace the living antecedents of a text.

I think Eliot should be juxtaposed and interpreted basically alongside Arnold and Irving Babbitt, Eliot's New Humanist teacher. Buckley's book on Eliot, Arnold, and Leavis (1959) has already been discussed, and his evidence that words like moral and artistic are functionally identical concepts in all three of these critics. Eliot stands for the same humane tradition upheld by Irving Babbitt, and continues the same polemic against atheistic naturalism and the innocent humanism of Rousseau and romanticism. He differs from Babbitt in his express adherence to Christian dogma, a position undoubtedly influenced by T. E. Hulme. The romantic view of man, Hulme wrote in 1913 (1936, pp. 111–40), has implied that man is good, spoilt by circumstance; the classical view that man is intrinsically limited, disciplined by order and tradition, is enunciated in the "sane classical dogma of original sin." Eliot himself says he split with Babbitt because the New Humanism was an ersatz religion that could not be sustained without a basis in historical Christian dogma. Babbitt could not "take the religious view—that is to say that he cannot accept any dogma or revelation," and his "humanism is the alternative to religion" (1932, p. 384). This assessment illustrates pointedly Eliot's rejection of another critic's inclusive functional religion because it does not conform to Eliot's own particular constrictive notion of religion. It is ironic that Babbitt's thematic criticism today often shows a religious comprehensiveness absent from the narrow textual formalism of his adversaries (McKean, 1961; R. Ruland, 1967, pp. 11–56; Levin, 1966, pp. 321–48).

Eliot's latest essays adopt a modest overview of all his previous work as critic, with a plea that his most categorical aphorisms be seasoned by recalling the date of their context, and interpreted only as handy conceptual symbols for emotional preferences of a poet turned critic. *To Criticize the Critic* (1965) categorizes Leavis as a moralist and I. A. Richards and Empson as philosophical critics. Eliot believes it "impossible to fence off *literary* criticism from criticism on other grounds, and that moral, religious, and social judgments cannot be wholly excluded." His essay "The Frontiers of Criticism" (1956) gives an unexpected parody of the explication de texte method characteristic of the tiresome "lemon-squeezer school of criticism," teasing and pressing out every drop of meaning, line by line, without a reference to the author or his corpus. Eliot's own applied criticism almost never tarries over careful textual detail—I count this a sluggish deficiency in him—but usually seizes deftly upon the metaphysic of a work, the trend in an author's entire sensibility, an illuminating comparison between texts and personalities. His essays on the Metaphysicals, the French Symbolists, and Dante are inimitable. He constantly evaluates, especially in his controversial peremptory denunciations of Milton, Shelley, and Lawrence. It is possible to view a good portion of Eliot's career as a progressive refinement of his early position on the poetry and belief theme (Smidt, 1961; Wellek, 1956, pp. 410f.).

I. A. RICHARDS. At first I. A. Richards seems the antithesis to Eliot's religious humanism, especially in his neopositivist separation of scientific referential language from poetic and religious emotive language. This distinction seems to deprive both poetry and religion of cognitive content, much in the manner of analytic philosopher A. J. Ayer's tendentious diffidence toward the status of all value language. What we easily overlook is Richards's intent, by this distinction, to preserve the integrity of both literature and religion in an age of scientific monism, so that the scientist will not treat them as sheer confused, deficient referential language. In *Principles of Literary Criticism* he asserts his conviction that "the arts are our storehouse of recorded values" (1926, p. 32). Actually this is Arnold again, and also Babbitt, desperately clinging to the values of literature when church dogma and all other beliefs seem demolished.

Eliot characteristically accuses Richards, Pound, and Babbitt of "a deracination from the Christian tradition," notably because of their immersion into Chinese philosophy (1933, p. 132). But Confucianism is broadly religious, we need not remind ourselves, and Richards shows special deference to Confucius by basing his earlier aesthetic theory in *The Foundations of Aesthetics* (1925) professedly on Confucius's *Chung Yung*. After a jejune, slipshod, often cocky survey of different aesthetic approaches, Richards and his coauthors opt for "synaesthesis," which defines the greatest art as that which contains a Confucian equilibrium of complex values and impulses, summoning all the human faculties. Here is the religious origin of that preoccupation with paradox, tension, and irony by Richards in his stimulating explications collected in *Practical Criticism* (1929), which has influenced most figures in the Anglo-American school. A few excellent specimens of Richards's ability to explicate intensively and yet reach beyond the text are his criticism of the passage from Shakespeare's *Antony and Cleopatra* (1936, pp. 64–65), Denham's "Lines on the Thames" (1936, pp. 120–23), and the implied normative reading of a Hopkins lyric (1929, pp. 80–90).

It is principally Richards who initiated the interminable debate on belief and poetry within the rhetorician school, which has almost always been carried on within the framework and terminology of his original faulty statement of the problem. Let me try to conjecture how the confusion arises, without repeating my personal solution to the problem, which I have already outlined in chapter 4. First, Richards virtually identifies the religious impulse with the literary experience, and treats both of them as noncognitive—I think this is the basic presupposition that must be controverted. Next, he views a person's beliefs as a set of cognitive referential sentences detachable from the noncognitive religious impulse itself. Yet in later years during this discussion, especially under the impact of his Coleridge studies, Richards seems occasionally to imply the religious experience, or the literary—or both—might be cognitive. Richards's conceptualization of the problem leads his followers into a series of dead ends, pleonasms, and dogged wearisome debates (Isenberg, 1968; Price, 1968; Aiken, 1967; F. Foster, 1962, pp. 47–63, 133–50). On the other hand, with conscious fidelity to the implications of Richards's original impulse and purpose, Jerome Schiller (1969) has expanded and improved the theory to include multiple perspectives on belief, especially when explicating works other than simple lyrics.

F. R. LEAVIS AND IVOR WINTERS. The moral humanism of F. R. Leavis has been mentioned recurrently in the preceding discussion, and his touchstones of discipline, maturity, and moral seriousness that he struggles to protect from the deteriorating commercialization of modern life. I find his stinging vindictive manner, as though trapped in an eternal bear pit, far more exciting than the substance of almost anything he has written. It is paradoxical to see him sparring with the formalist Wellek, accusing him of being too philosophical a critic. Wellek rips Shelley's belief out of the poem to be explicated, generalizing too quickly on Shelley's philosophy (Bentley, 1948, pp. 23ff.). Yet Leavis is outraged that he himself should be grouped with a formalist like Cleanth Brooks—"I have paid considerably more attention to relating literary criticism with other studies and disciplines, and . . . with the problems of contemporary civilization than he has done" (1953b, p. 180).

Another critic very similar to Leavis in his ethical emphasis and quarrelsome temperament—dogmatic, too, in a patronizing, surly way that I actively dislike—is Ivor Winters. He is always ranking poets, drawing up canons of poems, and attempting to liquidate imagined adversaries. His *Function of Criticism* (1957) affirms the principle that is apparent on almost every page of his applied criticism. Each literary work consists of a moral judgment with a content that is rationally apprehensible.

ALLEN TATE AND CLEANTH BROOKS. The Southern agrarians as a group are more dignified and mannerly in controversy than Leavis and Winters. Allen Tate in *The Forlorn Demon* offers two very capable essays in applied religious criticism, his studies on the themes and aesthetic sensibility of Poe and Dante. In "Ezra Pound and the Bollingen Prize" from the same collection (1953, pp. 156–60), Tate wrestles bravely with the ambiguities of his decision to vote in favor of Pound's *Pisan Cantos* despite their fascist, anti-Semitic ideas. He acknowledges that nothing comes to us as pure poetry, and thus the medium cannot be extricated from the disagreeable subject matter. In a rather slippery distinction, Tate privately rejects the philosophy but still publicly, in his role as a judge in the poetry contest, endorses the superior quality of the poetry. The Pound essay is followed by "A Note on Critical 'Autotelism'" (pp. 161–64), constituting a repudiation of a systematized critical methodology like Kenneth Burke's. Tate prefers a large loose frame of reference like Eliot's, an approach improvised and tentative.

Among the Anglo-American rhetorical critics probably the most broadly influential in the university classroom is Cleanth Brooks, especially through the Brooks and R. P. Warren *Understanding Poetry* (1960) and *Understanding Fiction* (1959) anthologies, with their compact provocative explications. A study of the three successive editions of *Understanding Poetry* itself gives evidence of Brooks's progressive odyssey. For instance, in the 1950 edition the editors remark that twelve years after the book's exclusive attention to the poem itself, they have decided to modify the book, adding an extended commentary on Eliot's *Waste Land,* and in other ways to show how history is related to poetic meaning. If Brooks's *Well Wrought Urn* (1947) has a pronounced autotelist flavor, there is scarcely anything implicit about the Christian religious stance in his later *Hidden God: Studies in Hemingway, Faulkner, Yeats, Eliot, and Warren* (1963a) and *William Faulkner* (1963b), besides the heavy religious coloration in much of his anthology *Tragic Themes in Western Literature* (1955).

In "A Concluding Note" to *Hidden God* (pp. 128–32), Brooks echoes the worries of Eliot about the tragic modern dissolution of the Christian synthesis. Now "we read literary works not so much for instruction in ideas as to learn—through a kind of dramatic presentation—what it feels like to hold certain beliefs, including the pressures exerted against belief." This sentence is a delicately phrased effort to preserve the hypothetical world of the relationally autonomous symbol, and yet make it philosophically available. Here he also quotes Tillich on modern literature as a voice of prophecy against dehumanization. Faulkner is approached as a "residual Christian," a phrase I find very appropriate, suggesting as it does that Faulkner perhaps reenacts unconsciously and remotely nearly as much of the Christian experience as certain pre-Christian writers were once said to have anticipated. Brooks's succinct essay on "Christianity, Myth, and the Symbolism of Poetry" (1962a) insists with Eliot against Arnold that literature cannot give us salvation, but it is "the prime instrument for understanding other men and other cultures and other value systems." As we would anticipate, the lens it holds up to nature is only *as if*—a distortion mirror, lens, or prism. Having advanced far beyond what a "Chicago Critic" once described as his "critical monism," Brooks calls attention to the fictionality of fiction, but concedes generously, "we surely have the right to study a work of art in any way that interests us or that makes sense of it."

ELISEO VIVAS. I suppose the most undisguised conversion within the Anglo-American rhetoricians is the career of Eliseo Vivas. In *The Moral Life and the Ethical Life* (1950) he recounts how World War II introduced the dimension of tragic irony into his shallow optimistic naturalism. He left his earlier formalist aestheticism and, under the influence of Bergson, Kierkegaard, Dostoevsky, Kafka, and Bernanos, turned to a passionately engaged moral-religious style of criticism. Although Vivas's theory of literary criticism is parceled into short essays throughout *Creation and Discovery* (1955) and *The Artistic Transaction* (1963), I think its premises can be epitomized. First, he supports the semblance theory of Langer I have already expounded, measuring the poet's ability to transmute artistically his raw subject matter into an icon of virtual feeling. The literary symbol gives us not direct conceptual knowledge of the world, but a dramatized intransitive ecstasy, a Joycean epiphany, with a meaning essentially immanent and reflexive in Dewey's sense. Vivas claims he derives this theory mostly from A. C. Bradley's distinction between the matter for and the substance of a literary work (1960, p. 286). Second, he expects the critic to go further than this, to grasp the values, the vision of the world or the moral conflict embodied in a work.

Since this second point is more crucial to our discussion, let me develop it with more precision. Vivas prepares himself by learning all he can about the rhetorical, psychological, political, and religious context of the novel to be interpreted. But he must then read the novel *intransitively*, committing himself to the aesthetic transaction, unlike those who "judge the poem by what they know of reality, instead of submitting their knowledge of reality to the frequently unpleasant, because unflattering, but usually enlarging operation of letting the poem judge their knowledge" (1963, p. 91). *King Lear*, for example, can be sidestepped as a threatening confrontation "for the person who takes too easily for granted the providential nature of God. To grasp fully the challenge involved in *King Lear*, it must be approached in the aesthetic mode" (p. 150). Vivas intends the critic after this aesthetic immersion to pass religious or political judgment on the drama, as long as he can recognize his grounds for doing so. This latter phase of criticism tries most of all to elucidate the values held by the novelist as a human being, his philosophy and attitudes prompting him to "turn from some subjects and to choose others, to misinterpret some values and to neglect others, while often doing full justice to some" (p. 200).

We have watched critics like Buckley, Glicksberg, and especially Langer winnowing literary works according to the Jamesian formula of rendering felt life, Bullough's appropriate distancing—not crudely forcing personal feeling and philosophy into the art form, but informing, trans-substancing, dramatizing. This is the indomitable theme of Vivas's applied criticism, and it is startling to observe him wring so many worthwhile insights out of it. Silone's *Fontamara* and O'Neill's *Desire under the Elms* are written according to formula, Melville's *Pierre* is a poor psychological case study, but the *Divine Comedy,* of course, is ideally semblanced. Every successful theory contains germs of a lavish reductio ad absurdum, and Vivas's *D. H. Lawrence: The Failure and the Triumph of Art* (1960) is such a parody—a clumsy, preachy, astonishingly undisciplined book. Trying to mediate between Eliot's negative and Leavis's positive assessments of Lawrence, Vivas first admits he finds most of Lawrence's ideas sophomoric and pernicious. But the Birkin-Gamekeeper primitive sexual characters are rendered successfully, whereas the Clifford-Gerald impotent types survive merely as undramatized abstractions. This thesis seems feasible, but Vivas repeats its premises incessantly, always scolding and fretting about the effect of Lawrence's ideas on the impressionable reader. There are commonplace paraphrases to commemorate Lawrence's moments of achievement, but a shrill moralistic excursus whenever the naked unsemblanced philosophy obtrudes on the surface of the text. *Lady Chatterly* is a calculated incitement to venereal pleasure, lacking artistic distance. *Plumed Serpent* is a silly conceptual tract, "pure corn," especially inaccurate in its reportage of Mexican ethnic and church customs. *Aaron's Rod* again gives proof that Lawrence has not "digested the subject he has to transmute to substance." These artistic flaws are pursued back relentlessly to deficiencies in Lawrence's personality and vitalist philosophy.

Three outstanding essays of Vivas's applied religious criticism are "Kafka's Distorted Mask," "The Two Dimensions of Reality in *The Brothers Karamazov,*" and "Dreiser, An Inconsistent Mechanist." To my taste, they combine superb intuitive attempts to reach the religious dynamic of a corpus or single work, with intensive scrutiny of specific passages. For example, Vivas analyzes *The Castle* and *The Trial*, then conjectures about Kafka's conception of existence, which Vivas differentiates from Kierkegaard's and also his own. He shows how Kafka remained inexorably faithful to the limitations of his own tragic empiricism (1955, pp. 29–46). In a quick resumé of Dreiser's corpus, he follows the author's voice as philosophic editor insisting reality is meaningless, yet Vivas contrasts this with another aspect in Dreiser that lets his characters espouse values he apparently supports with genuine secret feeling (pp. 47–72). Vivas distinguishes in *Brothers Karamazov* between Dostoevsky's actual metaphysics, and the way he dramatizes his ideas psychologically, testing them on the lips of one character, stacking up odds against them, inverting and distorting them (pp. 3–13).

PHENOMENOLOGICAL CRITICISM

Until a recent profusion of translations and commentaries, the French phenomenological critics have been relatively inaccessible to most American readers (Oxenhandler, 1960; LeSage, 1967; Fowlie, 1968). I have already noted the similarities between this group and the Anglo-American rhetoricians; there is also a deeply significant difference. The Anglo-American group seems to be straining arduously beyond an initial affirmation of the literary work's existence as a separate entity. Cautiously maneuvering between the affectivity and intentionality pitfalls, they are attempting to reclaim the detached aesthetic object within the matrix of man's unconscious life and the broader circle of his cultural tradition.

The French school seems to begin with assumptions different from these, based more on Heidegger and Merleau-Ponty than on Aristotle and the Scholastics. Almost impassive to the affectivity-intentionality warnings, they establish a firm continuum of consciousness between poet-poem-critic, much like the one elaborated before in my own critical theory, and view the work as a semiotic moment in consciousness. When I approach *Brothers Karamazov* as a critic, for example, I would not search for organizing metaphors within the novel itself, but aim first to give it a life in my own consciousness, and then attempt to describe the transaction between my own experience and this new life in my own mind. The creative act of producing the novel, the dynamic organism of the novel itself, and the moment of experience within the critic—all are an almost undistinguishable flow of consciousness. This permits the critic a tremendous release, given the scope to draw on any knowledge and critical methods available, the privilege to co-create alongside the author and repossess the literary work in each critic's own idiosyncratic way. The danger, of course, is an arrogant *eis*-egesis ("reading-in" from outside) instead of exegesis, subordinating a great work to the claustrophobic subjectivity of a second-rate critical mind. But the prospects are an unpredictably imaginative personalized style of literary criticism, instead of the detached, bookish, colorless models habitually proposed for veneration.

I observed before how J. Hillis Miller analyzes the consciousness of space and time that readers experience in meeting a figure like Hardy, for example. In a phenomenological analysis of distended space, Miller evokes a sense of emotional void, disembodiment, separation from an "Infinite Will" that is always in reserve, keeping its distance. This is the method employed by the French critics, a suggestive description of the configuration of metaphors grasped in the literary experience, the distortions and jolts and uninterrupted flow. Wallace Fowlie (1968) calls this a search for the concealed intent of a literary text, what I have described before as the functional religious dynamic. It is not a question of computing the frequency of a specific recurring theme, but an intuitive, vigilant prowling for areas in the work where its profound significance is concentrated. It probes the secret of the writer's obsessions, some original relationship between the text, its author, the modern sensibility. Structuralism at its purest is an organicism, requiring that any detail must always be referred to the intentionality of the whole. The ideal explication of a specific passage would imply the ability to catch the resonances concentrically of an entire work, of a corpus, of an era. Laurent LeSage (1967) introduces an interesting critical statement by Roland Barthes that describes this method as immanent analysis, in terms that initially sound indistinguishable from those of the Anglo-American rhetoricians. Criticism is a study "that locates itself *within* the work and establishes its connection with the world only after having described it fully from inside."

The most outstanding example I know of this creative phenomenological method, besides J. Hillis Miller's applied criticism, is Sartre's *Saint Genet, Actor and Martyr* (1963), a literate, overwhelmingly vivid portrait of Genet's total world view. Genet's very birth was a blunder and rejection, and therefore he resolutely transforms himself into this "No," with a conscious resentment and anger directed against all patronizing sympathetic readers, especially those trying to approach him only on an aesthetic level. A taboo agent for everyone, he becomes a sacred object for himself, and in a gesture of bravado invites being gazed upon as a passive object. This is a highly imaginative existential psychology, cleansed of the dogmatic pyrotechnical clichés of classical psychoanalysis. Wallace Fowlie suggests similar perspectives on a writer's entire corpus—Blanchot on Lautréaumont, Barthes on Michet, Goldmann on Racine, Richard on Mallarmé.

Another genre characteristic of the phenomenological critics is the long evocative essay on a familiar existentialist category interlaced with strings of impressionistic quotes from literature. I have in mind Georges Poulet's *Studies in Human Time* (1956) and *The Interior Distance* (1959) as especially abortive specimens. There is a web of lyrical rhetoric swirling around disjointed generalizations about man's feeling of time in different historical epochs, and attempts to synthesize in a few paragraphs the intricate corpus of major literary figures in rapid succession. Gaston Bachelard is far better, notably in *The Poetics of Space* (1964a), which employs fables and poems to help conjure up the mysterious feelings associated with corners, nests, drawers, wardrobes, and other spatial realities about which most of us probably never suspected anything could be articulated. In *The Psychoanalysis of Fire* (1964b), from a set of four books on each of the elements with a spirited introduction by Northrop Frye, Bachelard presents some intriguing slants on myth patterns, and especially the use of fire archetypes in romantics like Poe and Hoffmann. One dialectic employed is the Prometheus Complex of seizing fire versus the Empedocles Complex of giving oneself to fire (Kushner, 1963).

GEOFFREY HARTMAN. Georges Poulet is also given ungracious treatment by Geoffrey Hartman who himself professes an explicit kinship with the French phenomenologists. Poulet's analysis of Henry James's fiction superimposes his own theory of a progressively improving consciousness onto James instead of trying to discover what James is actually trying to say. Hartman's *Unmediated Vision: An Interpretation of Wordsworth, Hopkins, Rilke, and Valéry* (1954) tries to devise a method beyond the many limited partisan approaches to literature, a complete interpretation of the text that reaffirms the radical unity of human knowledge. Of the four selected poets, Hartman centers on a single poem by each, and through that poem touching the rest of the author's work, and also interpreting the poet as an expression of a particular moment of history. This book adds another supporting voice to Scott, Miller, R. W. B. Lewis, Abrams, Frye, and others in their rediscovery of an authentic religious vein in romanticism. The romantics found a sacral dimension in nature, the body, and human consciousness that was unmediated, founded not on the biblical revelation but only on the spiritual authority of their own experience. Hartman's method follows Northrop Frye's fivefold categories of interpretation.

His later book, *Beyond Formalism* (1970), continues Hartman's same approach, with a few deserving samples of practical criticism. He wants a deeper formalism than previously realized, "to redeem the word from the superstition of the word," beyond the elementary preliminaries of textual explication, situating the text "in the life of the artist, his culture, and the human community." The ideal methodology is French formalist, seeking the larger structures of consciousness, the release of a work's repressed or hidden content, what Levi-Strauss calls *mythèmes* and Frye *archetypes.* But the Anglo-American rhetoricians' respect for the objective reality of the literary symbol is a needed corrective here, for an excess of the phenomenological tendency dissolves art into a simple mirror of consciousness or social process. "Camus and Malraux: The Common Ground" (pp. 85–92) associates Camus's austere style and idealization of the desert with his antipathy to religious rhetoric and secular parodies of hope. "Hopkins Revisited" (pp. 231–46) is a skillful correlation of Hopkins's diction with his religious vision—his style shows the strain of address, attempting to get first the right pitch and immediacy in words so that he can later achieve full religious possession. "Marvell, St. Paul, and the Body of Hope" (pp. 151–72) interprets the fifth and sixth stanzas of "The Garden" in the light of Romans 8:19 and 1:20, a Pauline description of nature's contingency and yearning for redemption. Hartman shows a sophisticated awareness of the complexity here by attributing Marvell's sources not directly to the New Testament but to Renaissance influences that indirectly include Scripture. *Wordsworth's Poetry 1787–1814* (1964) presents further talented explications of individual poems. Hartman constructs out of this material a drama of Wordsworth's consciousness and maturation, with a diagnosis of the reasons for artistic flaws in *The Excursion* and his conflicts of identity as a poet.

7

ORTHO-CULTURAL CRITICISM

THE WORD *culture* in my third category, "ortho-cultural criticism," means the inclusive phenomenon that Lionel Trilling and others describe as "a people's technology, its manners and customs, its religious beliefs and organization, its systems of valuation, whether expressed or implicit" (1965, p. xi). A cultural critic accepts the literary work in all its *relatedness,* as a product of all the social and intellectual forces surrounding it—in all its *historicity* within a specific context of space and time. By the term *ortho-cultural* I want to emphasize the actively creative and normative, more than the merely descriptive function of this approach. The ortho-cultural critic attempts to repeat in the Kierkegaardian sense or to reenact the ideal context. He summons forth the model public needed to comprehend this particular literary work, the ideas and attitudes its author took for granted or felt compelled to emphasize. George Steiner says the authentically historical critic "will 'feel ahead,' he will lean over the horizon and prepare the context of future recognition." He will ask, for instance, what a new work "contributes to or detracts from the dwindled reserves of moral intelligence. What is the measure of man this work purposes?" (1967, pp. 8–9).

David Daiches has argued that since the literary experience is only one activity among many carried on by man in society, the critic's responsibility is "as much to point the way to social conditions under which literature can more adequately fulfill its function (once he has decided what that function is) as to pass judgment on works which have already been produced" (1938, pp. 277–78). We have seen this emphasis in the humanist semiotic critics, especially when they speak of recovering the moral verities and the humane tradition, or educating the reader to ask the appropriate questions of explication. But the ortho-cultural critics make this their undeviating concern. I shall split them for convenience into two divisions, the less and the more *ortho,* or consciously judicial. The first group I can describe as historical with the overtones given this term by Dilthey and modern historicist philosophers of history. Their literary historiography is not a dispassionately accurate chronicle, of course, but an imaginative reconstruction, an explication of conjectured relationships between the poet, poem, and critic in an ambience constantly fluctuating and in need of ongoing reinterpretation. I shall call the second group political, in the stricter sense of a political ideology—Liberal, Socialist, Marxist, the Left, generally with a religious creed of naturalistic humanism—but more widely, too, in the sense of an Aristotelian *polis,* and thus comprehensively social and sociological.

HISTORICAL CRITICISM

There are a staggering number of critics whose work falls under the designation historical, from vast *Kulturgeschichte* tracts to tight explications of a single literary passage, expressly dependent on scholarly footnotes and the *Oxford English Dictionary* to fix a word's limited range of meaning in a definite historical era (Colie, 1967; Edel, 1964). After skimming through the many varieties of historical criticism, Douglas Bush states his own preference for a criticism with less background and more textual emphasis, that tries to "re-create the mental worlds of the authors it deals with" (1966). Helen Gardner, too, has shown a recalcitrant concreteness in her applied criticism instead of the careless digression one might fear from the historical critic. Explicating a passage from *Macbeth* to expose the distortions in Cleanth Brooks's too inventive interpretation of the same lines in historical isolation, she beats him at his own exacting game. Gardner reminds him to begin not with his own subjectivity but with the text itself in its historical actuality, and only then turn away to find resonances in the other plays, the Bible, the mystics, and elsewhere. She trusts the significant paradox that the more I establish a work in its historical context, both the more its unique individuality will be apprehended, and the less it will seem merely an unexceptionable period piece (1959). If the historical critic's basic temptation is to wander beyond the resident artistic values in literature, then an exemplary unconscious parody of this occurs in Will and Ariel Durant's popular *Interpretations of Life: A Survey of Contemporary Literature* (1970). In a style of unmitigated gusto, they introduce details about the authors' lives because the Durants admit writers frequently seem more interesting than the characters in their works. And poems are treated ingenuously as philosophical statements often unhappily obscured by tricky imagery and diction.

As an extended illustration of the countless shapes of historical criticism, I shall select a group of examples, almost all of which deal with manifest religious content. They will be distributed under five arbitrary headings, progressing from a text's immediate ambience to a broad cultural history. First, there is the historical critic who researches into an author's notes, letters, prefaces, and obiter dicta to help grasp the genesis and undigested ingredients of the literary work. Edward Wasiolek's prefaces to each of the collected Dostoevsky *Notebooks* (1967–71) summarize the evidence and give amazingly informative clues to interpreting the novels. Stavrogin in *The Possessed,* for example, in earlier drafts of the novel mouths many of Dostoevsky's favorite religious ideas, yet in the final text appears almost spilled out and silent, the residue of his former ideas now split dialectically and parceled out to different characters, expressly contrived to stand as Doubles for disparate phases of Stavrogin's growth. Wasiolek's own book *Dostoevsky: The Major Fiction* (1971) gives this material an even more literate, coherent development, with a sure intuitive grasp of Dostoevsky's metaphysic. Further examples in this first category would also include some types of critical biography, especially those which emphasize the correlation between biographical and literary symbolism. Leon Edel suggests that the very form Hawthorne gives to *Scarlet Letter,* "the manner in which he has related it to history, the words he has used, his choice of phrase and color, and above all his symbolic images, are all, in the end, symbols of himself, signatures of his inner being" (1967).

My second set of examples point to the wider historical context behind a total corpus or a single work. Naresh Guha's *W. B. Yeats: An Indian Approach* (1968) unearths a range of Indian religious influences on Yeats besides the customary Neoplatonism, Kabbala, alchemy, Swedenborg, and Böhme background. His evidence includes Yeats's themes, aspects of his symbolism, his correspondence with Tagore, and his early interest in Theosophy. A similar, more relentlessly detailed comparison occurs in *Joyce and Aquinas* by William Noon (1957), which investigates Joyce's texts, notebooks, correspondence, to find out not only his earlier obvious applied Aquinas, but also the later, better assimilated affinities of outlook between these two figures. Noon is careful to show how Joyce modifies the Aquinas strain by perspectives derived from Vico and neo-Kantians. Martin Kallich's *Other End of the Egg: Religious Satire in Gulliver's Travels* (1970) does not miss the political, moral, and literary dimension of this partially realized fantasy, but concentrates mostly upon the implied viewpoints on doctrine, ritual, and church polity that Swift attacks.

In the third category I shall include criticism that reconstructs within a group of writers the corporate context behind them. George Steiner's *Tolstoy or Dostoevsky* (1959) plays upon the philosophical dialectic between these two rival figures. He suggests the tenuous possibility that specific fictive characters in the work of each novelist actually lampooned progressive stages in the other novelist's development. Helen White's *Metaphysical Poets* (1936) devotes a few chapters to each poet, offering generous historical and biographical materials interspersed with scattered explications. There are separate essays on "Mysticism and Poetry," "The Intellectual Climate," and "The Religious Climate." Unlike the present century, the arena of sectarian church controversy in an era like the seventeenth century is so prominent that explicit religious can be more neatly separated from other intellectual influences. Robert Petersson's *The Art of Ecstasy: Teresa, Bernini, and Crashaw* (1970), with especially fine plates on the sculpture, bridges three disciplines and three national cultures to establish a common zeitgeist, an idiosyncratic baroque sense of movement and style, notably its devices to represent Teresa transported outside of time (cf. Praz, 1958). Martha England and John Sparrow in *Hymns Unbidden: Donne, Herbert, Blake, Emily Dickinson, and the Hymnographers* (1966) introduce a topic literary historians usually neglect, the influence of hymns and oratory on the diction and often ironic religious tone of specific poets. Watts and the Wesleys themselves shaped earlier poems of the metaphysicals into hymns. Just as Donne's stylistic mannerisms register his deep sense of incoherence and disorder around him, so Dickinson records her anxieties by rough antitheses, abrupt breaks in meaning, lapses from rhyme, frequent usage of the dash to preserve paradox and involuted syntax. In the same way that she rejected the religious practices of her family, so the skeptical themes of her lyrics and the twisting of conventional hymnody rhymes and meters express her religious questioning and rebellion. Brian Dendle's *Spanish Novel of Religious Thesis, 1876–1937* (1968) establishes a background of anarchism and anticlericalism during this period, and after sampling characteristic themes decides that the novel with an agnostic perspective is generally more successful artistically than the thesis novel. As anticipated, the doctrinaire novelist is often betrayed into nonsemblance, an ingenuous recourse to direct authorial comment, stock mouthpiece characters, and bungling satire to peddle his philosophy.

The fourth group of samples attempt to map out the wider milieu of an entire literary period. Meyer H. Abrams's definitive *Mirror and the Lamp: Romantic Theory and the Critical Tradition* (1958b), for instance, follows the line of romantic ideas in aesthetics, "philosophy, ethics, theology, and in the theories and discoveries of the natural sciences." He associates the shift in style from Johnsonian neoclassical to Coleridgean romantic literary criticism, with a paradigm revolution that pictures the human mind as a creative projector rather than a passive reflector. His *Natural Supernaturalism: Tradition and Revolution in Romantic Literature* (1971) is a magisterial synthesis, although the theme has become a recent commonplace, as I have shown in discussing Scott, R. W. B. Lewis, Hartman, and others. Wordsworth is taken as the examplar of a group ranging from Blake and Coleridge to Hegel, Schiller, and Hölderlin, with common themes, styles, and ways of feeling and imagining. They preserved a religious anthropology but reinterpreted it in terms of the prevailing ego and nonego dialectic. They attempted a metaphysics of reconciliation, which involved a personal odyssey from the opposed fragments of experience to an organic synthesis. Most of these romantics in their apocalyptic yearnings for a new earth and moral utopia moved from an earlier stance of political revolution to an interiorized revolution of the imagination, from political to imaginative radicalism. Abram's interpretation of Hegel's *Phenomenology of Spirit* as an ambitious *Bildungsroman* autobiography is an especially talented reading of a complex and demanding book.

Other illustrations of this fourth category include Perry Miller's books on the Puritan epoch, especially *Errand into the Wilderness* (1956). The essay "From Edwards to Emerson" I consider a landmark in articulating essentially this same transition from biblical to natural religion described by Abrams. Emerson is a Puritan discarding the husks of dogma, with the same passionate need to worship that gripped Edwards the theologian. Edwards thought God's glory so dominant that man could scarcely be distinguished as an entity separate from the divine mind. It is a short step from this near-monism to the pantheism or panentheism of Emerson's immanent "Oversoul"—flavored, of course, by German idealism, Swedenborg, and the *Bhagavad-Gita*. Miller's chapter on "The End of the World" about apocalyptic themes and imagery in the Puritan imagination also deserves to be read alongside Abrams's chapter on the New Earth utopic vision of the romantics. Miller covers the romantics more specifically in other books, especially in *Nature's Nation* (1967). Like Perry Miller, Basil Willey is fascinated by the religious dimensions of seventeenth and nineteenth century literature (1934 and 1949), notably in the philosophy of Arnold and Carlyle, and in the spiritual aeneid of George Eliot as a symbol of the era's vicissitudes in belief. In a little-known but perspicacious essay on "Christianity and Literature," Willey complains that so-called Christian critics are too apt to start being Christian before they have finished being critical (1958). They need a wider concept of Christian religion that embraces values such as sincerity, wit, and technical mastery.

The fifth and last category of historical criticism comprises what has been called "History of Ideas" criticism, tracking the evolution of a specific theme within one period or in a longer tradition. Here a dialectical stream of ideas occupies the foreground of attention rather than their specific embodiment in concrete literary works or in other sources. The most obvious name associated with this type of literary criticism is Arthur Lovejoy, principally in *The Great Chain of Being* (1961) and *Essays in the History of Ideas* (1960), which pursue a theme through literature, religion, politics, science, and attempt to test its presence at the root of popular tastes, pieties, and prejudices. Lovejoy has claimed that his exploration centers not so much on the obvious words or phrases naming an idea as on the functional conditions prior to the formulation of an idea. He looks for dispositions, poses, intellectual fashions, susceptibilities, the "implicit or incompletely explicit assumptions, or more or less unconscious mental habits, operating in the thought of an individual or a generation" (1961). This is an apt description of the concealed intent upon which the French phenomenologist critics focus. The history of ideas is elusive territory, of course, especially thorny to verify, but I find Lovejoy reliable more for his sound intuitions than the cogency of his method. Lovejoy's *Essays* book develops religious implications in themes like primitivism, pride, Milton and the paradox of the "Fortunate Fall," concluding with a complete Lovejoy bibliography. Herbert Weisinger (1964, pp. 13–25) has discredited Lovejoy's method as too atomistic and ingenuous, especially if applied beyond the eighteenth century, when ideas are no longer so clearly visible on the surface of the text. Marjorie Nicolson's *Science and Imagination* (1962) and *Mountain Gloom and Mountain Glory* (1963) should be included here to illustrate the Lovejoy and Whitehead vein of intellectual history. Her first book traces the effects of the telescope and microscope on the literary imagination, theology, and other areas of experience. The second shows how a fascination with rugged mountains, vast space, the terrible and sublime developed gradually as a new category of aesthetic pleasure during the eighteenth century.

This same broad historical approach has been extended to include all the fine arts. André Malraux's *Metamorphosis of the Gods* (1960) studies different period styles of portraying the divine, gradually shoved into the background as a specific subject matter and replaced by an epiphany of ordinary physical realities. Malraux has a wide following, but I think his applied criticism indulges in the most random and vacuous generalities. Erwin Panofsky is more empirical and rigorous, to my taste. His *Meaning in the Visual Arts* (1955) distinguishes in method between pre-iconographical description, iconographical analysis, and iconographical interpretation. In the first, I observe the triangular or rectangular scheme of DaVinci's *Last Supper;* in the second, I focus on specific images and allegories, such as the way to distinguish Judas from Christ and John in the picture; in the third, I try to understand the *Last Supper* as a symbol of DaVinci's personality, of Italian High Renaissance culture, or of a specific religious attitude. Panofsky's expansive theory of art criticism could provide a necessary aesthetic supplement to the excessively autotelist art theory of Susanne Langer. His *Studies in Iconology* (1939) explores among other motifs the Blind Cupid and Father Time symbols in painting and literature. Suggesting important parallels with the religious poet's dilemma, the two-volume set of *Albrecht Dürer* (1948) shows some of the distanced, ambiguous ways a great painter copes with overt religious subject matter.

HARRY LEVIN. Often the comparative literature mantle has been an excuse for gossipy anecdotes of literary biography and artsy pedantic commentary on period styles and national temperaments. Harry Levin in *Refractions: Essays in Comparative Literature* (1966) and *Contexts of Criticism* (1957) tries to formulate an exacting methodology that reconciles aesthetics and ethics, balancing a strict formalism and an indiscriminate historical dilettantism. The ideal historical critic, then, ought to embody this basic paradox from the essay "Criticism in Crisis" (1957, pp. 251–68): "By understanding the context in which a given work was originally framed, we can detach it without undue violence and bring it into the differing contexts of our own experience. Knowledge of history leads to control of history." The historian's footnotes are not irrelevances but attempts to remove the encrustations of time. Levin's *Gates of Horn* (1963) develops this argument further. Literature is an institution, like law or the church; it is accessible to the main currents of life at large, but translates them into its own terms and peculiar forms. Literature does not reflect or reproduce ideas but refracts them. Themes are an intrinsic component of artistic structure, no less so than are lines and color.

As applied critic, Levin specializes in literary biography and the analysis of an author's entire corpus. In a series of essays on Stendhal, Balzac, Flaubert, Zola, and Proust, especially their reactions to middle class attitudes, *Gates of Horn* distills such characteristic themes as the declining Napoleonic heroic image, the woman in quest of roles beyond the merely sexual and familial, the machine, the underworld, the artist's consciousness. For each of the five novelists, Levin presents a brief literary biography and a description of the corpus, with significant remarks on each individual work. There is information on the artistic genesis and critical reception of *Bovary*, for example, a discussion of hospital and cathedral symbols in the book, its dramatic movement and theme. *James Joyce* (1960), on the other hand, is an undistinguished rambling book, which fumbles in its resolute attempts to place Joyce in literary history, stressing both his independence and the debt to tradition. *The Overreacher: A Study of Christopher Marlowe* (1952) reveals a competent grasp of Marlowe's metaphysic, the pervasive theme that also epitomizes his characteristic style—hyperbole, "the overreaching image, reinforced by the mighty line." Tamburlaine's domination, Barabbas's policy, Edward's infatuation, Faust's knowledge, all are tragedies of acting and willing to excess. Each work is amply explicated, with exhaustive statistical computations of a recurring word or image, and the use of perceptive modern counterparts to elucidate themes and characterization.

DAVID DAICHES. Unlike so many other critics, David Daiches is both first-rate theoretician and applied critic. Observe the practical critic at work in "Guilt and Justice in Shakespeare" (1967, pp. 1–25) and "Walt Whitman's Philosophy" (pp. 62–87) from his *Literary Essays*. The first gives a compressed illustration of Daiches's method, explaining his moves step by step. He wishes to mediate between extremes of reading each Shakespeare play only in its formalist autonomy, and the excessive appeal to an Elizabethan *Weltanschauung*. Accordingly, he first runs through the plays, trying to hear each one in its integrity, using his knowledge of the period as contributory or corrective only where needed. Next, he works from individual plays to "a larger view of how Shakespeare's mind and imagination were moving during certain periods of his career," then back again to each play with heightened interest and understanding. In the Whitman essay Daiches explicates individual poems, and constructs on this evidence a synthesis of Whitman's vision of man and its relation to the poet himself, society, nature, language. At the center of Whitman's poetry is a metaphysic that can be symbolized in a gesture of embracing, hailing, pointing.

In his revised second edition of *Virginia Woolf* Daiches returns to this work after twenty years, convinced that he lost himself in the technical devices of her novels, but "did not sufficiently explain what those devices were employed *for*." In other words, Daiches's conscious perspective has become progressively more teleological, closer to the religious dimension. The explications here are routine, except for his analysis of *To the Lighthouse*, which makes sense of the symbols, character groupings, use of time, the problem of communication. Disinterested in Woolf's biography, he focuses on her vision or attitude toward experience. At the center of this is her recognition of an unresolved paradox between a person's need for individuality yet also for solidarity with others. The justification for Daiches's critical focus on her metaphysic is his conviction that "whatever else literary value may be it may certainly in some of its aspects include the philosophical" (1963, p. 12).

Willa Cather (1951) I find more impressive as practical criticism. In his preface Daiches calls it a work of literary criticism and appreciation, not *Kulturgeschichte*. His tack is to see how he can structurally justify the significant portions of every work he analyzes, and to determine whether Cather successfully dominates or renders what is always an excessive richness of material. Her central vision is the conflict between pioneer and connoisseur values, how the heroic can create an appropriate culture embodying discrimination as well as zest. *Milton* is also a satisfying book. He disdains controversies over Milton's theological heterodoxy or orthodoxy, but concentrates on each work and its essential background in Milton's sensibility. Two close explicatory sections illustrate Daiches at his best: the discussion of *Samson Agonistes*, its critical reception, genre, theme, psychological and dramatic development, the poetic and symbolic aspects. Also, Daiches follows sensitively the progress of thought and feeling from stanza to stanza of the "Nativity Ode." With a sort of michievous reductionist humanism, Daiches sticks to reading Milton's corpus as a celebration of the tragic ambiguity of man. Thus he believes Milton uses his complex theological framework simply as a cosmolological metaphor of man's condition. Predictably, then, Daiches concludes that *Paradise Lost* is least artistically effective when Milton confuses his framework with the fiber of the poem. "Milton, operating as a poet rather than as a theologian, probes more deeply into man's fate than his formal scheme would seem to allow" (1957, p. 212).

I think Edwin Muir (1965, pp. 134–42) successfully catches Daiches in further instances of this same reductionism. He lists passages where Daiches refuses to interpret Joyce in terms of his anti-Catholicism or burlesque Catholicism but only as a humanist, or boils down Eliot's Anglicanism to that of the thwarted classicist, groping for order and authority. Muir retorts: first understand the item in its integrity, second agree or disagree, but do not "transform it into something else and then assess it as something else." Yet my own comment on this point is that Daiches at least confronts the functional religious issue, even if he too peremptorily translates it into the concepts of his own humanist religion. Daiches has addressed this problem in a consistent theory that can be pieced together from three random essays on religion and poetry (1952, pp. 73–95; 1964, pp. 212–26; 1967, pp. 206–25). Summarily, it is useless to grieve that Yeats had worse material to work with than Dante. For the poet must concentrate on the significant patterning of his experience, which is never confined to mere symbolic systems but always is lived outside and beyond all systems. The poet needs, not ready-made myths, "not so much a faith as a poetic principle to enable him to counterpoint against each other the different aspects of knowledge of which the modern world has made him aware" (1967, pp. 222–23). Any myths will work for the poet as long as they are complex enough to contain the tensions he experiences. As I would express it, Daiches in theory does not want the literary work to be measured against a dogmatic religious canon superimposed from the outside. The critic must accept the work and its vision, judge it artistically as a symbolic construct, and search for its metaphysic, its own functional religious dynamic. Daiches in practice, however, can be faulted for unconsciously superimposing his own extrinsic doctrinaire humanist canon.

Some of Daiches's most valuable theoretical essays occur in *A Study of Literature for Readers and Critics* (1964), *Literary Essays* (1967), and *Critical Approaches to Literature* (1956). In "The Nature of Poetry" (1964, pp. 135–95) he gives a superior explication of Milton's *Lycidas*, emphasizing the paradoxes, but insisting, too, that poetry is more than paradox. As an illustration, he stages an implied attack against formalist critics' fixation on irony, by doing a parody explication of the many paradoxes in Kilmer's "Trees," with abstruse references to Spinoza. I have shown Daiches's intense concern for the autonomy of literature. At the same time, he makes constant Arnoldian affirmations like the following: "At its highest, literary activity becomes at once comment on and epitome of all that is of value in human life" (1938, p. 12), or literature is "a unique way of communicating unique insights into the nature of human experience" (1964, p. 229). He expects the best critic to use "any means at his disposal—analytic, descriptive, histrionic, yes, even historical—to arouse alert interest, to produce that communicative impact without which all further critical discussion is useless" (1967, p. 176). Most important of all, every critical approach for Daiches, no matter how theoretically inclusive it may appear, is always tentative, partial, approximate in practice.

POLITICAL CRITICISM

In a discussion on literature and belief I. A. Richards once quipped that if we worry too much about this problem while reading a work we cease to be literary critics and become theologians or moralists. George Steiner's comment on this statement (1967) is "No, we have become men." Steiner then denounces the neutral humanism of a man who publishes 300 pages on some past writer without expressing one opinion why he should be worth reading today. The best criticism is an act "of pivotal social intelligence," moving "outward from the particular literary instance to the far reaches of moral and political argument. . . . Art is, even at its most formal remove, a critique of values, a counterproposal to life in the name of deeper possibility." This plea for an engaged criticism, passionately committed and responsible and value-oriented, is the distinguishing badge of the *political* literary critic. He does not simply tolerate the assessment of centrifugal values in a text; he believes such an act of judging is indispensable to an authentic criticism. Another characteristic of this approach that must be noted is the emphasis on the grubby concreteness of a work, its transitory, penultimate values. Thus, some of the most representative political criticism is written for periodicals as a book review or brief rebuttal in the heat of an ephemeral controversy. I have expressed difficulty before in my attempt to define a dimension of ultimate value, the religious dynamic. But this political middle range of value I am now trying to describe is what John Sirjamaki, Clyde Kluckholm, and Ruth Benedict mean by the configuration of a culture (1948, pp. 464–70), the moral patterns of behavior, deducible functionally from observing these actions empirically, the immediate this-worldly units of a specific value system or ethos. Unlike an absolute ethics, these value units provide more detailed models for appropriate everyday life, the meaning and sanctions for eating, working, human relationships. I would say that political critics in theory focus more on these immediate configurations, but in actual performance often explicitly—and always by implication—reach the level of a deeper ethics or the religious dynamic. Their preferences differ, too, in the intensity of normative, judicial passion they express about the specific social relations under discussion.

An articulate manifesto for the political critic can be found in Leo Lowenthal's *Literature and the Image of Man: Sociological Studies of the European Drama and Novel, 1600–1900* (1957), where literature is approached as an "explicit picture of man's orientation to his society: privileges and responsibilities of classes; conceptions of work, love, and friendship, of religion, nature, and art." The poet does not merely chronicle a society, but in his creative act defies or justifies its values, often helping society to reach a better understanding of itself. The critic's responsibility is essentially to translate a work's private equation of themes and stylistic norms into social equations. Lowenthal's applied criticism here is average, occasionally quite adept, as in an anlysis of the emerging island society in Shakespeare's *Tempest,* a microcosm of Renaissance configurations related to work, sleep, learning, language, and sexuality (cf. Lowenthal, 1967; Roberts; Gray). Daiches (1956) cites books by Humphrey House and John Danby to illustrate the resourceful transaction between criticism and sociology. House traces the final stability of Pip in *Great Expectations* to Dickens's unquestioned assumption about England's current economic security and the transformative power of money. And Danby shows how Spenser's concept of his insecure social place required that he hustle to display a command of all the poetic crafts, whereas Sidney's work exudes the serene private devotion to truth characteristic of a man securely at the top.

There is an outer limit to this type of literary criticism that shades into what Dwight MacDonald calls "social-cultural reportage" to describe his own work, which treats literature as one among many cultural expressions. In *Memoirs of a Revolutionist: Essays in Political Criticism* (1957), *Against the American Grain* (1962), and *Dwight MacDonald on Movies* (1969), he examines the phenomena of high culture and mass culture. Representative topics are the Hutchins-Adler "Great Books" program, the Book of the Month Club, Bible translations, parodies, dictionaries, the art film, the underground film, or the "Doris Day Syndrome" of asexual wholesomeness. Irritated to find himself relegated by *Time* magazine to its "Religion" section, he reaffirms his conversion from Marxism to MacDonald's own moral philosophy, not to any organized religion. His interest now is primarily not in whether there will be a financial depression or the United States will get along with Russia, but in the questions asked today only by the so-called religious people: What is the good life, what are the criteria of good and bad, what are the basic human needs, who am I, how can I live truthfully and lovingly? The tenor of MacDonald's practical criticism can be gathered from two perceptive movie reviews of the overambitious goals and crudity of technique in *The Pawnbroker,* the corrupt sentimentality of *Ballad of a Soldier* (1969), and two essays on the fusion of style and personality in both James Agee (1969) and Hemingway (1962).

Susan Sontag resembles MacDonald as a critic of social taste, outdistancing him in the specific literary intent and fine texture of her work. Her main books are *Against Interpretation* (1967) and *Styles of Radical Will* (1969), much of which are composed effectively in the mode of the French phenomenological critics. By the attack against interpretation she means we need less distanced, judicial academic talk about the literary text. The function of criticism should be to show how a literary work "is what it is, even that it is what it is, rather than to show what it means." She calls for an erotics of art, not just a hermeneutics. Sontag describes her work as "meta-criticism," not so much scrutinizing the work as clarifying the assumptions underlying specific judgments and tastes. Yet the intense formalistic explication of Bergman's *Persona* is inimitable (1969, pp. 123–46), her classics on pop art and science fiction have been deservedly influential in forming contemporary taste, not just in reporting it (1967). "The Aesthetics of Silence" (1969, pp. 3–34) is a complex impressionistic grasp of that moment in art when it tends toward anti-art, an elimination of the image, the mediacy and treachery of words. Sontag can be profitably read in conjunction with a similar description of art's mystical *Via Negativa* in Van der Leeuw's work already discussed. It is startling to confront the presence of religious imagery in pornographic art, a phenomenon that Sontag in "The Pornographic Imagination" (1969, pp. 35–73) explains shrewdly. Forms of total imagination, whenever we experience at the most serious, ardent, enthusiastic level, can scarcely hold off the language of transcendence, or religious encapsulation.

An absorbing controversy of the last five decades has centered on how engaged the poet and literary critic should be. Victor Erlich (1955) chronicles the uneven battle in Russia between formalists and the doctrinaire Marxists whose theory of literature seems to have overlooked the refined taste and humanism of Marx and Trotsky. Literature becomes simply an incitement to social action, a mirror of what society is or should be. A pointed illustration of what can now be recognized as a Soviet stereotype is Nikolai Bukharin's "Poetry and Society" (1953, pp. 498–514), which excoriates pure art as lifeless and decadently bourgeois, and holds a mere aesthetic criticism blameworthy of ripping the work of literature from its vital social context. Rebelling against this Stalinist dogmatism, Georg Lukács's realist criticism offers more nuanced alternatives. In *Realism in Our Time: Literature and the Class Struggle* (1962) he explores literature to find "the view of the world, the ideology or *Weltanschauung* underlying a writer's work." The individual ontological existence of *Anna Karenina*, for instance, cannot be distinguished from the social and historical context in which this novel was created. Lukács's political thesis is that a capitalist economy caused the decline from nineteenth-century interpersonal realism to the thing-fixations of naturalism. A resolute defense of Lukács's literary criticism occurs in George Steiner's "Marxism and Literature" set of essays (1967, pp. 305–92), but Sontag sees in the later Lukács only a crude variation on the mimetic theory (1967, pp. 90–99).

In the French scene LeSage portrays an era after World War II when critics were especially anxious to orient the young toward a new society. Literary criticism could only be polemical, as figures like Sartre,

Albérès, Picon, Simon practiced it, before the accession of the *Nouveau Roman* and a later generation of less political structuralists (1967, pp. 3–26; and Adereth, 1968). John Mander's *The Writer and Commitment* (1961) extends this same discussion to British literature, especially Auden and Orwell, although the activist Left never achieved the dominance it did in France. One of Mander's basic conclusions is that Auden succeeds artistically when his poetry addresses friends in an actual social context, but founders when it speaks to the entire world or a generic society.

The American version of this conflict can be traced in Daniel Aaron's *Writers on the Left: Episodes in American Literary Communism* (1961). Much of the excitement can be epitomized in the stormy history of magazines like the *Partisan Review*. Levin (1957, pp. 251–68) says the *Review*'s history from the thirties to the fifties has been a long groveling recantation of Marxism; "such militance as it still musters is centered less on causes than on personalities." MacDonald (1957, pp. 3–32, 369–72) feels he must defend whatever genuine shred of religiosity that is his own against the attacks of Sidney Hook and the *Partisan* secular radicals. Howe (1970, pp. 211–65) calls attention rather to a group predominantly Jewish, ranging beyond this magazine but whose names frequently appear in its pages, including Howe himself, Philip Rahv, Lionel Trilling, Alfred Kazin, Delmore Schwartz, Paul Goodman, Saul Bellow, and Meyer Shapiro. Their style of political criticism can be deftly characterized: a fondness for dispute and dazzling connoisseurship, a personal tone but impersonal vocabulary, an antispecialist self-conscious bravura, "melding notions about literature and politics, sometimes announcing itself as a study of a writer or literary group, but usually taut with a pressure to 'go beyond' its subject, toward some encompassing moral or social observation."

Howe gives an astute explanation for the distinctively partisan, bellicose tone in this group of critics, a style I usually find stimulating, but sometimes recklessly vengeful and carping, soured by Nietzschean *ressentiment*. The Marxism gives bite and edge to their style long after they have disavowed it. "There is something, perhaps a quasi-religious dynamism, about an ideology, even a lapsed ideology that everyone says has reached its end, which yields force and coherence to those who have experienced it. A lapsed Catholic has technical advantages in his apostasy which a lifelong skeptic does not have" (p. 246). What Howe describes so well as a quasi-religious dynamism is what I would call the functionally religious drive itself, always more encompassing and vital than any of its limited dogmatic or conceptual expressions. In this post-Marxist conversion the group sloughed off a particular dogmatic framework that had finally become constrictive of the authentic dynamism it was supposed to nurture. A favorite strategy in the literary criticism of Howe, Rahv, and others in this circle is to draw upon their conversion insight. They can recognize their own basic religious dynamism in others professing an express Christian dogmatic framework or some other specific ideology. They can identify with the drive yet repudiate its specific ideological label. I have already mentioned Hyatt Waggoner's effective rebuttal against Howe, demonstrating the way Howe's naturalistic humanism operates as a covert dogma (1967, pp. 47–58).

IRVING HOWE. Howe is an exemplary practical critic and theoretician. It is difficult to equal his description of that complex reality I have described as the religious dynamic. In *Decline of the New* he says it is an "intermediary area, between overarching ideology and local style, which has to do with [the poets'] deepest sense of human existence: their biases, insights, emotions, barely articulated values. In trying to locate this area we speak, awkwardly but perhaps unavoidably, of a writer's vision, that quality of his work for the description of which ideological pattern is too gross and stylistic detail too fine" (1970, p. 40). The introduction to *A World More Attractive* (1963, pp. 59–76) defends his own style of criticism, trying to balance careful scrutiny with a concern for "the characteristic qualities, the defining mode of vision, by which a writer can be recognized and valued; I have hoped to isolate the terms through which he confronts the experience of our time." Seeking the "moral style" of Hemingway, Faulkner, and Fitzgerald, Howe enters deeply into their work to find the "series of gestures and rituals made to serve as a substitute for a moral outlook that could no longer be summoned."

In practice, Howe's proficient discovery of this dynamic resists simple illustration, for often the flow of a whole essay consists in a nuanced exfoliation of a writer's metaphysic. The process is an indispensable part of the results. Howe sees George Orwell, for instance, as driven by a passion to correct errors, persuade, straighten things out in his own mind and in the world, and his prose therefore becomes an urgent voice, stripped of mannerisms, the issue at stake allowing no room for virtuosity or beauty. *Politics and the Novel* (1957) strings together a series of Howe's dispersed prefaces to novels, the best of which expose complex moral signatures in Dostoevsky's *Possessed* and James's *Bostonians.* From *A World More Attractive* (1963), the essay on Robert Frost (pp. 144–57) offers convincing textual explications to distinguish between the woodsy pseudo-pastoral Frost and the ironic, troubled figure of the best lyrics. Wallace Stevens's poetry is permeated with a ruthless prodding demand for joy, exploring every possible way to attempt living when freed from gods and the crisis of unbelief (pp. 158–67). In "T. E. Lawrence: The Problem of Heroism" (pp. 1–39) Howe sees Lawrence as the prototype of contemporary man, straining in *Seven Pillars* with a vision of heroism he can neither realize nor abandon. Lawrence tries to express in this book his experience as a fable of heroism, and "assign a scheme of purpose to hesitant improvisations which in the end did come to bear such purpose." Howe investigates Lawrence's correspondence to find statements of his actual motives viewed before, during, and after the revolt, a different truth than that later retrojected by the writer himself. Lawrence's book becomes a work of fierce unmasking, forcing an emergence of self in the very process of composition, trying to name some enlarging selfless purpose he never actually found. In his later years, suffering the aftermath of heroism, he experienced a sense of contingency and desolation, purely secular, that used to be associated with an era of religion.

Certainly Howe's best work is *William Faulkner.* He explicates each novel skillfully, with a separate essay on the short stories, and gradually reconstructs Faulkner's moral vision, a topic to which Howe devotes an entire chapter. The Faulknerian gesture is his characters' mark of distinct self-definition, whether of defiant outrage or submission in the face of death. "At its greatest, the gesture suggests that for Faulkner heroism signifies exposure, the taking and enduring and resisting of everything that comes between birth and death" (1952, p. 106). I favor Howe's description of the Faulknerian religious vision as post-Christian, appearing as an occasional standard of judging, a force to repudiate, a memory that troubles, a "belief picking at its own bones."

PHILIP RAHV. Rahv has a far more limited output of applied criticism than Howe. In *Image and Idea* (1949), *The Myth and the Powerhouse* (1965), and *Literature and the Sixth Sense* (1969), there appear three Dostoevsky essays investigating his intellectual development, and the political, ecclesiastical, and literary milieu behind *Crime and Punishment* and *Possessed.* "The Legend of the Grand Inquisitor" is an especially capable explication of Dostoevsky's most famous literary conundrum, not in textual isolation but as a product of Ivan's consciousness in the interplay of drama and ideology throughout the wider novel. Rahv also commends Tolstoy's creative tact, when in his greatest fiction he lets dogma interact with the "irreducible quality of life" (1969, pp. 134–49). But *Resurrection* and later fiction, of course, are casualties of Tolstoy's moral proselytism. One of Rahv's most accomplished essays is "The Death of Ivan Ilyitch and Joseph K.," which explores the world views of these two antiheroes, representing the opposed religious styles of Tolstoy and Kafka. In studies on the heroines of Hawthorne and James,

Rahv states his conviction that Hawthorne's religious attitude contrasts unfavorably with Dostoevsky's more authentic metaphysical and religious consciousness. The inherited beliefs that Hawthorne portrays are mere psychological spectres, not real moral or religious passions.

Literary criticism, as Rahv explains and practices it, must center itself on larger, more controversial problems than close textual explication—"issues of value, of belief and ideological conflict." He asks for a criticism in the synoptic mode, which employs every appropriate formalist and extratextual approach, a mode he thinks best achieved by his colleagues Howe, Trilling, and Wilson. His own bristling polemicism is a conscious attribute, which along with his hopeful realism, historical awareness, and "a measure of social and ideological commitment" he traces back to his early training in Marxism (1969, p. vii; 1965, p. 61f). Rahv's tone is often peremptory and virulent, as though he feels personally betrayed by figures like Leslie Fiedler and Norman Mailer, and threatened by beat poets and swinging young reviewers, by the new porno-aesthetics, phony avant-gardism, and any theory of criticism trying to separate morality from literature. This radical of yesterday ironically seems outmaneuvered in a game where players are now far more radical and iconoclastic than before. Irving Howe, with more disciplined composure, echoes this chagrin over the McLuhan-Marcuse-Norman Brown fad, the coarse surface hedonism and rhetoric of violence, those who merely accept the new sensibility without a willingness to judge it (1970, pp. 211–65). The problem for Liberals like himself, Howe concludes, is that the capacity for self-doubt, ambiguity, self-irony, "the reward of decades of experience, renders them susceptible to the simplistic cries of the new. . . . One may have to face intellectual isolation and perhaps dismissal, and there are moments when it must seem as if the best course is to be promiscuously 'receptive,' swinging along with a grin of resignation."

As a context for Rahv's critique of religion, I suggest his colleague Sidney Hook's *Quest for Being* (1961), notably its essays on the new failure of nerve and his debate with Van den Haag. Hook believes that the massive threat in confronting the authoritarianism of Hitler and Stalin frightened many Liberals of the forties and fifties into abandoning democratic methods of compromise and free inquiry, which so far have remained largely untried. These Liberals surrender what Howe calls their humane irony and self-doubt. Instead they have staged a cowardly escape into the protective arms of an authoritarian crisis-religion, preaching man's intellectual and moral insufficiency, his need for an extrinsic divine authority, a Kierkegaardian leap of faith. There is no doubt that the published Van den Haag rejoinder to Hook, for example, suggests a "Grand Inquisitor" use of religion as an opportunistic anodyne to comfort and consolidate the masses against a worse totalitarian secular chaos. Hook recommends his own modest style of naturalistic humanism, seeking to better the human condition without contriving a substitute secular messianism, and without acknowledging any absolutes except the right to unhindered inquiry.

Now Rahv's biting essay on "Religion and the Intellectuals" (1965, pp. 22–32) presents an argument almost identical to Hook's. Many of the Anglo-American rhetoricians first showed a failure of nerve by their ostrich-like formalism, and when this failed, they parroted variations on Eliot's escape into royalism and Anglican authoritarianism. Such a religion is suspect, for it often prizes an idolatrous tradition, church institution and dogma, and the aesthetic High Church candle more than an authentic religious experience. Rahv shrewdly suggests that their reactivated emphasis on Original Sin is probably an aesthetic demonology, a mystification about the ubiquity of evil, so that we can wash our hands irresponsibly of something irredeemable. It is understandable, with these partially justifiable suspicions in mind, that Rahv and other secular radicals adopt so defensive a stance on the express religious dimension of the literary text or the process of critical judgment. They intend to guarantee that the religion under discussion is not a cowardly dishonest substitute, a religion that believes nothing in particular, but a strictly defined, constrictive notion of religion opposed to the more inclusive theory I have tried to defend on other grounds. Rahv would be comfortable negotiating mostly with the neoorthodox Christian or the strictest supranaturalist. For he distrusts attempts "to reinterpret the concept of the divine as pure transcendence, or as the absolute ground of existence (an absolute of which nothing, however, can be demonstrably known), or, more mildly still, as a perspective uniting the real and the ideal. All such notions are wretched substitutes for the *mysterium tremendum* of a dying and rising god" (1965, pp. 23–4). In Rahv's first sentence here, three modish theological descriptions of God can be recognized successively: an excessive early Barthian notion, Tillich's "Ulitimate Concern," and Dewey's "union of ideal ends and actual conditions."

LIONEL TRILLING. The word religion has a less explosive and controversial resonance in the criticism of Lionel Trilling than in Rahv's. Trilling thinks students approach literature today mostly to explore and appropriate an authentic human impulse or organizing principle, style, consciousness, or moral sensibility. Accordingly, the literary work "now stands virtually in the place of religion and may even be thought of as itself a religion." The word spiritual is defined by Trilling as the contemporary prophetic impulse to destroy evil and specious good, questioning the mores and values of a bourgeois world (1965, pp. 57–88). Deferring to the willingness of Hawthorne and Melville, Faulkner and Hemingway to wait on a negative capability, a modest but intellectually active uncertainty, Trilling prefers to apply to them Allen Tate's word piety instead of religion. Piety implies a quality of engagement and transcendence, rather than belief in any actually formulated doctrine (pp. 209–34). As he explains in *The Liberal Imagination,* "religion in its decline leaves a detritus of pieties, of strong assumptions, which afford a particularly fortunate condition for certain kinds of literature; these pieties carry a strong charge of intellect, or perhaps it would be more accurate to say that they tend to stimulate the mind in a powerful way" (1950, p. 300).

Trilling's favorite terms are moral and cultural, which he shares consciously within the tradition of Arnold and Leavis. "Dr. Leavis and the Moral Tradition" (1956, pp. 101–106) and *The Opposing Self* essays (1955) endorse Arnold's dictum that great literature is a criticism of life. The poet quarrels with the culture by confronting it with surprise, freedom, and elevation. Or Leavis says literature gives us a "vital capacity for experience, a kind of reverent openness before life, and a marked moral intensity." The questions Trilling addresses to every literary work are these: "Is this true, is this to be believed, is this to shape our future judgments of experience?" Even if the work itself signals clearly that such questions are irrelevant, then the critic still asks, "What is being implied about logic and truth by this willful departure from logic and truth?" For "the judgment of literature is overtly and explicitly a moral and intellectual judgment. The cogency, appositeness, the logicality, the *truth* of ideas must always be passed upon by literary criticism" (1956, p. 135). Trilling does not hesitate, for instance, to indict writers like O'Neill, Dos Passos, and Thomas Wolfe for the disproportion between their passion of utterance and a deficient intellectual capital. He thinks the aesthetic achievement depends partially "upon the amount and recalcitrance of the material the mind works on, and upon the mind's success in mastering the large material" (1950, p. 295).

We can select four skillful brief explications to show the quality of Trilling's applied criticism: Wordsworth's "Immortality Ode," Wharton's *Ethan Frome,* Tolstoy's *Anna Karenina,* and James's *Princess Casamassima.* The text of the "Ode" is closely analyzed, linked with Wordsworth's philosophy, his era, his opinion of himself as an artist, and is contrasted with Coleridge's parallel "Ode." Wordsworth's experience of preexistence is described by Trilling as a serious conceit vested with delimited belief, a currently popular idea with suggestive validity (1950, pp. 129–59). Trilling believes *Ethan Frome* the result of a purely literary impulse, in the worst sense of that word. It embodies a morality of biology, inertia, necessitated suffering, an ethic of mere superficial social demand, lacking depth and authentic tragedy (1956, pp. 31–40). Tolstoy's moral imagination or moral vision consists of a steady equalized affection for every one of his characters, all at the mercy of the actual and trivial, which is of the greatest but not final importance (1955, pp. 66–75). Trilling associates the James novel with a wide context of nineteenth-century anarchist political activity, and analyzes his technique of indirection that generates the imagination of disaster (1950, pp. 58–92).

"A biography of Arnold's mind" is Trilling's description of *Matthew Arnold* (1939), and this phrase also could characterize *E. M. Forster* (1943). His purpose is to present Arnold's thought in its complex unity, without the distortion of composing it into a system, and to relate it to the historical and intellectual background. Human isolation, religious doubt, the experience of nature—Trilling draws these themes from the poetry and essays, to articulate Arnold's vision or philosophy. The metaphysic reconstructed in *Forster*, a far more satisfying book than *Arnold*, is the relaxed will, the paradox of comic seriousness. Forster teases and plays with his characters to uncover what is most deeply human underneath the shibboleths. A conflict that begins between two moral absolutes usually develops by suggesting ambiguity on both sides, undermining any heroism. *Passage to India* receives an especially fine analysis, notably on the ultimate dimension of the book's central problem—is Hinduism or any religion able to heal divided relationships, once Mrs. Moore discovers that Christianity is inadequate? Forster's achievement, in Trilling's final interpretation, is to accept man in the world without the sentimentality either of rationalism or cynicism.

EDMUND WILSON. Wilson clearly has become an institution, basically unshaken by decades of oscillating ideologies and critical fashions around him. In "Thoughts on Being Bibliographed" (1950, pp. 105–20) he calls himself only a journalist, analyzing and shaping forms of current public taste, expressing himself in topical reviews that are provisional, expecting later revisions. The two earliest goals of his career were to introduce Marxism and the "new" literature of Joyce, Eliot, and Proust. The inscription-dedication to Christian Gause in *Axel's Castle* (1934) asserts what would become Wilson's motto of literary criticism: "a history of man's ideas and imaginings in the setting of the conditions that have shaped them." He sees himself in the tradition of Vico, Herder, Taine, DeQuincey, Poe, and Shaw. Like so many of the great critics in this epoch, Wilson impatiently carves his path midway between autotelism and artless extratextual social commentary. He does not want detached aesthetic appreciation, especially when it is artificially restricted only to the field of lyric verse, but a criticism that raises the crucial moral and political issues, and terminates after historical and biographical study in an assessment of a work's full value (1952, pp. 243–55). Yet he reproaches the party hack who forces literature to conform to mechanical partisan slogans. In "The Economic Interpretation of Wilder" (1952a, pp. 500–503), written in 1930, he spots the banal Marxist presuppositions behind a critical impeachment of Thornton Wilder by Michael Gold. Wilson's "Marxism and Literature" (1952a, pp. 266–89) underscores Engel's intuition that the great novelist allows his political ideas to remain hidden in the work of art. Marxism can tell the critic little about the artistic value of a work, except to throw light on its origin and social significance. Short-range literature propagandizes, but long-range literature can trap a Leftist critic capable only of extracting the overt moral and not the real purport. It is usually true "in works of the highest order that the purport is not a simple message, but a complex vision of things, which is not explicit but implicit." The essay "André Malraux" (1952a, pp. 566–74) synthesizes Wilson's approach to a text in the form of these fundamental questions: Where is the author's own center? What is his frame of reference? What is his view of the human situation?

This complex vision is Wilson's term for the metaphysic, the quest for which can be demonstrated in a few of his most brilliant, widely anthologized essays in practical criticism. *Axel's Castle* gives the quintessence of a whole epoch in the image of Villier's Axel, a solitary Faustian character insulated in his castle, fearing to risk disillusioning confrontation. The recent symbolists had turned not to love, politics, travel, but to the interior kingdom of the imagination, the autotelic art object itself. "Dickens: The Two Scrooges" (1947, pp. 1–104), after a superior sketch of the social and psychological background, and the progressive emergence of each novel from this context, uncovers a manic-depressive impulse at the root of Dickens's heightened appetite for melodrama. Dickens's corpus can be interpreted as an incomplete effort at self-dramatization. In the earlier books, characters manifest extremes of good and evil, with the evil often reformed, whereas in a late novel like *Edwin Drood,* Dickens manages to turn one of the principal characters into a Raskolnikov dual personality. "Philoctetes: The Wound and the Bow" (pp. 272–95) is an especially thorough scrutiny into this Sophocles play—its unusual genre, the modern relevance of its symbolism, the characteristic dionysian psychology at work in this and other Sophoclean plays, and finally a mythic interpretation of the play itself.

A familiar attribute of Wilson's criticism is its stubborn contrariety. He is often accrediting a neglected historical anomaly, or dethroning a figure canonized by fellow critics or by mass culture. Aldous Huxley and Scott Fitzgerald lack sufficient intelligence and experience of life. Hemingway discovered Marx rather late, something bigger than hunting and bullfighting, but in retrospect his whole corpus seems a courageous response to every pressure of the era's moral atmosphere. The neglected late Kipling developed far beyond the romantic jingoism of his earlier popular fiction. Especially significant are a few of Wilson's express religious judgments. In "A Dissenting Opinion on Kafka" (1950, pp. 383–92) Wilson refuses to accept Kafka as either a great artist or a moral guide. With a pronounced dislike for his childish respect and fear, the stuffy atmosphere of bourgeois family life and boring commercial activity, Wilson prefers to read Kafka as a satire on bureaucrats and parasites, rather than a parable of man before God. Critics should stick to the human rather than the divine dimension here.

"Spendors and Miseries of Evelyn Waugh" (1950, pp. 298–305) is a demolishing critque of *Brideshead Revisited.* When Waugh loses his satiric veneer, the snobbery and sentimentality become shamelessly uncontrollable. Wilson himself, "unsympathetic by conviction with the point of view of the Catholic convert," suspects that in the final scene of *Brideshead* mere nostalgia for the aristocratic past evokes a meretricious sense of religious reverence. The novel is a Catholic tract insufficiently rendered. In *A Piece of My Mind: Reflections at Sixty* (1956, pp. 1–18) Wilson replies to Christian theologian critics of his *Dead Sea Scrolls* book (1969) by pitting against each other a dishonest review versus a favorable review, both by Catholics, and then another supportive review by a Presbyterian. Wilson finally expresses relief at his own freedom from these authoritarian church shackles that limit the intellectual integrity of those attacking him. He ridicules the modern Christian who professes orthodox conformity and yet, as a human being, must trim down credal absurdities to broad humane rationalizations.

8

PSYCHO-MYTHIC CRITICISM

My FOURTH and final category, "psycho-mythic," embraces critics with the most ambitious purposes of all. Little about them is petty; even their failures are colossal self-parodies. Bruce Harkness's "The Secret of *The Secret Sharer* Bared" is a clever satire on the traps awaiting the psycho-mythic critic. Conrad's novelette becomes a morass of homosexual ambiguities, which Harkness with a sort of manic sleuthing exploits and reduces to the Hyacinthine archetype. Phallic symbols are ubiquitous, there are significant repetitions of the word "queer." "Cramp," a word Conrad employs, could easily be mistaken at sea for "camp." Harkness asserts confidently that the Captain is Apollo and his Double is Hyacinth. Any obvious major detour from these mythic parallels is lamely explained as "more powerful for its lack of closeness to the original myth" (1969, pp. 91–101).

Just as semiotic critics are incipiently, sometimes emphatically orthocultural, so most of the critics already discussed in part 2 are psychomythic insofar as they achieve an encompassing perspective *in-depth.* The overt focus in this criticism is psychological, in the most comprehensive sense of an individual and social psychology: an analysis of all the significant inner forces within the literary work's total context. This includes first the novelist's creative act in relation to its genesis in his own conscious and unconscious life, and in his whole society. Second are the patterns of meaning in the work itself as an integral symbol of his imagination, and most obviously, the forces influencing character behavior in fiction. Third is the critic's experience of the work as an act of identification, displacement, projection, catharsis, and as an activation of social archetypal drives and expectations. I consciously reject the name "psychoanalytic" in describing this psychological criticism because its accurate usage is to define classical Freudian analysis, and it often tends to exclude alternative approaches. Freud's theory of personality, art, and culture has an experimental verifiability no more authoritative than the psychology of Jung, Adler, the functional and behavioral schools, and especially the "third force" contemporary humanistic, existential, phenomenological movements in psychology. The influence of none of these schools ought to be minimized simply because of doctrinaire polemics.

In his essay "Cultural Anthropology and Contemporary Literary Criticism" (1966, pp. 129–36) Haskell Block complains justifiably that "myth" is one of the most muddled, abused terms in our critical vocabulary. "It is perhaps an important feature of our modern mythomania that its converts are willfully obscure." To clarify at least a few assumptions, I shall define myth as a symbol, usually in the pattern of a narrative or dramatic ritual, expressive of the deepest meaning of microcosm and macrocosm. Unlike Rudolf Bultmann's famous definition of myth, this does not necessarily suggest a two-story universe, or the portrayal of supranatural beings. The word "expressive" in my definition toys with an epistemological ambiguity—one myth may actually express this meaning in a specific historical culture, whereas an apparently nonmythic literary work, for example, may function as a myth, and thus be potentially expressive to the critic able to create the appropriate responsive context. Myth implies an actual or potential framework of collective belief. When the critic speaks of Faulkner's myth, for example, he intends to reenact it in a new imaginary social context or bring it to the foreground as the actualization of an archetype in the Jungian collective unconscious.

I would describe as psycho-mythic, then, the critic who in his conscious orientation draws upon the contributory sciences of psychology and anthropology to explore this inner individual-social meaning in a literary work. My arbitrary division of these critics will be the familiar psychological and mythic classifications. More analytic in style, focusing mostly on a scrutiny of the individual person, the first group employs a more explicit psychological vocabulary, usually Freudian. The second group, interested more in play, cult, ritual, and archetypes, uses rather the language of Jung, transactional social psychology, and anthropology. It seeks a perspective more global, comparative, architectonic.

PSYCHOLOGICAL CRITICISM

The parodies of criticism in this first classification are especially keen, and instructive to analyze. Frederick Crews, a scholar in the field of psychological criticism, in his "A. A. Milne's Honey-Balloon-Pit-Gun-Tail-Bathtubcomplex" (1969) imitates the bombastic, self-important style of an awkward translation from the German. He begins by conscripting Freud's support for the artist, quoting favorably and trying to reinterpret Freud's grossest statements about art as a neurotic defense. The task is to search the literary work for traces of the author's crudest perversions that he would have manifested if he had not sublimated them by artistic activity. When no evidence is found for a specific tendency, one verifies that this tendency is present but repressed. Milne's delight in bears is interpreted as a denial of a primal scene fear of being castrated and devoured by bears. Far more incredible is an unconscious self-parody by the psychiatrist Rudolph Friedman, whose "*Struwelpeter,* a Psychoanalytical Interpretation" (1960, pp. 493–502) gets trapped in its own arrogant rhetoric, leaping dizzily from one sensational catastrophe to another. The reader is introduced immediately to the picture of a little girl—"and, of course, the missing penis in the shape of an umbrella and a teapot." In a tone that always assumes his interpretations are self-evident, Friedman piles one unsubstantiated insight upon another: the little boy's "hair is a luminous halo of uncombed black and yellow out of which a frightened feminine face tries to gaze with schizoid severity and direction to compensate for the lost and holy genital eye which alone can see in the vagina of life and the coffin of death." A bowl of soup the boy dislikes is masturbatory excretion, he is lifted into the air by his flapping umbrella because he has become so light from masturbation. The boy's hands are outstretched and scratched, which Friedman interprets as stigmata, "a tragic commentary on the impending fate of the German nation" (pp. 495–96). Here are all the basic fallacies: an inflated dependence on the Freudian analytic style and jargon, the scarcely verifiable projective interpretation of a text by critics with apparently pansexual obsessions. There is also a feverish exposé of complex and even catastrophic patterns in purportedly simple material, and the presumption that a literary work's significance is reducible to conjectures about its psychological origins.

The most judicious introductions to this type of criticism are a few theoretical essays offering balanced overview and appraisal, without partisan apologetics. William Griffin's "Use and Abuse of Psychoanalysis in the Study of Literature" (1966, pp. 19–36) points to errors like those discussed above, especially the critic's simplistic reductionism and attitude of medical superiority. Rejecting narrow stereotyped conceptions both of criticism and of psychology, Griffin cites a few pieces he considers authentic applied psychological criticism, mostly the work of Maud Bodkin and Kenneth Burke. Simon Lesser's "Note on the Use of Scientific Psychological Knowledge in Literary Study" (1957, pp. 294–308) redefines the problem not as use or disuse of psychology, but whether to avail oneself of the empirical knowledge accumulated by psychologists for half a century or to rely on one's own implicit common sense psychology. This essay is an appendix to Lesser's *Fiction and the Unconscious,* a book that analyzes the reader's unconscious presuppositions and feelings in responding to a work of literature. Frederick Crews in "Anaesthetic Criticism" (1967) supports the better types of psychological criticism, illustrated in a fine selective bibliography, styles which refuse to reduce significant tensions in reader and text by a dishonest anaesthesia, while Herbert Weisinger in "The Hard Vision of Freud" (1964) suggests future directions for Freudian literary criticism. Louis Fraiberg's *Psychoanalysis and American Literary Criticism* (1960) contrasts the naive and incompetent use of Freud by Krutch and Van Wyck Brooks, with the more subtle integration of Freudian categories into the criticism of Trilling, Wilson, and Kenneth Burke.

Most of the standard pieces by psychological critics, such as the essay on *Hamlet* by Ernest Jones, recur in the more popular anthologies on psychology and literature (Phillips, 1957; Ruitenbeeck, 1964; and Manheim, 1966). Claudia Morrison (1968) has compiled an exhaustive descriptive bibliography of these critics, especially during the 1910–30 period, with a biting commentary on the simplicism and obscurity of most exponents. Frederick Hoffman's *Freudianism and the Literary Mind* (1957), after an extensive summary of Freud's ideas and their direct influence on Joyce, Lawrence, Kafka, and Mann, explores the mature use of Freud by Herbert Read, Wilson, and Kenneth Burke. Hoffman defends the type of literary critic able to approach the text in ways as various and complex as the material itself, enlisting whatever contributory knowledges available, no matter how mutually exclusive the claims asserted by all their proponents. Incidentally, Hoffman's own critical performance illustrates this principle quite well. He tries out the impressionistic French phenomenological mode with moderate success in *The Mortal NO* (1964), but an unfortunately banal religious-literary style in *The Imagination's New Beginning: Theology and Modern Literature* (1967; cf. Melvin Friedman, 1970).

Among most psychological critics, it is apparent that theory far outdistances practice. A few of the better examples of applied criticism are surely Leslie Fiedler's *Love and Death in the American Novel* (1967), especially its erratic but nevertheless brilliant insights into American heroine types. Although Fiedler prefers a tack more mythic than most other psychological critics, he has five provocative essays on the psychology of the child in *No! in Thunder,* ranging from the biblical Christ Child portrait to Peter Pan, Little Orphan Annie, and the corrupted innocents of *Lord of the Flies.* Fiedler says he does not center attention on religion but on what he calls natural piety, the Wordsworthian condition of wonder (1960, pp. 251–94). Robert Rogers's *A Psychoanalytic Study of the Double in Literature* (1970) gives some imaginative readings of Shakespeare, Melville, Dostoevsky, and Hesse based on Rogers's use of the Double as a flexible heuristic device, which reflects endemic dualistic tendencies of the human mind. Two apparently autonomous characters in a novel are viewed as components of the single dream product from the author's dialectical imagination. Ernst Kris's fine essay on "Prince Hal's Conflict," beginning with the actual *Henry V* material available to Shakespeare, analyzes the artistic decisions necessary to confront the unresolved conflicts in this historical figure, especially Hal's relationship with his various "fathers" (1965, pp. 273–90).

HERBERT READ. Read is a British version of Edmund Wilson, a dominant personality beyond petty critical controversies, the prophet and arbiter of most significant new cultural trends arising in the last five decades. "I have been gradually drawn towards a psychological type of literary criticism," he frequently asserts, but defends himself against Anglo-American rhetorical critics' charges that his interest in psychoanalysis seduces him away from the work itself. "Form is a psychological fact. My whole critical purpose has been to show that form is an organic, indeed a biological phenomenon. I have been in need of psychology to define form" (1967, p. 27). It is paradoxical to watch Read in *The Forms of Things Unknown* (1960) derive his own psychological theory of art as self-revelation from the more autotelist symbolic theory of Cassirer and Susanne Langer.

His title essay in *The Nature of Criticism* I find the clearest assertion of his total position. Literary criticism is essentially the valuation of a poem by an aesthetic standard. Yet Read recognizes it is impossible to apply such a standard without bringing in questions of value which are basically social or ethical. The psychological orientation must not be abused to reduce a work to its origins; analysis profanes, whereas the aesthetic sense of wonder arises when a work is intuited as a synthesis. First, Read views the psychological critic in a Jungian as well as Freudian perspective. This critic tests the social validity of the symbol, the extent to which a novel embodies fantasies of universal appeal to primal images and impulses. Second, his psychological knowledge of a specific creative process gives the critic an appreciation of the "fruitfulness, the richness, and the range of mind behind the symbol," and helps him verify that a given neurotic tendency has perhaps been sublimated. This provides collateral support for his textual interpretation tentatively formed on more intrinsic grounds. Third, a psychological bent ought to make a critic even more ideally tolerant a critic than others, opening up his initial crystallized attitudes, prepared to search into strange, unfamiliar reaches of human experience (1956, pp. 124–46).

In "The Tree of Life" (1963, pp. 180–97) and *The Cult of Sincerity* (1968) Read describes himself, with the parallel Eliot dictum in mind, as "a romanticist in literature, an anarchist in politics, and an agnostic in religion," influenced mostly by the philosophy of Bergson, Whitehead, Santayana, Kierkegaard, Jung, and Buber. His "politics of the unpolitical" is directed against philistinism and technology, rationalism, and a strong centralized state. He relishes the freedom of the divine irresponsibility, which Keats calls negative capability. "This Heraclitean principle of flux, of chance, of fortuity issues out of the tragedy of war, and is basic to my anarchism and romanticism. . . . I hate all monolithic systems, all logical categories, all pretences to truth and inevitability" (1968, p. 55). Recounting his own loss of Christian faith during adolescence, Read characterizes his present attitude not as active disbelief but as waiting on God, as Simone Weil would put it, with his own private myth, a separate fantasy, which he suspects even members of dogmatic churches implicitly construct out of the public symbols and ideas transmitted to them. Read, in other words, is religious in his stance of unconditioned waiting, concerned to explore what Acton called the "latent background of conviction" embodied in each literary work (1967, p. 11). In his *Wordsworth* (1949) Read defends his stress on the poet's private religious philosophy, because he is convinced that "the strong sense of personal beliefs will tincture the whole utterance of a poet, determining his very imagery and vocabulary." But we shall see that Read interprets these beliefs further as an elaborate defensive framework of rationalization in Wordsworth's own life.

I believe Read's finest pieces are three brief essays, without the digressive repetitiveness of his longer lectures or full-length books, which sometimes suggest he never had a thought he did not publish twice (cf. Gerving, 1969). The first sample is "The Nature of Criticism," which I have already paraphrased. "Myth, Dream, and Poem" (1956, pp. 101–16) presents a superb demonstration of an actual dream and Read's own efforts to express it in an original poem, the "immediate translation of the dream into its verbal equivalents." The process illustrated is as instructive as the commentary spun around it, on topics such as the nature of poetic versus discursive language, and the length of time elapsing between the dream experience and its poetic embodiment in poets as diverse as Blake and Dryden. "The Later Yeats" compares two versions of a lyric "The Sorrow of Love," the 1893 and 1933 revision, emphasizing the apparent changes in diction. In a line-by-line explication, Read explains why he prefers the earlier version, and gives a plausible account of the changes in structure caused by the later, more stripped diction (1945, pp. 208–12).

Read's forays into more express psychological materials are often adequate applied criticism, but lack the mastery of style and purpose exhibited in the essays above. The essay "Gerard Manley Hopkins" confirms anticipations that Read would prefer Hopkins's secular nature lyrics and poems of agonized doubt, to the poetry attempting a direct expression of Hopkins's religious beliefs (1956, pp. 331–53). "The Creative Experience in Poetry" tracks material in Coleridge's "Ode" back to his biography and state of mind (1960, pp. 124–40). Distinguishing between contingent public literature and a purer intrinsic type, the essay "Swift" places Swift in the former category, his artistic intent solidly conditioned by the immediate political and social circumstances. Drawing upon his satires and correspondence, Read offers a coherent reconstruction of Swift's self-understanding as writer, politician, and churchman (1956, pp. 196–219). Unlike Read's earlier book that concentrates on Shelley's personality, the later essay "Shelley," in rebuttal to T. S. Eliot and other unsympathetic critics, tries to defend the maturity and coherence of Shelley's philosophy as a prophetic, unsystematic version of Godwinism, with messianic intuitions similar to those behind Marxism and Judaeo-Christianity (1945, pp. 119–28). *Wordsworth* is a bloated work of unsteady purpose, filled with repeated pleas that its hypotheses be entertained, yet lacking the rigorous textual explication or analytical biography requisite. Read's thesis is that ten fertile creative years in Wordsworth's life spring from the love affair with Annette Vallon and its termination, and that his intellectual fluctuations in this period are simply a structure of rationalization and sublimation covering these emotional changes. In a surprisingly narrow contraction of his own romantic agnostic perspective, Read judges Wordsworth's ethics essentially insincere, his political ideas prejudiced, his religious philosophy of nature inconsistent. Wordsworth adopted a strategy of supernaturalism without God to "hide the heretical significance of his philosophy of nature under a screen of orthodox beliefs" (1949).

NORMAN HOLLAND. Almost nothing else encountered in psychological criticism foreshadows what Norman Holland has achieved in this style. His theory and practice unquestionably surpass anything else in the psychological vein, and in many other critical styles, too. The applied criticism in "Psychological Depths and 'Dover Beach'" reveals all the essentials of his method. First there is a tight explication of the Arnold lyric. And then Holland begins to ponder his own conflicting feelings: a reaction of peace even though the material seems despairing. He reasons that if by analyzing his own reactions he can discover drives the poem stirs up in him and defenses the poem presents for dealing with those drives, then he can understand the different reactions of others to the poem for whom those defenses are less adequate. Next, he details the images and other strategies offered as subtle defences by "Dover Beach," tapping one's earliest childhood experiences, evoking the child's trust that he shall be nurtured. Finally, Holland passes above this one poem to generalize on the major Victorian modes of defense (1968, pp. 248–67). Approaching the literary work as impulse and defense, then, Holland's method is principally to analyze the emotional underpinnings of his own informed reactions to the literary experience.

An even more vivid compact example is Holland's summary explication of *Macbeth* in *Psychoanalysis and Shakespeare.* After listing a series of fundamental themes running through the play, he formulates an intellectual statement of the essential *Macbeth* quality—the uncertain perception of the manner in which supernatural, natural, and unnatural mingle in a man's mind and breed outward. In his personal reactions to *Macbeth,* Holland takes account of ambivalent feelings, reflected in the play's dualistic patterns and its ambiguous use of gender, blood, and darkness symbolism. These he correlates with primal conflicts, such as the distinction between ego and nonego, the child's gradual progression from obeying and blaming others to an acceptance of responsibility himself. Reinterpreting *Macbeth,* then, in terms of a central nuclear fantasy, Holland experiences it as an interaction of oedipal impulses. A person attempting to resolve incompatible attitudes to a father employs his obedience to preternatural authorities as an excuse for killing the father king. What Holland calls the *Macbeth* quality "translates into a wish to act aggressively, justified by obedience to a parent, poised against a fear of dependence and subsequent betrayal of a libidinal kind. In short, the psychoanalytic reading can tell us in a more or less scientific way how the unconscious conflicts and fears buried in us find in the fictitious events and intellectual issues of the tragedy emotional power" (1966, p. 326).

These two inductive accounts, I believe, present a clear exposition of Holland's critical method. In *The Dynamics of Literary Response* (1968a) he describes literature as "an introjected transformation." By this he means the literary text provides me with a fantasy I introject or experience as though it were my own, supplying my own associations to it. These interiorized creative fantasies are disciplined by some outside control, of course, which is presented by the work itself. Formal devices in the work pass into my consciousness to guide me in "transforming the fantasy toward ego-acceptable meanings—something like sublimation." Elsewhere he calls the literary work "a multiple projection or symbolization or stimulus of unconscious impulses of the audience, interacting through such primary thought processes as identification, condensation, displacement, and the like" (1966, p. 313). Holland's theory of criticism is best understood as a theory of responses to literature, with meaning partially embodied in the literary work and partially contributed by each reader's mind. This approach is almost indistinguishable from I. A. Richards's core-context explanation of a poem's meaning in terms of the multiple ideal reader responses, although Holland's paradigm is more psychoanalytic. It is the critic's own mind, then, which must stretch his literary experience in the two following directions: "a literary text has implicit in it two dimensions—one reaches 'up,' toward the world of social, intellectual, moral, and religious concerns; the other reaches 'down,' to the dark, chthonic, primitive, bodily part of our mental life."

The last two chapters of *Psychoanalysis and Shakespeare* (1966, pp. 294–349) explore three types of psychoanalytic criticism—critical autobiography or reading toward the author's mind, character analysis or reading toward the fictive character's mind, and Holland's own criticism of affect or reading toward the audience's mind. Problems with the first type, especially in trying to comprehend a figure like Shakespeare, include a lack of extratextual biographical knowledge and the inability to sift out an idiosyncratic style from the unknown conventions employed. The second, character analysis, founders on the dilemma of literary naturalism, that homo fictus is not homo sapiens, that literature here cannot compete with the more immediate and verifiable knowledge gained from case histories of real people. Holland's argument for the third type is convincing. A criticism of affect can salvage with more plausibility the best insights of the first two approaches. Moreover, since the psychological critic basically charts continuities between the literary work and the psychoanalytic description of some mind, and since the work itself cannot be analyzed separately from the analyzer, there seems no better mind to work with than one's own.

Holland testifies that his present style of psychoanalytic criticism emerged only recently, after long strenuous experimentation. In his teaching he began with the organic unity of the work itself and its implicit meanings; then he tried to formulate these themes in contexts of specific concern to him and his audience, moral or Christian or Marxist. In the preface to his *Dynamics of Literary Response* (1968a, pp. vii–xviii), he explains his gradual progression from mythically, religiously, thematically to psychoanalytically, or to the deepest nuclear fantasy, the inner experience of the text. *Psychoanalysis and Shakespeare* is itself a twice-born book, first based on a mere reading knowledge of Freud, and then entirely rewritten after Holland entered a training program in the Boston Psychoanalytic Institute, and experienced the psychoanalytic method "in the pulse." A third of this book summarizes Freud's theories on the artist, the work, and reader response; another third samples and evaluates most of the psychoanalytic criticism of Shakespeare up to 1964. Holland pounces upon every trace of *Vulgarfreudismus*, probably the very heresy which Holland escaped by the decisive revision of his book—detaching Freudian themes from their living experimental therapeutic context and inflating them into a tendentious theory of art and culture. The basic questions to which Holland thinks a psychoanalytic criticism ought to contribute special insight are: What are my critical assumptions? How do I willingly suspend disbelief and identify with certain characters? Can I offer a more than commonsense humanist understanding of catharsis, negative capability, stock responses, irony, and emotions like love and courage?

In his less pronounced psychoanalytic style, Holland uses other types of language to describe the nuclear fantasy in a literary work. *The Shakespearean Imagination* (1964) is a collection of lucid simplified television lectures on the poet's vision, the poetic world of each play and the whole corpus, the informing principle or essence or center of each work. That which makes the play what it is he calls the *Macbeth*-principle or the *Tempest*-principle. With the same skillful explications that characterize both Shakespeare books, *The First Modern Comedies: The Significance of Etherege, Wycherley, and Congreve* (1959) gives a thorough reading of eleven plays, and discovers in them an appearance-reality dialectic Holland also tracks down in Restoration politics, cosmology, court pranks, and literary criticism. Here he searches in each play for the unifying principle that informs the whole, and his thesis stresses an implied moral dimension in what is customarily interpreted as the amoral comic style of this period. Corrupt social patterns are of less consequence than individual personal relationships, a theme expressed in prevalent mirror and mask imagery, the absence of retribution for the rake-villain character, the disappearance of Elizabethan cosmic symbols.

MYTHIC CRITICISM

Norman Holland refers somewhat distastefully to myth and ritual criticism as a convenient marriage "of Jungian psychology to folkloric anthropology (for example, the Germanic successors to the brothers

Grimm or such writers as Sir James Frazer or Gilbert Murray (1966, p. 77). In his spirited introduction to the anthology *Myth and Literature* (1966), John Vickery describes the movement as a blend of psychoanalysis and the Cambridge School of Anthropology, notably Frazer's *Golden Bough*, Jane Harrison's *Themis*, Freud's *Totem and Taboo*, and Jung's *Psychology of the Unconscious*. From these classics emerged patterns of the dying and reviving god, scapegoat, heroic quest, ritual drama, and the cyclical nature of existence—archetypes that preoccupy Bodkin, Campbell, Wheelwright, Chase, Fergusson, Frye, and the other principal myth critics. Each has his characteristic emphasis: Frye usually discovers traces of fertility rites, Campbell the monomythic quest, Fergusson the outlines of early dithyrambic ritual. It is significant that Fergusson claims his theory behind *The Idea of a Theater* derives not only from Cornford, Harrison, Murray, and the Cambridge School, but notably from Kenneth Burke (1953, pp. 2f.).

The baroque and meretricious quality of much standard mythic criticism can be tested by sampling a few of the practical critiques in Vickery's anthology, quite inferior to most of the excellent theoretical material presented. An explication of *Nostromo* would pass for a spoof of the crudest religious-literary criticism, with its excitement over the Edenic landscape, snakes, the blue and white boudoir of Mrs. Gould who significantly venerates a statue of the Virgin Mary, Mr. Holroyd as holy-rod or a god figure. We are told that the conflict between Zenobia and Priscilla for Hollingsworth in *The Blithedale Romance* recalls the mythical battle between Aphrodite and Persephone for Adonis, and that Hollingsworth is "figured forth" as Vulcan, Moodie ambivalently as both Zeus and Hades. Douglas Bush in his charming parody "Mrs. Bennet and the Dark Gods: The Key to Jane Austen" captures these stylistic pretensions admirably. One mythic pattern is said to shade into and suggest another. Each character yields mythic overtones. Mr. Bennet is clearly Adonis, the father of all forms, Mrs. Bennet is "Informed Matter," Collins "the axis of several polarities" (1966, pp. 20–26). "Once you begin to look," Norman Holland remarks, "you can find under every literary bush a vegetarian god or great earth mother, coupled or separate."

There seem to be three recognizable variations on the mythic style of criticism. The first is merely an extrinsic comparison, what Joseph Blotner means by "laying a colored transparency over a sheet covered with a maze of hues to reveal the orderly pattern which otherwise resides within them unperceived" (1966, p. 244). In this way Blotner can superimpose myths of Oedipus and Demeter on a novel that seems almost plotless, such as Woolf's *To the Lighthouse*, and discover clear and coherent strands of narrative that he would otherwise have overlooked by a purely autotelist criticism. A second mythic approach traces the direct transmission and conscious reinterpretation of earlier mythical patterns within the creative process of writers like Joyce, Mann, Lawrence, Yeats, and Eliot. A competent illustration of this type is John Vickery's "Myth and Ritual in the Shorter Fiction of D. H. Lawrence" (1966, pp. 299–313), which simply tracks down the overt allusions to primitive beliefs and behavior. A third approach is the most daring and fallible, a search into the unconscious depths for an archetypal pattern of the Jungian collective racial memory, or what Read calls the "social validity of symbols," or Holland "the dark chthonic primitive part of our mental life." It is not necessary to endorse Jung's theory of the collective unconscious here, but merely to concede that a few definite symbolic patterns are endemic to the human creative act and its constructs whenever a person tries to express his feelings of celebration, tragedy, hope, love.

The distortions that plague the unwary myth critic, especially in his venturesome pursuit of this third approach, are significant. C. S. Lewis argues that Greek myth sources begin to usurp attention that should be given to the text itself. The work is treated like rubble left over from the ruins of more stately buildings, whereas the anthropological material is more likely the rubble from which a new cathedral has been constructed. For every step away from the dark origins is an advance in coherence, in suggestion, in imaginative power" (1969b, p. 306). Another objection is that an emphatic mythic criterion renders me incapable of evaluating the superior artistic value of *Lycidas* over a nursery rhyme or folk tale, all of which may embody the same archetype. The most serious complaint is that preoccupation with timelessly recurring myths and archetypes can lead to an escape from the important historicity and temporal relationships of the work itself. Philip Rahv in *The Myth and the Powerhouse* (1965) denounces this current myth-obsession as a shortcut to transcendence, a fear of the hazards of everyday freedom. This can be a traditionalist escape backwards into an ideal primitive condition, or else a freezing of all change within a world of permanent Platonic forms. He finds this tendency simply a pompous, even more abstract new version of the old literary autotelism, both of which styles of criticism insulate the critic from live contemporary issues of value, belief, and ideological conflict.

I shall try to assemble some of the more plausible responses to these objections. The better myth critics have applied this archetypal perspective with shrewd flexibility or, as one among many critical methods, have expanded it into a macroscopic framework embracing every conceivable style of literary criticism. The prototype for this last strategy is Dante, who in his famous letter to Can Grande della Scala suggested four levels of meaning operative throughout the *Divine Comedy*, transposing to literary studies an outline prevalent in theological discourse. Dante's hell as literal narrative, for example, is a remedial vision of life beyond death; as allegory it is the living hell of the social and political milieu in his century; as tropology it exposes the private moral hell within each living person; as anagoge it represents the mystery of all evil. Kenneth Burke and especially Northrop Frye have followed Dante's architectonic impulse to create an inclusive pluralistic theory, although I shall challenge the thoroughness of Frye's synthesis later. A crucial proviso must be asserted here. The critic should not allow himself to be wafted from the literal to the broad anagogic implications of a text without laboring through the middle two dimensions, the specific configural, penultimate level that preoccupies the ortho-cultural critics.

Another theoretical way to shield oneself against these difficulties is to exploit the protean ambiguities in the term myth itself. Wallace Douglas has an engaging essay on "The Meanings of 'Myth' in Modern Criticism" (1966, pp. 119–28), documenting a spread in its denotation, from illusion through belief to higher truth. Most often Douglas uncovers presuppositions of a dichotomy between mythos and logos, Richards's distinction between emotive and referential language, with an implied preference for the mythic as more primitive, comprehensive, spiritually profound. Locating the myth in a text is frequently no more than a disguise "by which critics can indicate their approval of the doctrine they find in whatever work they happen to be exploring." A myth can mean a symbolic version of human wisdom; a basic social or class convention; an historical or metaphysical reality invested with human meaning and values as worthy of commitment; a repository of unconsciously held social memories and lost collective rituals that enable the race to function; an oracle of divine revelation. With a few woo-woo noises we can associate the content and form of myth with any passionate human intuition, with dreams and the unconscious, echoes of the primordial mystery, the uncanny world of value and spirit.

I disagree with Douglas's strictures against importing so inclusive and slippery a term into contemporary literary criticism. My criterion is the simple pragmatic one I have employed before—if a critic's specific concept of myth enables him to reach more insight into the literary text, let it survive as a functional heuristic tool, unless it could be replaced by something more productive for him. A strict, rigorous clarity can be even more detrimental than fuzzy protean concepts for unfolding and assessing a complex literary symbol. I think mythic criticism at its best is scarcely distinguishable from religious-literary criticism, for myth and religion refer to the deepest metaphysic of a literary work, if both terms are understood in the comprehensive functional sense already discussed. Yet John Vickery claims that myth and ritual, the key terms in mythic criticism, "encompass that out of which literature emerged; therefore, [this criticism] is aligned with literature essentially, not accidentally, and in a way that social, political, philosophical, and religious concepts are not (1966, p. x). Vickery's opinion directly contradicts the express religious descriptions by numerous leading myth critics, especially the Cambridge anthropologists, and my own definitions of both the terms religion and myth. Vickery perhaps forgets that literature in man's historical evolution was once religious liturgy and dance, charms and oracles. And religion has been perennially lived as cult and mores before its credal hymns solidify into institutional dogmas.

As a further response to charges of mythomania, some myth critics have consciously reaffirmed the historical particularity of each literary work. Northrop Frye distinguishes between the myth or inherited convention, and its displacement in a particular work. He calls literature a "reconstructed mythology" (1963, pp. 36–38). Leslie Fiedler's distinction between archetype and signature implies that a work of literature comes into existence whenever a new signature is imposed upon a common mythos (1960, pp. 295–328). By archetype he means the mythos, a characteristic response to human situations of celebration, dying, fear of the unknown. It is a pattern belonging to the Jungian collective unconscious, or Platonic "World of Ideas," the infra- or meta-personal, the community at its preconscious level of acceptance. The signature is the totality of differentiating factors in a specific work. It is the mark of Jung's individuated self and persona, or of Freud's ego and superego—the joint product of both one's own personal idiom and the conventional expectations of a particular era. In other words, a great novelist turns to such debased popular archetypes as the detective story, western, science fiction, and renders his material through subtle, complex signatures. Maud Bodkin contrives a similar distinction in her *Archetypal Patterns in Poetry* (1934). Each poet has a distinctive *Weltanschauung*, an "individual vision, or perspective of reality, determined by his own nature and the main events and conditions of his life." The paradigms which are commonly accepted in an era, ingeniously varied in individual appropriation, she calls "stereotypes." A poet's belief begins as only a stereotype, but later becomes an embodied archetype when properly rendered, or becomes a "passionate apprehension of reality which the poet communicates through that framework."

The best representative applied myth criticism seems to occur in extensive comparative studies of genre or thematic patterns, rather than in the intensive analysis of a single text. Francis Fergusson's *Idea of a Theatre* (1953) interprets each drama in its total literary and social context as an implicit ritual performance. Each dramatist works within a set of social ritual expectations, so that Oedipus can be viewed as enacting the role of both king and scapegoat to lead the audience in a ritual purification of the state, or Hamlet and his audience as straining to expiate rottenness in the state of Denmark. This approach deemphasizes the more introspective interpretations of these dramas, and makes plausible the otherwise frequently misunderstood conclusions to many Shakespearean tragedies, where a new figure arrives to reconstitute political control, a symbol of divine cosmic order that the characters and audience together have recovered. *The Nature of Narrative* (1966) by Robert Scholes and Robert Kellogg, studied alongside the former's anthology *Approaches to the Novel* (1966a), surveys a wide history of narrative forms and their roots in the oral tradition of the ballad, epic, and other preliterary situations. The intent here is to approach works like *Ulysses* and *Magic Mountain* with flexible modern narrative canons, liberated from the procrustean framework of the nineteenth-century realist paradigm, but closer to the broader philosophical-rhetorical genres familiar to Chaucer. A similar widened encyclopedic perspective is brought to the philosophical lyric by William Empson in his evocative *Some Versions of Pastoral* (1950).

Philip Wheelwright's *Burning Fountain* includes an essay on "The Cosmic Fire," which explores the Bible, the Vedas, Buddha's Fire Sermon, Heraclitus, and the most varied sources to demonstrate the range of possible meaning, especially the full religious depth-meaning when the fire symbol operates at greatest semantic intensity. Wheelwright's fierce attention to the imagery in literary works is consonant with his theory that the theme in an artistically rendered poem ought to be fused with the rhythm and imagery. "Philosophical ideas in poetry should be like those sculptures of Rodin's where the unfinished human or animal figure is left continuous with the unhewn stone" (1954, p. 331). Herbert Weisinger's *Tragedy and the Paradox of the Fortunate Fall* (1953) begins with a psychological analysis of the rebirth archetype in human experience. Then he demonstrates its complex appearance in the human myths attempting to express Near Eastern and

Judaeo-Christian religious experiences. Finally, he speculates that Shakespearean tragedy is probably based on a secularized version of this same pattern. Our depth-reaction to tragedy, then, possesses all these human reverberations, many of which we associate with our religious experiences. Weisinger's scholarly concentration on the basic religious dynamic behind both the Christian phenomenon and the tragic Shakespearean phenomenon is so much more tenable than theories like Auerbach's and Driver's discussed earlier, which presume to detect horizontal influences between Christianity and the specific later works.

Maud Bodkin's *Archetypal Patterns* (1934) and *Studies of Type: Images in Poetry, Religion, and Philosophy* develop themes around such symbols as God, hell, heroes, women, gardens, storms. *Archetypal Patterns* is rich and germinative, especially in Bodkin's efforts to correlate great images appearing in religious experience with stock poetic archetypes, like "the divine man, the divine mother, Heaven and Hell, rebirth from death to life." But the later *Studies* book is a wretched dead end, a meandering pastiche of thin personal impressions, obsessed with the wartime Nazi menace. Its homiletic tone can be somewhat explained by her theory that Whitehead's "Divine Persuasion" lures us to probe beneath religious dogmas and literature to locate the archetypes themselves. She rewrites Matthew Arnold into a mythic argot, hoping that man "may yet in his encounter through literature with thinkers past and present, or in personal relation with present-day leaders and friends, so realize the archetypes of saving wisdom and spiritual rebirth as to share in the religious life and fellowship that to others has been mediated by the Christian churches, or the great religions of the East" (1951, p. 175).

NORTHROP FRYE. Among literary critics today the name of Northrop Frye is often uttered in the same tone of hushed sacrality that only a generation ago was reserved for an aphorism from T. S. Eliot. I think many of us have experienced a new literary complexity and depth since we read Frye's *Anatomy of Criticism* (1966), just as most poetry seemed frought with irony and paradox after we first struggled through William Empson's *Seven Types of Ambiguity* fifteen years before (1947). The commentators assembled in Krieger's *Northrop Frye in Modern Criticism* (1966) give an impression of the Frye phenomenon and the controversial heat it generates, especially in Wimsatt's "Northrop Frye: Criticism as Myth" (pp. 75–108), which includes a useful selective bibliography. In addition to the customary broadsides against extratextual detours, Wimsatt scores perceptively against Frye's inconsistent and pretentious terminology, the cluttering biblical and classicist window-dressing, the obscurity, the cute paradox in language. Frye's response to Wimsatt and his other colleagues is mostly a defence of systematization in the *Anatomy*. The system is there for the sake of the insights, not the insights for the sake of the system. "In the muddled mythology of stock response, the system-builder is the spider who spins nets out of his bowels, as contrasted with the bee who flits empirically from flower to flower and staggers home under his burden of sweetness and light" (1966, p. 136). The tone and nature of Frye's response bear the unmistakable signature of his style as a literary critic: magisterial, dry and bookish, aloof, urbanely playful.

Frye's most impressive work of applied criticism is *Fearful Symmetry: A Study of William Blake* (1962), with convincing sections on Blake's epistemology, religious ideas, his ethical and political philosophy. From this data Frye sketches the shape of his central myth, and shows how the symbolism in individual works plausibly supports this vision. He is determined to link Blake with typically poetic thinking and British conventions, so that Blake is not simply tolerated as a unique religious freak. At the end of this study Frye ranges throughout the history of poetry to find archetypal parallels to Blake's themes and poetic style. *Fearful Symmetry* is an essential book in unlocking Frye, because the *Anatomy* actually evolved out of problems only partially resolved in the method of this earlier work, as Frye himself explains in "The Road of Excess" (1963c, pp. 3–20). More recently he says that his disgust with the antiromanticism and fascism of Pound and Eliot prompted him to select Blake as a fighter for causes still alive, a poet "the opposite in all respects to what Eliot thought he [himself] was" (1973, p. 18). It is significant to recall that Frye in the last decade has become one of the leaders in a reversal of fashion counter to the ideological classicism supported by the humanist semiotic critics. In the foreword to his anthology, *Romanticism Reconsidered* (1963b), with a qualified selection of essays by Frye, Abrams, Trilling, and others, Frye proclaims, "The anti-Romantic movement in criticism, which in Britain and America followed the Hulme-Eliot-Pound broadsides of the early twenties, is now over and done with. . . ."

The *Anatomy* can be read profitably alongside Frye's "Archetypes of Literature" (1963a, pp. 7–20), an earlier "summarized statement of the critical program worked out in that book," and "Literature as Context: Milton's 'Lycidas' " (1963a, pp. 119–29), containing a set of basic *Anatomy* categories applied to a concrete text. Otherwise, a reader can lose the essential outline and issues, because so many inconsequential aspects of this huge framework get emphasized. In the analysis of

"Lycidas" Frye observes our need to avoid autotelism and, at the other extreme, not to turn the poem into a scissors-and-paste collection of allusions. Both methods are reductionist; the one too inverted, the second merely amplifying other poets' echoes. The purpose of the *Anatomy* is to furnish a principle that holds these two tendencies together, the centripetal and centrifugal. The principle can be stated simply but its implications are incredibly complicated: each literary work means the whole corpus of its possible commentary, and all of literature is a single organism or anatomy.

By this anatomy or "imaginatively coherent body of experience," Frye has in mind Shelley's "great poem, which all poets, like the co-operating thoughts of one great mind, have built up since the beginning of the world," or Eliot's familiar concept of tradition in which every new creative work alters and is shaped by the organic history of literature. More prosaically, each literary work bears a potential or hypothetical relationship with all reality and especially with other works of literature. A reader approaches "Lycidas" with certain presuppositions about all poems, about the creative process of writing poetry, about the history and categorization of literature, about genre conventions and the predictable favored archetypal patterns in the pastoral—shepherds, death, winter, sunset, decaying flowers. He needs a sound critical taxonomy to reach the heart of "Lycidas" itself: "We need to know much more than we do about the structural principles of literature, about myth and metaphor, conventions and genres, before we can distinguish with any authority a real from an imaginary line of influence, an illuminating from a misleading analogy. . . ." (1963a, p. 129). The intent of the *Anatomy* is to provide this exhaustive taxonomy, categories of the generalizations that can be made about *all* winter symbolism, for example, or plays in the low mimetic mode, or heroes in the ironic mode.

In the Frye fivefold typology that expands Dante's four levels of interpretation, a literary work's meaning is literal, descriptive, formal, archetypal, and anagogic. Thus, I can interpret it pluralistically, first of all as an intricate verbal texture, in autotelist criticism. Or in progressive degrees outward, through the various critical styles, I back away from the painting to see composition instead of brushwork, until I can eventually interpret the work essentially as a monad of all literature. The work ultimately becomes a microcosm "of the total order of words," of everything literary, conceived as existing in its "own universe, no longer a commentary on life or reality, but containing life and reality in a system of verbal relationships" (1966, pp. 121–22). I shall later question what ontological reality this abstracted universe of possible forms possesses, and whether this commentary or referential relational aspect can be identified with the religious dynamic in a work. Frye asserts that literary criticism "has an end in the structure of literature as a total form, as well as a beginning in the text studied. . . . One may develop a primary body of commentary around the obvious meaning, then a secondary body about the unconscious meaning, then a third body around the conventions and external relations of the poem, and so on indefinitely" (p. 342). The task of the critic is commentary, comparison, and Kierkegaardian repetition, which latter concept Frye articulates with admirable clarity: the "recovery of function, not of course the restoration of an original function, which is out of the question, but the recreation of function in a new context" (p. 345).

Besides *Fearful Symmetry* and the essay on "Lycidas," I have not discovered an applied criticism in Frye commensurate with his staggering theoretical ambitions. Such works, of course, would have to be dazzling encyclopedic studies of a major writer's corpus or of a dominant archetypal pattern—but a critic has only one life to write huge books as inimitable as the *Anatomy* and *Fearful Symmetry* anyway. There are countless applied insights scattered eliptically throughout the *Anatomy* that make it the inventive, fertile book it is. The problem with Frye's categories so often is that one grasps three parts of a fivefold taxonomy and cannot find any use for the remaining structure unless one gets appropriate illustrations. *Fables of Identity* (1963a) Frye says should be read as part of the work in practical criticism he promised in his *Anatomy*, and there are indeed a few essays worthy of comment there.

In *Fables*, "The Structure of Imagery in *The Fairie Queene*" (pp. 69–87) seeks the vision, a general structure of imagery in this total poem, correlated with the "axioms and assumptions which Spenser and his public shared, and which form the basis of its imaginative communication." Frye touches upon the politics of the era, biblical myths, a cyclical nature archetypal pattern, and Spenser's moral dialectic. "How True a Twain" (pp. 88–106) gives an interesting reading of Shakespeare's sonnets as an organic sequence, with a sensitive discrimination between love conventions in the genre—"a sort of creative yoga," —and the conjectured personal feelings of the individual poet. "Quest and Cycle in *Finnegans Wake*" (pp. 256–64) is a remarkably lucid and brief comparison between the Joycean myth of Finnegan and Blake's myth of Albion. Devoting a third of the essay to her role as a deeply religious poet, Frye's "Emily Dickinson" essay (pp. 193–217) reconstructs her vision, "the larger structure of her imagination," "the bent of her mind," and compares her philosophy with Blake's. "The Realistic

Oriole: A Study of Wallace Stevens" (pp. 238–55) is a proficient synthesis of his major themes, following the development of his metaphysic throughout the corpus. There is a resourceful comparison with Yeats, Eliot, and Rilke in their moods of religious extremity. "Such language may or may not go with a religious commitment: in itself it is simply poetry speaking as poetry must when it gets to a certain pitch of metaphorical concentration."

In Frye's criticism there is a central set of contradictions, evasions, and muddled paradoxes that I confess I cannot get beyond. First, in the *Anatomy* he separates subordination and value judgments from the act of criticism itself, which must essentially be "coordination and description" (1966, p. 26)—a naive and untenable pose of neutrality, as I have indicated in expounding my own theory. Anyway, Frye makes the constant value judgments we would expect of all critics in practice, patently in his pert side-comments during almost every explication, which are the characteristic feature of his style. Or a more specific example is his polemical reason for selecting Blake as his constant touchstone, as mentioned before. Frye does endorse an ethical-historical criticism that *transvalues* civilization, because he works for the "goal of social effort, the idea of complete and classless civilization" as "an implicit moral standard" (p. 348). But the next moment, he defends literature as a self-contained literary universe without external goals. However, this assertion then causes him misgivings that perhaps "we merely restored the aesthetic view on a gigantic scale, substituting Poetry for a mass of poems, aesthetic mysticism for aesthetic empiricism" (p. 350). This statement could be no better paraphrase of Rahv's very impeachment of the myth-evasion cited before. But a paragraph later, Frye expands a literary anatomy or verbal universe beyond purely literary works to include philosophy, science, religion. Besides his intent to protect the relational autonomy of the semiotic literary work, and his anxiety to resist Arnoldian tendencies to make the work revelatory and morally normative, the gist of these contiguous avowals and disavowals is simply confused. Frye does not confront rigorously this basic question: Does a literal-descriptive-formal-archetypal-anagogic interpretation of "Lycidas" include first, a judicial moment in criticism; and second, an interpretation of this poem not only in relationship to all literature but as a virtual microcosm of *all* knowledge and being? In other words, is Frye's theory truly pluralistic, does his archetypal-anagogic interpretation get beyond the pure literariness of literature, and sanction an ortho-cultural, psycho-mythic, religious criticism in the inclusive sense I have defined?

I do not think Frye has ever resolved this paradox stated in *The*

Well-Tempered Critic: "When we speak of actual human life, or the actual environment of nature, we speak of something of which literature is only a part, and a ridiculously small part at that. But when we speak of literature, we speak of a total imaginative form which is, in the context, *bigger* than either nature or human life, because it contains them, the actual being only a part of the possible" (1963c, p. 154). And the *Anatomy* says that religion affirms "this is," whereas poetry adds hypothetically "but suppose *this* is." Purportedly religion comes to a poet qua poet only as a metaphor. The critic qua critic can only treat every religion as a human hypothesis, the divine as the unlimited or projected human (pp. 125–28). As recently as 1973, after sufficient time to clarify or retract this position, Frye asserts again that his background in extensive theological studies helped him introduce the Bible into literary criticism, "not because it represented a religious 'position' congenial to my own, but . . . it illustrated the imaginative assumptions on which Western poets had proceeded; consequently the study of it pointed the way towards a phenomenological criticism which would be as far as possible free of presuppositions. I am not by any means sure that it is possible really to get free of presuppositions . . ." (1973, p. 21). Here his theory provides an inadequate basis to describe his own best practice. Frye's concept of religion seems divorced from what I have called the work's religious dynamic, and is relegated to an eschatological realm of merely possible imaginative essences. Frye sets up the old autotelist chasm between the poet qua poet and the poet qua man, the critic's aesthetic judgments and his value judgments. The work is artifically separated from its immediate engaged centrifugal context, myth from reality, religion from literature, the possible from the actual. The basic impulse and outline of the *Anatomy* would be improved if every one of these major fallacies could be exposed and discarded, none of which I believe is essential to the basic thesis, scope, and methodology of the book.

KENNETH BURKE. A proficient taxonomist himself, Kenneth Burke seems too massive a phenomenon to fit anyone else's classification. Stanley Hyman has served him well as clarifying apologist in "Kenneth Burke and the Criticism of Symbolic Action" (1948, pp. 347–94), following the development of his principal themes from book to book, and in editing the accessible Burke sampler *Perspectives by Incongruity* (1964a) and *Terms for Order* (1964b). Daniel Aaron fails in repeated efforts to categorize Burke's ideological vagaries, concluding that Burke judges both communism and capitalism with cold professorial detachment as merely two rival social strategies (1961, pp. 287–92). Finally, Burke himself in a few "Curriculum Criticum" notes from the third edition of *Counter-Statement* hints at the diverging critical styles through which he has progressed. Most important, Burke justifies the scarcity of applied criticism in his books by explaining that his scope is the wider symbolic and linguistic domain. Such "analysis of language and of human motives at some points overlaps upon literary criticism in the strict sense of the term, at many other points it leads into inquiries not central to literary criticism" (1953, p. 219). We are dealing not with literary criticism alone, then, but with what Hyman facetiously calls "Burkology," a meta-criticism that combines semantics, economics, sociology, social psychology, and philosophy (Knox, 1957; Rueckert, 1963 and 1969).

If Burke is to be associated with the name of any movement in psychology, it would not be Freud or Jung so much as G. H. Meade, Dewey, and transactional social psychology. The principal models employed are not the Freudian checks and balances mechanistic system, but Meade's game and role-playing paradigms and Dewey's biological model of the mutual conditioning interaction between an organism and its context. The literary work is always viewed as functional and relational, doing something for the poet and his audience. What I especially admire is Burke's skill in reaching behind the paradigm of archetypes as more or less timeless static Platonic forms, to the recurring dynamic *situations* that prompt human beings to devise similar archetypal patterns for coping with them. In other words, Burke's situational immediacy could provide a sound corrective to Frye's eternal world of literary forms. Whenever Burke experiences a literary work, he attempts to take it back to its "alchemic center," the "ground of its existence, the logical substance that is its causal ancestor" (1945, p. xviii). Fiedler's requisite distinction between archetype and signature can be expanded in Burke to cover a wider human phenomenon: certain situations are perennial, the strategies of response can succeed or fail artistically. "A given human relationship may be at one time named in terms of foxes and lions, if there are foxes and lions about; or it may be named in terms of salesmanship, advertising, the tactics of politicians, etc. But beneath the change in particulars, we may often discover the naming of one situation" (1964a, p. 107).

This approach avoids the extremes of autotelism and mythomanic generalizations; it rivets the literary work to its total living, evolving context. *A Grammar of Motives* (1945, pp. 365f.) presents an outstanding symbol of this contextual dynamism. Imagine a statue of two fencers, one lunging forward with his sword aimed at the shoulders, the other fencer raising his sword to deflect the blow. The latter figure of the pair is lost, and a new type of dueler is substituted, a man with a pistol aimed at the stomach. It is misleading to try reconciling the posture of the surviving swordsman's parry to the posture of the gunman, or to memorialize the first gesture as an eternal, universal parry, as capable of meeting the gunman's action as it was to meet the former swordsman's. The literary work memorializes this first parry, after the removal of the opponent whose thrust called forth the gesture. "What, then, is the parry an answer to, when in the course of time a new opponent, with his own different style of thrust, has arisen to take the place of the former opponent?" This illustration points up each critic's responsibility first to grasp the full original situation out of which the work emerged, and second to translate and reenact it within a new hermeneutical situation.

Literary criticism, then, must be sociological in Burke's sense of the term. Critics should attempt to codify the characteristic strategies poets have developed to name and respond to situations. Tearing down barriers erected around art as a specialized phenomenon, Burke approaches literary works as "strategies for selecting enemies and allies, for socializing losses, for warding off evil eye, for purification, propitiation, and desanctification, consolation and vengeance, admonition and exhortation, implicit commands or instructions . . ." (1964a, p. 109). In the impetuous essay "Ritual Drama as Hub," Burke suggests ritual drama as a culminating form, a paradigm from which the philosopher could draw a calculus, vocabulary, and set of coordinates to integrate all the social sciences (1964b, pp. 119–44). The most familiar set of coordinates in his literary criticism are the pentad of act-scene-agent-agency-purpose, and the triad of chart-prayer-dream, the latter division corresponding roughly to the grammar-rhetoric-symbolic books in Burke's corpus. Burke employs the pentad to expound the central insight in his practical criticism: settings explain and are explained by the actions that occur in them. The triad is a blueprint of Burke's critical theory as a coherent system. The literary poem in itself is chart (grammar); the poem related to its public is prayer, proverb, oracle, or spell (rhetoric); the poem related to the poet is dream (symbolic).

Two famous examples of Burke's practical criticism illustrate convincingly his architectonic and transactional emphasis. The " 'Socioanagogic' Interpretation of *Venus and Adonis*" (1950, pp. 212–21) redefines Dante's four levels of interpretation, widens these to encompass all the major styles of literary criticism, and then ranges through these to give a very compressed explication of the poem. Moral or tropological criticism becomes a name for the mode associated most commonly with Burke—*Venus* as a ritual forming, stabilizing, heartening, purifying, sacralizing for the poet and reader. Allegorical criticism is equivalent to a psychoanalytic interpretation of Venus as mother-figure, and a sociological criticism of the economic and social classes symbolized in each of the characters. "Socioanagogic" is Burke's equivalent term for Dante's eternal glory anagoge, and Frye's apocalyptic. He consciously secularizes the divine resonances into worldly glory, the social or hieratic human mystery. This is "the principle of secular divinity, with its range of embarrassment, courtship, modified insult, standoffishness, . . . its scenic embodiment in the worldly equivalent of temples, ritual vestments, rare charismatic vessels. . . ." The most popularly anthologized Burke selection is the brilliant essay "Antony in Behalf of the Play" in *The Philosophy of Literary Form* (1957). The moment in which Antony addresses the mob becomes a commentary on the ritual significance of an entire drama. Just as we have identified ourselves with the forces that destroy the Caesar-principle—symbolized in the phrase "et tu" and the ritual blood purification—now in a tremendous rhetorical peripety Antony convinces us that the Brutus-principle must also be destroyed to expiate our guilt. Burke lets each psychological ploy used by Antony in this single speech radiate outwards to expose the most hidden forces at work throughout the play.

Another explication, more diffuse but of comparable quality, is "*Othello:* An Essay to Illustrate a Method" (1964a, pp. 152–95). Burke interprets each action as the initiation into a mystery, emphasizing the magic ritual aspects of Desdemona's handkerchief, and her "Willow Song" and prayers as sacrificial preparations. Recurrent images are knit together by elaborate psychological associations, and Iago and Desdemona are sometimes approached as symbolic Doubles corresponding to aspects of Othello's own interiority. Burke always tries to get a perspective of synthesis, and then measure how individual items embody and in turn develop it. At the end of this explication he moves beyond *Othello* to the Shakespearean corpus, "in search of an over-all motivational scheme that might account for the shifts from one work to another." A rambling explication, with desultory moments of genuine insight, is the essay "Symbolic Action in a Poem by Keats" (1945, pp. 447–64). Keats's "Ode on a Grecian Urn" is read dramatistically, as one compact rhetorical situation centering on the final oracle identifying truth and beauty. Burke concentrates especially on the transcendental fever that enables us to rise above mortality and also to reflect on the metaphysical basis for this act. In "Fact, Inference, and Proof in the Analysis of Literary Symbolism" (1954, pp. 283–306), Burke gives a close interpretation of Joyce's *Portrait,* with animadversions on the critical methods Burke is trying out in the process. A more conventional sociological and psychological approach is adopted in "The Rhetoric of Hitler's *Battle*" (1964b, pp. 95–110). Originally published in 1939, this analysis of *Mein Kampf* emphasizes effects of the book on its audience, and especially its terms of demonic religious symbolization.

I have used the term religious as Burke himself does to characterize demonic symbolism. Burke has elsewhere drawn attention to a common strategy in literature "reflecting a shift from the religious passion to the romantic (or sexual) passion (the extremes being perhaps the varied imagery of self-crucifixion that characterizes much nineteenth-century literary Satanism)" (1954, p. 296). To handle this shift, Burke has desacralized Dante's term *anagogic,* as I observed before, to pick up the more immediate reverberations of human transcendence. This process of secular-religious language transformation is what I extract as the insightful central theme in *The Rhetoric of Religion* (1961), an otherwise uneven garrulous book, particularly bungling in its capricious biblical exegesis. Man's language about the ineffable God derives from three orders of human experience: natural ("His powerful arm"), sociopolitical ("lord and father"), and linguistic ("The Word"). But man's religious language is situated in what Burke calls an upward and downward Platonist dialectic. There is an upward derivation from empirical data to a transcendent supernatural term, then a reversal back to these lower terms, now viewed as modified by and sharing in the unitary principle encountered en route. Analogies thus fold back on themselves. We are almost overfamiliar with the secularization of religious modes, as in Joyce, when Dedalus transforms the Catholic background of his youth into a jesuitry and priesthood of art. Buck Mulligan in *Ulysses* mocks this as "the cursed jesuit strain . . . only it is injected the wrong way." But the contrary movement must not be overlooked, by which symbols, secular in the beginning, become set apart religiously. Church vestments, at one time borrowed from sheer secular styles, for instance, were abstracted for ritualistic use after fashions changed. The word "vestment" itself, once connoting general clothing, now suggests only religious dress.

Burke has touched something important here, as he so frequently does, with almost casual genius. My repeated complaint in part 1 of this study has been that religious critics often cart out unexamined theological categories like grace and redemption and paste them on scenes and symbols in the literary work. I imagine Burke's impulse would be to analyze first the genesis of the term *grace* from human situations of favoring, giving, forgiving, as analogues of the human experience of God's acceptance; and then compare how religious strategies themselves and the strategies in a literary text being explicated encompass similar situations. Burke develops this technique further in his essay "A Theory of Terminology" (1967, pp. 83–102), suggesting the philosophy of Shakespeare, Kant, or the critic himself be conceived as the product of a graduated series of motives. Some of the possible ultimate motives behind specific styles of philosophical and scientific speculation are dread and terror, play, wonder, Veblen's idle curiosity. A person's religion could thus be a defensive strategy of cowardice or courage, for example, or a pledge of gratitude. Although similar to the Freudian perspective on religion and art as illusion, neurosis, reaction formation, Burke's motive theory seems more flexible and imaginative in its emphasis on wider contexts of social interaction shaping the religious drive.

9

TWO NEW RELIGIOUS-LITERARY SCENARIOS

I BEGAN part 2 with my own theory of functional religious-literary criticism in chapter 4. It has become the basis for the subsequent four chapters outlining what I consider the most significant trends in modern literary criticism. To each applied critic I addressed the question: how productively does he grasp the religious dynamic in a literary work? And what are the full religious implications of his actual practice, whether this be supported by his theory or not? As a fallibilist like C. S. Peirce, I recognize that practice may transcend theory, and that error can have fruitful social purposes. An interpretation based on a deficient theory can still be at minimum partially insightful, and at best intuitively exact.

However, I have addressed the following question to the critical theory itself: what factors in this particular aesthetics enhance or diminish the embodiment of the ideal functional criticism I have sketched? For example, in an attempt to confront Northrop Frye's apparent theoretical evasions, I sought unsuccessfully for further evidence that it could sanction my own type of religious criticism. Is his systematic theory open to literature as a microcosm of *all* being, does it not just tolerate but actively encourage the judicial moment in criticism, is it a genuinely pluralistic system?

From all the evidence assembled in this inquiry, a few conclusions about the nature of religious-literary criticism can be articulated. Most important, there are now two scenarios that have to be overhauled. The first portrays our threatened and solitary religious critic, pleading for minimal recognition before an authoritative established academy of autotelist literary critics. Instead, I have now drawn a picture dominated by humanist semiotic, ortho-cultural, and psycho-mythic critics, with the stricter autotelists in a distinct but legitimate minority. Almost every major critic analyzed here has been striving for a mediatory position between the extremes of centripetal and centrifugal interpretation. The significant issue is no longer the legitimacy of centrifugal criticism.

What matters now is the rigor of its method, the comprehensiveness of its vision, and its capacity to mature beyond lightweight common sense and social commentary into a more profound religious philosophy.

The second scenario to be replaced is the simplified framework I constructed in part 1. It was a nominal group portrait of those critics describing themselves as explicitly religious or theological, with their field of study, major issues, achievements and perhaps even some of their failures. In the sociology of knowledge we ought always to begin by scrutinizing the sphere of evolving self-definition before any attempt to improve on this from outside. My own new scenario replaces this somewhat organized self-defined portrait with an abstractionist collage, superimposing faces in fluid interaction, breaking up neat established religious-literary outlines, party labels, recognized canons of books, programs of study. My functional blueprint of an ideal religious-literary criticism apparently favors some critics nominally political or psychological over some nominally religious. I think the new paradigm suggests a functional criticism more inventive, profound, and diversified, recovering the best charismatic moments in earlier religion and literature interdisciplinary exchanges before an institutionalized paralysis occurred.

There is scarcely a dilemma in methodology broached by explicit religious-literary critics in part 1 that has not been handled also by all the critics introduced in part 2. I have indicated that the three major problem areas stated summarily at the conclusion of part 1 have all been addressed here, independently of the pronounced religious emphasis. The parodies on psychological and myth criticism dramatize the same gaucherie familiar to readers of nominal religious-literary criticism. We have the same dogmatic *eis*-egesis, a reductionism of complex fictive events to a few sterile technical formulas, a mythomania and pansexual obsession that have their counterparts in what I have called spiritual monomania. The critique by Weisinger of Lovejoy's facile recovery of the mere surface ideas in a text recalls the religious critic's tendency to pick up obvious God-talk or Christ symbolism, yet overlook the functionally significant religious pseudonym. Rahv's complaint that archetypal critics float above historical actualities into an abstract Platonic realm repeats the theme of R. W. B. Lewis's "Huckleberry Bushes." Pious readers soar too quickly into transcendent generalities.

Among all these present literary critics, too, we can recognize the crucial interaction between an evolving critical method and the choice of a specific text or problem for analysis. So much explicit religious-literary criticism centers on the corpus of Dante, Milton, Dostoevsky, Joyce, or Graham Greene, for the pronounced religious symbolism in these figures embarrasses the critic incapable of at least a cursory religious commentary. Moreover, is it valid to test the resiliency and integrity of religious criticism by demanding that it render an impressive interpretation of the hen-coop world in Jane Austen's novels? The autotelist critic, at the opposite extreme, has restricted his dazzling repertoire to explicating a safe range of cerebral lyrics or formalist novels. The names of Kafka, Dostoevsky, Faulkner, Wallace Stevens, and others have reappeared with noticeable frequency in part 2. No doubt the religious impulse in literary criticism begins to awaken whenever a critic, no matter what his theory, attempts to transcend himself by grappling with an entire corpus, or bridging a number of works with thematic parallels, or a total genre. His religious imagination intensifies, too, when he searches exhaustively for the deeper metaphysic, especially in texts by combined writer-theologians like Dante, Milton, Goethe, Melville, Yeats, Dostoevsky, Tolstoy, Kafka, Mann, Sartre, and Beckett.

PART 3

LITERARY ASPECTS OF RELIGIOUS THOUGHT

10

TOWARD A FUNCTIONAL RELIGIOUS HUMANISM

THERE ARE at least five purposes behind these final six chapters on modern religious thought. First, in part 2, I consciously selected major critics whose theory and performance supported my own paradigm of religious-literary criticism in chapter 4. So now, I shall sift out important tendencies in contemporary theology sanctioning the principal assumptions behind this same religious-literary theory, especially my cornerstone notion of functional religion. For the sake of a manageable outline capitalizing on my own strengths, I shall restrict my perspective to the religious thought of the West, mostly Christian and para-Christian, just as I have already limited myself only to critics of Western literature.

Second, this study makes no pretence about offering even as thorough a précis, for example, of Karl Rahner's convoluted theology, as I presented for David Daiches's relatively transparent critical theory. But I shall focus almost exclusively upon those features in Rahner and other significant figures that sustain a comprehensive theology of culture and literature, and notably whatever explicit literary criticism that might emerge.

My third purpose is an attempt to take soundings in these currents of religious thought according to the same fourfold classification I applied to literary criticism—autotelist, humanist semiotic, ortho-cultural, and psycho-mythic. Some instructive parallels between literary criticism and theology will, I hope, become apparent, and each correlative tendency in criticism ought to be apprehended more firmly once its corresponding implicit theological foundations are more rigorously explored.

Fourth and conversely, if the tendencies in literary criticism are now better understood, my fourfold classification will seem more feasible in its own right—productive too, perhaps, for an initiatory overview of the intricate variations in modern religious thought. But the classifications suggest misleading analogies as well, for they approach the totality of religious thought as a macrocosmic symbolic system of *homo religiosus*.

Yet the purport of a religious symbol is by my own definition always more than mere human symbolization.

My fifth and most significant purpose is to summon all literary critics to a new scrutiny of the crypto-theological roots underneath their characteristic value judgments, and acquaint them with the broad range of theological options available to them.

Before presenting this overview of theological approaches, I shall clarify three preliminary assumptions in my own theological perspective—about an inclusive style of theologizing, the context and scope of contemporary theologies, and the bellicose dialectic between the humanist's religion and the theist's humanism.

AN INCLUSIVE THEOLOGICAL STYLE

Norman Holland contrasts the two psychological methods in his first and second drafts of *Psychoanalysis and Shakespeare* (1966), the first based on a mere reading knowledge of Freud, the second on his lived experience of Freud in the psychoanalysis of himself and others during a training program at the Boston Psychoanalytic Institute. His earlier stance represents a mentality casually applying Freud to the tragedies, Jung to the comedies, and Adler to the histories, all in an atmosphere of detached eclecticism. The second is a passionate commitment—his personal appropriation of Freud's style and vision "in the pulse." Holland's conversion here can be described as an odyssey from notional to real assent, from the faith described in the Epistle of James, a sheer intellectual assent, capable of existing without works, to the comprehensive justifying faith expounded in Paul's Letter to the Romans.

The same problem confronts us in exploring the divergent theological positions within these four categories. My personal religious commitment to a particular historical revelation may inhibit the use of the psycho-mythic style, for example, or it may support a wide humanism embracing all four approaches. Each person must distinguish between a theology endorsed because it gives best coherence to his own personal faith, and a theology recognized as the most productive basis for literary criticism. These two theological options may coincide or diverge, depending on each person, but the multiple styles themselves are always more than four conceptual tools for the resourceful literary critic. An authentic theology cannot be merely an impersonal academic game. Karl Barth has insisted repeatedly that a real theology must not be about God but toward God, and can be performed only in an act of prayer and wonder. Luther says a person becomes a theologian by living, dying, and being damned, not by reading and speculating. More accurately, I think the authentic theologian must fully experience *and* speculate.

In his popular essay "Where Are We in Theology?" (1972, pp. 27–38) O. C. Thomas discriminates sharply between the tasks of prophecy and theology, only to settle finally for a combined prophetic theology. Prophecy discerns the signs of the times, the live fundamental issues in our private, public, and professional lives, the religious depth in current intellectual, artistic, and political movements. Theology is the critical testing, refining, systematic organizing of this prophetic vision. Prophecy alone is unsteady and transitory impulse; theology alone is futile and dessicating cerebration. All vital theology must be prophetic in this sense, just as I asked that an authentic literary criticism combine an attitude of subjective empathy with one of quasi-objective understanding and assessment, Whitehead's moment of romance and a moment of precision, participation and reflection. I therefore cannot accept the strictures by Edward Schillebeeckx against "a literary and phenomenological kind of theology." He exaggerates the dichotomy between faith itself, and the reflection about faith which "at a certain distance from life, precisely in order to fathom its meaning and to be able ultimately to give it a true direction, does not correspond exactly with lived life" (1968, p. 114).

Theology is essentially logos of theos, "God-talk," an insight into the holy, or what I have previously described as participatory reflection upon religious experience. Theology is defined by Paul Tillich in his *Systematic Theology* as "a rational interpretation of the religious substance of rites, symbols, and myths" (1967, I, p. 16); and by John Macquarrie in *Principles of Christian Theology* as "the study which, through participation and reflection upon a religious faith, seeks to express the content of this faith in the clearest and most coherent language available" (1966, p. 1). John Cobb's *Christian Natural Theology: Based on the Thought of Alfred North Whitehead* expects theologians to show some recognition of indebtedness to a community of shared conviction and faith, for theology is basically "any coherent statement about matters of ultimate concern that recognizes the perspective by which it is governed is received from a community of faith" (1965, p. 252). For Cobb, Macquarrie, and Tillich, what distinguishes a theologian from a philosopher is precisely this conscious solidarity with and spokesmanship for a community's religious experience. Macquarrie believes the philosopher speaks mostly as an individual investigator and pursues the universal religious phenomenon rather than a specific manifestation of it (pp. 2, 35). Although Tillich confuses the status of this discussion by usually equating a theologian with the specifically Christian theologian, the philosopher is distinguishable by his detached objectivity, his ability to transcend a particular faith tradition or theological circle, and his more direct relationship to the other human sciences (pp. 18–28). Cobb achieves flexibility in this dilemma by an elastic notion of community, so that he can talk about communist, naturalist, and humanist theologians, and the possibility of a Buddhist functioning as a Christian theologian by empathic and imaginative participation in a different faith. The act by which a person enters into a divergent faith-world suggests analogies with the suspension of disbelief and the adoption of new possibilities of consciousness, discussed before by literary critics confronting a differing belief system.

By the word "theologian" I imply a scope as comprehensive as that suggested by my notion of religious experience. Besides spokesmen deputized within a specific church tradition, the term includes all marginal philosophers who still view themselves in some relationship to these communities, and all those resolutely or unconsciously freed from particular confessional moorings who speak from a recognizable philosophic tradition or, in the widest extension, for the broader human community. "A full articulation, through systematic, historical, and comparative reflection, of a person's way of life"—this is how Michael Novak describes religious studies, or what I mean by theology (1971, p. xii). In a book review of Louis Dupré's *The Other Dimension* (1972), Langdon Gilkey argues that Dupré theologizes surreptitiously throughout his book and needlessly constricts its scope by capitalizing on the "traditional—and possibly still politically wise—Catholic distinction between philosophy and theology" (cf. Pegis, 1955, and deLubac, 1967). Gilkey's suggestion of Dupré's political motive here is shrewd, for it recalls the opportunism shown during the last half-century by numerous Christian theologians masquerading as philosophers to escape censorship by antimodernist ecclesiastics. Actually, my major precedent for reconstructing a fluid spectrum of religious experience-theology-philosophy is Karl Rahner's theology, which generally best articulates my own personal faith. His approach in "Philosophy and Theology" (1969) is that the religious revelation heard and believed is already a theology, insofar as it is appropriated within previous categories and horizons possessed from elsewhere, no matter how much the new experience may alter this framework. And "in every philosophy men already engage inevitably and unthematically in theology. . . ." For whether the specific philosopher consciously recognizes this or not, "the depth of the human abyss, which in a thousand ways is *the* theme of philosophy, is already the abyss which has been opened by God's grace and which stretches into the depths of God himself. . . ."

The theos upon which theo-logy focuses I have thus far described variously as God, the holy, religious experience, the ultimate organizing sentiment or value, the religious dynamic, the functional religious symbol or myth. I imagine any noticeable widening of this theos concept distresses both the traditional theist and atheist. For the former senses an erosion of clearly legitimated doctrinal boundaries, and the latter, experiencing the threat of an enveloping religious osmosis, must deny progressively more to maintain his recusant identity. It is easier to formulate a counterposition against a supranatural being, the superfather busybody God, than against ultimate concern, transcendent source, immanent spirit, universal consciousness, the absolute historical or life process, man's emerging transcendent self. By theos I refer gropingly to what Langdon Gilkey in *Naming the Whirlwind* (1969a) calls the source, ground, horizon, and limit of who and what I am, the ultimate context within which all meaning is supported. It is not *a* being, but the prior enabling condition of letting-be, "not what is known as an object so much as the basis of knowing, not an object of value but the ground of valuing, . . . the presupposition and basis of all we are and do, of our experience of things, persons, and ourselves, and that which appears at the limits of our powers and capacities." J. A. T. Robinson's *Exploration into God* (1967) calls this approach "an apprehension of the transcendent as given in, with, and under the immanent," God's reality and the universe interpenetrating, but the former always more than and never exhausted by the latter. With a similar panentheist emphasis, Gregory Baum in an essay on "Divine Transcendence" (1971, pp. 120–36) speaks of God as the more-than-human in human life, the sovereign insider in the human situation, establishing time and overcoming it, never identical with, absorbed, or determined by human history. In the style of Rahner, Tillich, Macquarrie, and these other theologians, my own description of theos is *the radically transpersonal which alone can be unconditionally affirmed.* I enlist here the models of human personhood and judgment. The first model idealizes the highest personal attributes in preference to an impersonal paradigm, yet asserts God is still *trans* or beyond the personal. The second model calls attention to this absolute context of meaning I imply in making any meaningful human affirmation.

To grasp the import of this approach to theos and theology, it is essential to recognize the complex paradigm it implies. The model is developed in Wilfred Cantwell Smith's "Secularity and the History of Religions," Georg Simmel's "A Contribution to the Sociology of Religion" (1955, pp. 1–18), and Mircea Eliade's *Patterns in Comparative Religion* (1963, pp. 1–38, 410–36). My paradigm is not the secular-sacred division we have usually accepted as an unquestioned framework for viewing the history of the West—the Graeco-Roman tradition of law and government, science, philosophy, versus the Palestinian religious tradition. Not the correlative nor especially the exclusivist distinctions of church-state, clergy-layman, reason-faith, philosophy-theology, nor even the conceptual and administrative separation of law schools today from divinity schools within a university. Smith challenges such a perspective, especially by arguing for the essentially religious dimension of the original apparently secular Graeco-Roman phenomenon, and a coherent religious *Weltanschauung* behind both of the two separate jurisdictions in medieval Christian society (cf. Cornford, 1957; Dunham, 1947; and Jaeger, 1960).

The model which Smith proposes is an inclusive perspective, similar to the Dewey-Whitehead organic contextual approach to religious experience pervading this present book. In Buddhist, Hindu, Islamic, and ancient Egyptian life, religion is not a mere sector but a quality of all life. No separate chapters in their history can be accurately devoted to political, intellectual, and religious developments. The entire culture is permeated by the religious adverb and adjective—the genuine Hindu goes about his daily business and his cosmic business in religious Hindu ways; or authentic Buddhist life is specifically Buddhist in its center, derivatively Buddhist in all else. We can call religious this "organizing principle of the whole, this center, this part that holds the other parts together. Yet if one calls this part religious, one must not call the other parts not religious. They become nonreligious only when this part ceases to function" (1969, p. 40). When I give up my faith, religion may continue on as one separate factor in life, but no longer as the principle integrating all other factors, and life loses its deeper pattern and meaning.

Georg Simmel's methodology is to view the explicit religious factor in a civilization as a heightening, refinement, and completion of all apparently nonreligious phenomena but which Simmel treats as momenta of religion. His illustrations are the familiar Confucian *pietas* in family, civic, and work relationships, and especially the blend of moral, religious, and juridical sanctions in the Hindu *dharma,* Greek *themis,* and Latin *fas.* Simmel views all of life pervaded, then, by "religious feelings and impulses, . . . whose extreme development and differentiation is religion as an independent content of life" (1955, p. 2). In the language of myth and ritual, Eliade develops this same perspective. By a *primitive* culture. Eliade refers not to ancient chronology, of course, but to a transhistorical possibility in man's present experience. The idealized primitive man views sacred originating forces "once upon a time" in the mythical narrative as the foundation and precedent for everything of value in the profane activity of today—eating, sleeping, hunting, mating, or what I have defined before as penultimate configurations. The current models and exemplars, all morality and custom, "every ritual, and every meaningful act that man performs, repeats a mythical archetype . . . , is taken out of profane 'becoming,' and returns to the Great Time" (1963, pp. 429–30). Smith's religious organizing principle, Simmel's heightening, Eliade's mythical archetype in a total culture are the social counterpart to Gordon Allport's religious master sentiment, described in *The Individual and His Religion* (1950, pp. 54–74), and to what I have described as the religious dynamic in a work of literature.

CONTEXT AND SCOPE OF CONTEMPORARY THEOLOGIES

In "Literature as Equipment for Living" Kenneth Burke recognizes that his interdisciplinary style of criticism requires the demolishment of customary barriers erected around literary studies as a specialized pursuit. "The new alignment will outrage in particular those persons who take the division of faculties in our universities to be an exact replica of the way in which God himself divided up the universe" (1964, p. 109). Lionel Trilling has described how in his own university teaching he experimentally modified the orientation of his literature classes, and how this teaching metamorphosis later affected changes in his critical style. He began with an autotelist emphasis on the literariness and formal analysis of the text, but this Socratic questioning and explication required small groups, whereas his classes were large and the students also seemed disinterested in close textual scrutiny. In their other courses, no ideas which students encountered seemed to equal in force and sanction what they experienced in modern literature, so Trilling's approach became progressively more thematic. And because students lacked philosophical background to comprehend these modern themes, he eventually devoted a large portion of his course to prologomena from Freud, Nietzsche, and Frazer (1965, pp. 3–30). Northrop Frye in "The Search for Acceptable Words" measures the impact upon criticism and scholarship of influences from contemporary Ph.D. training, writing the dissertation, journal publication, requirements in language and philological studies, computer information retrieval, modern library resources, and the garrison mentality that isolates one university department from another (1973, pp. 11–26). These three illustrations alert us to factors in the sociology of knowledge conditioning the development of specific styles, unquestioned assumptions, biases in the literary critic.

Autotelist criticism, for example, can scarcely flourish except in an autonomous linguistics or English department, and in a relatively stable society. Similarly, the shape of theology, and especially religious-literary criticism, is influenced by the classroom clientele, university departmental structures, contemporary reading and publishing fashions, state strictures on religious education, and the oscillating criteria of scholarship.

It would be useful to expand on the accurate historical synopsis of Michael Novak (1971, pp. xi–xvi), suggesting the vicissitudes in theological studies within the last few centuries. First, there was a period of seminary theology for the professional training of clergymen, often in institutions deliberately insulated from contact with other university disciplines. Second, during the eighteenth and nineteenth centuries philosophy with the most grandiose self-confidence addressed itself to all the large religious questions, whereas theology tended to be more ecclesiastical and seminary-oriented. Third, in the last half-century many philosophers turned from religious issues, metaphysics, and all but the analytical foundations. At the same time, psychology, sociology, and the other human sciences, developing in an atmosphere often hostile to the religious factor, asserted a more positivist independence from both philosophy and theology. Finally, reacting against overspecialization and recent secular dogmatisms, there is a concern today about the neglected religious questions, which emerge in departments of social sciences, humanities, and religious studies, all emphasizing a broad humanistic, interdepartmental, and transcultural viewpoint. Perhaps in the light of this historical survey, we can realize the controversial implications of my attempt in this book to identify philosophy with an inclusive type of theology. Frequently the professed theologian is treated patronizingly as a relic of stage one by the crypto-theologian at stage two. Both figures are then arrogantly relegated to an inconsequential back corner by the positivists reigning in stage three, whereas stage four is the only climate in which vital religious-literary criticism becomes really feasible.

Fashions of mass culture influence the shape of theologies. Neoorthodoxy matched the atmosphere of catastrophe and tragic irony following the Depression and the two World Wars. And the convulsive sixties witnessed a bewildering succession of theological styles—radical secularity, the death of God, hope and celebration, revolution—almost suggestive of complex rationalizations for moods of corporate oedipal rebellion, narcissism, manic-depressive neurosis. Skimming through the nine anthologies of *New Theology* from the last eight years communicates an experience of these many divagations, remarkably recorded and even anticipated by Marty's and Peerman's editorship. In the field of Catholic book publishing, for example, the last decade since Vatican II brought first a flood of books, then a dramatic malaise. As ghetto concerns were displaced by wider ecumenical, lay, and social activist perspectives, many Catholics gradually lost interest in the explicit religious label, especially the sectarian imprimatur, in books and the press. I suspect that ecclesiastical problems are being elbowed aside by wider religious questions of meaning, vision, friendship and trust, leadership, social and cultural criticism, all human issues at the margins of the expressly religious. The public perhaps has recognized that books sold through general outlets might actually be more authentically religious than the items recommended in the religion section of a magazine, or circulated by a religious publisher and religious bookstore.

There is no dearth of recent studies on the educational matrix of theology. Milton McLean (1967) concludes his anthology with a survey of courses and programs, both graduate and undergraduate, majors or minors in religious studies, at 135 public and 11 private institutions. The statistics also show elective religious course offerings and indicate how much work is accepted from cognate departments. Robert Michaelsen (1965), of course, is much more thorough in his 10 case studies at major American universities, analyzing patterns of specialization, textbooks and topics emphasized, enrollment figures, faculty qualifications and publications, the history of each program, and relationships with other departments. One of his main goals is to speculate on the legal implications of each program, especially if the institution employs ordained clergymen on a state salary. Erich Walter (1958) introduces such topics as indoctrination and academic freedom problems in the classroom, counseling and campus life issues, interdisciplinary friction or compatibility between religion and the humanities, the social sciences, and the natural sciences. Clyde Holbrook's work (1963) is a defense of appropriate techniques in studying and teaching theology as a liberal discipline, concerned with religion mostly as it impinges upon political, literary, economic, and other cultural contexts. He includes analyses of various programs similar to Michaelsen's study, but also a list of representative scholars in religious studies "identified neither with departments of religion nor with seminaries," although he concedes that most influential scholarship seems to occur in seminaries affiliated with university centers.

The relevance of all this data to our present discussion can now be summarized. The U.S. tax-support structure in each state prompts institutions to articulate and often disguise specific types of theology programs. In some public and private situations, a student waives state tuition support if he majors in religious studies, nor can he attain teacher certification in this major. Also in some public universities there is a reluctance about paying ordained ministers of religion a direct salary, or about supporting a department of full-time teachers of religion. These hard realities, besides the tolerance exhibited by other academic departments, the caprices of administrative policy, public relations, student and faculty interest, and other factors lead often to the submergence of the explicit religious rubric. Religious studies occur in philosophy departments or humanities programs, sometimes taught by part-time inadequately qualified local clergymen, at other times by figures whose primary competence is in fields other than theology. This factor is a double-pronged advantage—the Bible can be taught clumsily as literature by one English teacher with crippling deficiencies in Greek, Hebrew, and theological scholarship, for example, yet the text can be explicated by another English scholar with more sensitivity and insight than shown by many less imaginative biblical exegetes with all their philological credentials. For, as Holbrook observes somewhat utopically about the study of two sacred texts, "the comparative appraisal of Buddhist and Christian analyses of the nature and goal of human existence demands no more or less unique devices than does the comparison of Mandeville's and Rousseau's outlooks on life" (1963, p. 37). At any rate, in this whole university situation, theology is forced into more intimate and varied interdisciplinary contexts, now emerging alongside—or metamorphosed into—an anthropology of religious myth and ritual, a psychology of religious experience, a history of religions, a sociology of American church patterns, a study of religion and literature. McLean thinks recent theologians like Tillich and the Niebuhrs have proved to a wide public that no liberal education can be complete without an appreciation of man's religious nature. And the recent expansions of anthropology, Asian, African, Latin-American, East European Studies, and other programs in the human sciences convince increasingly more university faculty and students of their incapacity to grasp remote cultures without understanding the religious values and behavior at the center of these cultures.

I think a fine concise introduction to contemporary Christian theological currents is Daniel Day Williams's *What Present-Day Theologians Are Thinking* (1967), suggesting the lines of dialogue with historians, psychologists, and anthropologists, and selecting five central dilemmas that continue to preoccupy theologians. Ved Mehta's *The New Theologian* (1965) interviews reputable theologians primarily concerning their approach to the J. A. T. Robinson "Honest to God" debate, with frivolous journalistic commentary, inhibited by Mehta's own stereotypes of Christian orthodoxy and of the church theologian's traditional image. To sense the range of topics and styles in Christian theology—confessional and marginal—and other particular theologies, I recommend skimming many anthologies in the paperback series *New Theology* (1964–73), edited by Martin Marty and Dean Peerman, and *New Directions in Theology Today*, under the general editorship of William Hordern. Volume 6 in the latter series is Roger Shinn's *Man: The New Humanism* (1968), a helpful account of interchanges between Christian theology, existentialism, Marxism, and the biological and social sciences, with their conflicting humanistic perspectives. A good survey of the international Christian theological situation from Barth and Jaspers in Germany, to British analytic religious philosophy, and Van Buren, Gibson Winter, Harvey Cox in America, is presented in Sperna Weiland's *New Ways in Theology* (1968). A very informative book gradually reaching beyond its specific Anglican emphasis is Robert Page's *New Directions in Anglican Theology: A Survey from Temple to Robinson* (1965), with a perceptive history of the British analytic movement. An intricate but productive analysis of the transition from Schleiermacher to Barth and the later recovery of immanence in Tillich, Hartshorne, and Wieman occurs in *Transcendence of God* (1960) by Edward Farley. *Religion in Philosophical and Cultural Perspective: A New Approach to the Philosophy of Religion through Cross-Disciplinary Studies* (1967), edited by Feaver and Horosz, presents sixteen articles as a tour de force on the multifaceted interdisciplinary phenomenon, in articles by a historian, psychoanalyst, scientific humanist, and process philosopher, among others.

DIALECTIC: THE HUMANIST'S RELIGION AND THE THEIST'S HUMANISM

Thus far in this book we have met a recurring situation of major importance. The avowed theist accuses explicit humanist critics of slyly trimming down the theistic context of a work and then evaluating it as deficient or adequate humanism manqué—such as C. S. Lewis on Leavis's Milton; Edwin Muir on Daiches's Milton, Eliot, and Joyce; Hyatt Waggoner on Irving Howe's Hawthorne. On the other hand, Northrop Frye argues that critics can only approach the religious dimension in literature as sheer projected human value, and Rahv suspects that behind much religious conversion lies concealed a traditionalist, pusillanimous failure of nerve, an escape from the demands of human immediacy. R. W. B. Lewis, too, has derided the theist who leaps into transcendent religious generalities without touching the concrete "huckleberry bushes." When C. S. Lewis and Leavis both read

Milton, then, do the humanist Leavis and theist Lewis perceive the same poetry but disagree only in their prior assumptions about the nature of man and human joy, and thus merely assess the total literary experience differently? Or more accurately, is not the initial gestalt of each critic divergent? I am convinced that the entire *Weltanschauung* of humanism or of theism pervades the act of perception itself. Consequently, I shall not babble about an ideal moment of detached phenomenological experience of the text, which precedes the judicial moment that is somehow less pure or trustworthy than the former. A specious dilemma thus far, you will say, for I have already assumed that an explicit humanist is an implicit theologian, actually in search of the religious dynamic, the search in which Lewis engages consciously. So Leavis covertly and Lewis overtly are up to the same business. I congratulate the humanist for his crypto-religious sensitivity, and he proclaims me in turn an extraordinary crypto-humanist. Is this just a fatuous language game, and if so, by whose rules shall we play?

More than semantics is involved here. First, I think Leavis and Lewis are both theologians, with divergent religious convictions about man's destiny, capacity, and the good life. And this religious faith, without diminution, can be permeated by enough empathy and tolerance to motivate as fresh and accurate a perception of the work as possible, a perception differing according to each critic's varying capacities of artistic sensitivity, spiritual consciousness, and informed inclusiveness of perspective. Second and more important, however, is the conflict illustrated here between two totalisms, from below and from above, reductivist and distensionist, the humanizing and divinizing tendencies. Resisting the immediate tendency to flatten out these sharp polarities, I shall attempt to understand the plausibility of each approach and its potential fallacies, so that I can work toward a position of controlled accommodation between both tendencies.

One of the clearest humanist prototypes is the explicit anti-theist Ludwig Feuerbach, who in *The Essence of Christianity* portrays how man, after alienating his highest human qualities from himself, projects and hypostatizes them, worships them, and pleas to regain them again subserviently as grace, forgiveness, divine moral commands. Thus, "religion is the disuniting of man from himself; he sets God before him as the antithesis of himself. . . . Theology is anthropology (1957, pp. xxvii, 33). And the purpose of Feuerbach's own theology is therefore "reduction of the extrahuman, supernatural, and antirational nature of God to the natural, immanent, inborn nature of man . . ." (p. 339). This position of Feuerbach has its most obvious aftermath in Marx's translation of religious history into its sheer economic components, and Freud's treatment of religion as an illusory projection. Besides retrojecting both gods and demons back into man's consciousness where they originated, Freud's principal concern in *The Future of an Illusion* (1953) is that a morality forbidding murder, not for reasons of intrinsic human conscience, but only because God arbitrarily prohibits it, will disintegrate chaotically in an era committed to a twilight of the gods.

Freud and Feuerbach contain the quintessence of anti-theist humanism: first, man's religious history has not been an encounter with the hidden God progressively revealing Himself, but a growth in human self-awareness from *homo absconditus* to *homo revelatus*. In the quip of Morris Cohen, "An honest God's the noblest work of man." Second, man's religions are therefore worthy of attention as a humanistic study of his moral ideals, fears, his own deepest self-understanding. Third, man has been duped, even debased and harmed by alienating his human worth and then despairing of this loss or groveling to recover it from authoritarian idols of his own unconscious contrivance. Fourth, "if God does not exist, then all is permitted," the recurring dictum in *Brothers Karamazov*, is a patent fallacy. For brotherhood and morality are to be valued in themselves, not requiring the support of religious dogmas about the sovereignty and fatherhood of God, especially since the lives of those believing them show so little evidence of moral superiority anyway. Instead, the churches and religious believers have been the source of persecution, intolerance, intellectual dishonesty, and human disunity. T. S. Eliot says, "If you remove from the word 'human' all that the belief in the supernatural has given to man, you can view him finally as no more than an extremely clever, adaptable, and mischievous little animal" (1932, p. 397). The naturalistic humanist would expose Eliot's partisan logic behind trumping up these two contrived exclusive alternatives, and the unworthy meretricious threats and bribes attempting to coerce belief.

As a paradigm of theistic humanism, on the contrary, I shall select the Christian humanists Karl Rahner and Teilhard de Chardin. A preliminary response to the anti-theist approach I have just summarized would be that the theos rejected is clearly a supranaturalist authoritarian anthropomorphic symbol, functionally *alienating* for some unfortunate individuals in the manner claimed. But the actual theos accepted to replace it is Feuerbach's natural, immanent inborn nature of man, or Freud's mature intrinsic human ethos, the scientific spirit, or what Freud in his *Future of an Illusion* calls a mature intrinsic human ethic, the scientific spirit, the god Logos. These factors cannot be identified simply with the concrete actuality of man, but are values that function normatively as religious master sentiments, ideals of self-transcendence.

Whereas Feuerbach's theology and anthropology are identified, Rahner's anthropology is an abbreviated Christology, an inchoate theology of Christ and Christian existence, or conversely, his Christology is a self-transcending anthropology. What is man? God's self-disclosure in Christ claims a man is actually more than could be discovered only by empirical means. Man, his person and artifacts, has within his innermost existence an openness toward the divine, an entelechy oriented toward Christ as final and formal dynamic, or as man's combined destiny, exemplar, and vital intrinsic impulse of self-transcendence. Everything human is an icon, the potential self-expression of God, who from the beginning has created the human with the intent that God Himself should someday become the perfectly human, Christ. To perceive man and his civilization in its inner relatedness to Christ is to experience the human phenomenon in its deepest particularity and genuine reality. In his essay "On the Theology of the Incarnation," Rahner asserts his famous conviction about anonymous or crypto-Christianity. Every man conscientiously searching, open, trying to fulfill the imperatives of his humanity at its best—no easy matter!—says "yes to Christ, even when he does not know that he does. For he who lets go and jumps, falls into the depths such as they are, and not such as he himself has sounded" (1966, p. 119). In "Christianity and Non-Christian Religions" (1963, pp. 112–35), Rahner clarifies further his attribution of potential crypto-Christianity to the express Buddhist, Hindu, naturalistic humanist, not simply for their humanness *despite* the non-Christian status, but specifically in their particular community identity as authentic Buddhists or humanists.

In this theology, there is less emphasis on the familiar historical details of Jesus Christ's public ministry, more on the resurrected Christ and Holy Spirit, the Lord of History, the Pantocrator Christ of the ancient basilicas, the immanent Christ of both Eastern and Western Christian mystics. The same themes occur in Teilhard de Chardin's more lyrical personal idiom. In *Building the Earth* (1958) and *Writings in Time of War* (1967), Teilhard declares the characteristic purpose of his work: to reconcile two poles of attraction, "the sense of Earth opening and flowering upwards in the sense of God, and the sense of God rooted and nourished below in the sense of earth" (1958, p. 77). Or he hopes so to experience Christ and the human situation, that "it is impossible for me to possess the one without embracing the other, to be in communion with the one without being absorbed into the other, to be absolutely Christian without being desperately human" (1967, p. 57). Alert to objections that this theological vision may foster a cosmic pantheism despising concrete experience and plunging immediately into the divine reality, Teilhard requires that a Christian "give things their highest possible degree of reality, whether it be in his knowledge of them, and his love for them, or in their proper being" (1967, p. 139). Or he addresses God, "Must not my love drive its roots into every single thing, since it is through the entire extension of the world that You offer Yourself to me, that so I may feel You and clasp You?" (1967, p. 126). Teilhard's description of God is a personalized counterpart to the immanent religion of Freud and Feuerbach: "the deeper I descend into myself, the more I find God at the heart of my being; the more I multiply the links that attach me to things, the more closely does He hold me—the God who pursues in me the task, as endless as the whole sum of centuries, of the Incarnation of His Son" (1967, p. 61).

Definitely pertinent to the discussion here, I believe, is an insight developed in Leslie Dewart's *Future of Belief* (1966, pp. 52–76). Marxist anti-theism is conditioned relatively by its prior commitment to humanism, which rejects a particular concept of theos because this seems incompatible with a specific understanding of man's autonomy and dignity. Christianity professes an anti-theism, too, relative to its self-critical theism, stripping itself iconoclastically of such theistic distortions as excessive belief, complacency, fanaticism, and the selfish preference for personal salvation rather than an uncompromising passion for the truth. In this context, Basil Mitchell also impugns an unconditional type of faith that clings to a belief "in such a way as to refuse in advance to reject it even if it should be shown to be false. The religious believer, as it were, erects madness into a principle" (1969, p. 187). Dewart thus concludes that Marxists and Christians often agree implicitly in their humanism and conditional anti-theism, although "that of Marxism is relative to its humanism; that of Christianity is relative to its theism. This is why Marxism finds in the human experience the *absence* of God, whereas Christianity finds in the same experience *both* the absence and presence of God" (p. 75).

Summarily, in this confrontation between professed humanists and professed theists, I can affirm a few crucial premises of my own. First, every theological symbol is also an implicit affirmation about the symbolizer, man, and every statement about man implicitly affirms something about his center of meaning, God. There is what Kenneth Burke calls an upward-downward dialectic in all these statements.

Second, I believe *all* the figures discussed throughout this book are theologians of various styles and ideological commitments, on a wide spectrum both of intensity and rigor in their search for the religious dynamic, and of varying self-understanding about their theological search and the community of faith for which they are implicit spokesmen.

Third, all are truly humanistic insofar as they stress the concrete historical particularity of the human person, civilization, and literary work confronted, listen as far as possible to its own authentic voice, and labor to detect and articulate the constant dialectic at work between their own religious world view and the religious dynamic in the person or object encountered. The goal is to achieve as open and comprehensive a humanism as possible.

Fourth, the genuine humanist must somehow symbolize or mythologize the theos as present and implicated within the human reality itself, not as a sheer extrinsic source of moral demands or a prospective destiny dissociated from the inner human dynamic. I do not reach the reality of the sacred by diminishing the human, nor vice versa, but I experience God in human history as a single human-divine phenomenon—in the style of the classical Chalcedonian formula for Christ's humanity-divinity, distinct but inseparable from the world.

Fifth, certain stereotyped broadsides ought to be renounced. The implicit theologian does not necessarily become a deeper humanist or theologian simply by conversion to a specific style of explicit religion or theology. Nor especially is his humanism emasculated because he rejects supranaturalist dogmatic foundations. Moreover, the hatred, fanaticism, and neuroses prompted by pathological theism are no more pertinent to this discussion than the cynicism, totalitarian intolerance, or invertebrate adaptability sanctioned in the name of various pathological humanisms.

Sixth, I do not discriminate against humanists like Philip Rahv, Sidney Hook, Irving Howe, David Daiches, and others by setting up a language game with inclusive protean definitions of terms like theologian, religious dynamic, or theos. I claim the distended or transcendental humanism I have described can endorse all they affirm explicitly, and also whatever can be affirmed implicitly beyond this. On the other hand, their reductivist humanism denies the central meaning and impulse in the religious-literary criticism and theology I affirm explicitly. In their most doctrinaire moments, they transvalue my theos into far less, whereas I embrace all they affirm in their own position, but support nothing that they deny. The full particularity and integrity of both our approaches must be preserved, and this can be accomplished in a mutually tolerant pluralism. If both positions are to be more deeply synthesized within a single system of concepts and values, this can never be accomplished by a unilateral reductionism, but only by inclusive and self-transcending categories such as those I have espoused.

11

AUTOTELIST RELIGIOUS THOUGHT

THE AUTOTELIST style was introduced in chapter 5 as the extreme limiting case in literary criticism, most aloof and impervious to a functional religious approach. I now apply the term autotelist to theologies exaggerating the autonomy and hegemony of specific methodologies or themes to such an extent that they undermine the type of comprehensive theology and literary theory I have proposed. The biblical text becomes the exclusive source of religious truth, for example, or the strict empirical methods of the positive sciences must replace theological and metaphysical reflection, or a type of messianic sociology ambitions to supplement all previous knowledges. Each of these three realms is treated as authoritative, autotelist, not accountable to criteria derived from sources outside its boundaries. Two of these tendencies I shall now isolate for further description, the strict positivist style of language analysis and of biblical theology.

ANALYTIC POSITIVISM

Under the heading of analytic positivism I want to distill the most antimetaphysical tendencies in the Vienna Circle of Moritz Schlick and Rudolph Carnap, the neopositivist school of G. E. Moore and Bertrand Russell, the disciples of Ludwig Wittgenstein at Cambridge, and the Oxford school of linguistic analysis (Ayer, 1959). Some of the most militant and also communicable examples of analytic language reductionism occur in A. J. Ayer's *Language, Truth, and Logic,* the Antony Flew contributions to the famous brief debate with R. M. Hare, Basil Mitchell, and I. M. Crombie in "Theology and Falsification" (1955), and Rudolf Carnap's essay on "The Elimination of Metaphysics through Logical Analysis of Language." Their basic reductionist strategy has been to divide meaningful propositions taxatively into two classes, according to the approach popularized in Hume's *Enquiry Concerning Human Understanding:* tautological formal propositions as in logic or mathematics, and factual propositions empirically verifiable. Theological or metaphysical statements fitting neither of these classes are denied any cognitive status, for they state nothing true or false, though they might be tolerated as emotive, attitudinal, poetic exclamations. "We may accordingly define a metaphysical sentence as a sentence which purports to express a genuine proposition, but does, in fact, express neither a tautology nor an empirical hypothesis," Ayer first proclaimed in 1936. "And as tautologies and empirical hypotheses form the entire class of significant propositions, we are justified in concluding that all metaphysical assertions are nonsensical" (1952, p. 41). This hostility to statements about the absolute or about man's destiny arises not because they are emotive—an attribute that can be urbanely patronized—but because they masquerade deceptively as something they cannot be. Recall the divagations in I. A. Richards's evolving position on the cognitive function of both poetry and religious belief. Also, Susanne Langer's autotelist aesthetic theory can be better appreciated in this present context as a brave assertion of the true cognitive import in emotive utterances, the semblanced logical forms of feeling. Her link with the analytic movement can be studied in Langer's interesting textbook, with clear informative illustrations, *An Introduction to Symbolic Logic* (1967), first published in 1937.

Carnap's antitheological polemic is far more aggressive than Ayer's. Metaphysical assertions are pseudo-statements of unspecified syntax, framed in evocative inexact terminology. He performs a dazzling reductio ad absurdum of Heidegger's "The Nothing itself nothings," Descarte's *cogito,* and such commonplace philosophical clichés as God, the unconditioned, the primordial basis, the being of being, Freud's nonego, Sartre's being-in-and-for-itself. Carnap pronounces a verdict of meaninglessness on any knowledge that pretends to reach above or behind empirical experience, especially "on any ethics or aesthetics as a normative discipline. . . . It is altogether impossible to make a [meaningful] statement that expresses a value-judgment" (1959, p. 77). Theology and poetry are essentially mythology, generating an illusion of theoretical content in the deceptive logic of truth and falsehood suggested by their sentence structure. Asserting nothing, they can only *express.* Metaphysics "arises from the need to give expression to a man's attitude in life, his emotional and volitional reaction to the environment, to society, to the tasks to which he devotes himself . . . ." This attitude could be far better expressed in a pure art like music, "entirely free from any reference to objects. . . . Metaphysicians are musicians without musical ability." They achieve "nothing for knowledge and something inadequate for the expression of attitude" (pp. 79–80). There could be no clearer apologia for pure poetry, and for interpreting literature according to the more autotelist models helpful in grasping the other fine arts. Perhaps Carnap's diminution of the prescriptive language in ethics and aesthetics into a set of attitudes purely descriptive and expressive could be modified along the lines of C. L. Stevenson's suggestions in "Emotive Meaning of Ethical Terms" (1959, pp. 264–81). Even though their normative weight cannot be empirically verified, all these value judgments not only give a neutral description of my values but also claim the power to influence, intensify, change the interests of others around me. In Dewey's sense, ethical terms are persuasive instruments used in the intricate transaction and readjustment of human interests.

Antony Flew contributes a significant brief corollary to this discussion. Ayer in his historical introduction to Logical Positivism has remarked that as this movement evolved, the demand that all meaningful statements pass the test of strict empirical verifiability gave way to Karl Popper's principle that these statements must at least be theoretically capable of being falsified by the introduction of empirical counter-examples. Later developments reduced the stringency of both verifiability and falsifiability criteria, so that eventually the empiricist could require only that a meaningful assertion must "be capable of being in some degree confirmed or disconfirmed by observation . . ." (1959, p. 14). This minimal canon of at least some public observability, accountability, and empirical verifiability, for example, is also the basis for Sidney Hook's pragmatist attack in *Quest for Being* (1961) against the privileged esoteric self-enclosures erected protectively around religious language. Flew's insight is simply that this erosion of the falsifiability canon must have some limit, especially in assertions about God's existence. Using John Wisdom's parable of the discovery of a cultivated garden in the wilderness attended or not by a hypothetical gardener, Flew demonstrates how an assertion of belief in the gardener's existence, confronted by repeated challenges to give empirical evidence, is modified progressively by claims that he must be invisible, intangible, imperceptible, unknowable. Eventually the believer can show no empirical difference between a nonexistent gardener and the concept of an existent gardener whittled away by this process of endless qualification. "A fine brash hypothesis may thus be killed by inches, the death by a thousand qualifications" (1955, p. 97). I find this simple argument a vivid illustration of the apophatic *via negativa* paradoxes implied in any positive assertions about God. An exact use of analogous language requires me to deny features in every similitude I affirm of God. G. M. Hare's response to Flew in this same discussion echoes

Carnap's treatment of theology as sheer lyrical attitude—the believer's claims are only his *blik*, his viewpoint or stance or style, as expressive of a personality as his smile or handshake, but not asserting anything of verifiable content.

BIBLICAL POSITIVISM

A product of the best humanist tradition in his own era, Martin Luther could pray for a harvest of poets and rhetoricians because "I am persuaded that without knowledge of literature pure theology cannot at all endure. . . . There has never been a great revelation of the Word of God unless He has first prepared the way by the rise and prosperity of languages and letters, as though they were John the Baptists" (Marty, 1966, p. 189). This favorable entente between theology and the human sciences has been challenged repeatedly in human history, especially during epochs when a specific religious position sees itself a threatened subcult. Tatian, Tertullian, and other early Christian apologists denounced the subtle pagan acculturation affected by the theater and schools of rhetoric. This prophetic reprimand has been reenacted in the Christian iconoclastic heresy, seventeenth-century Puritanism, and the more recent protests of strict evangelical sects and popular utopic counter-cultures.

I have previously described how the literary critic both questions the text and allows the text to question him, so that his very categories and assumptions are modified in the process of interpreting. Similarly, Rahner observes that the biblical exegete simultaneously interprets and is interpreted to himself, for he creatively appropriates a religious experience mediated by his own previous categories and horizons, but the new experience also changes and passes judgment on this entire framework. Here is the dilemma, then: to what extent shall the religious interpreter apply methods, themes, models derived from literary criticism, psychology, anthropology, and the other human sciences—an approach associated in the nineteenth century with the Higher Criticism—in explicating and later translating or remythologizing his experience of the sacred text? How far shall he let his cultural context modify what he perceives, and how far shall he let that context be prophetically modified? Two extremes immediately suggest themselves in the history of Christianity—the lifeless acculturated Christianity characteristic of state churches and of uncritical civil religion in the eighteenth and nineteenth centuries, and the fanatically reclusive sectarian Christianity of the seventeenth century.

In American folklore the Scopes Trial at Dayton, Tennessee, in the twenties is a travesty of this debate between Liberal and Fundamentalist Christians. If the Book of Genesis were literally God's word to man, then its apparently nonevolutionary science could not err, nor be displaced by any mere human perspective. This was the contention of William Jennings Bryan, in the face of Clarence Darrow's skeptical citations from the biblical Higher Critics. Fundamentalist theology written today perpetuates this same quarrel. The contributors to Philip Hughes's anthology *Creative Minds in Contemporary Theology* (1966) are introduced menacingly as "scholars of evangelical conviction who place themselves under the authority of Holy Scripture, wishing to bring every thought into captivity to the obedience of Christ" (p. 5). The similarities here between biblical and analytic positivists are quite pronounced: poetry and theology must submit, almost at the extremity of self-annihilation, to the captivity and authority of Scripture, rather than on the other hand to the scientific experimental method. Bultmann is attacked for exalting "the critical reason of man next to the Scriptures" (p. 159); Teilhard de Chardin's subversively humanistic religion affirms "two separate sources of revelation, namely that of the divine Word and that of 'natural' autonomous reason" (p. 436). In a chapter entitled "Modern Theology at the End of Its Tether," Carl Henry (1966) attacks Tillich, Bultmann, and their followers as "modern Athenians," distracting the contemporary Christian by "existential, linguistic, and secularistic" ploys away from an awareness of his sinfulness. The target for most intensive censure, Hughes also insists, is these theologians' "unbiblical humanism, which denies the sovereignty and otherness of God and affirms the adequacy and centrality of man."

A more sophisticated biblical fundamentalism occurs in the thought of Abraham Heschel, whose essay on "Symbolism and Jewish Faith" (1955, pp. 53–80) shows a sensitive wariness of the obsession with myth and symbol among both contemporary critics and theologians. Rabbi Heschel fears the cognitive content and actual reality of God's biblical self-disclosure will disappear in a symbolic hall of mirrors, where man ends up discovering only his own face, reducing "beliefs to make-believes, observance to ceremony, prophecy to literature, theology to aesthetics." Heschel wants to constrict the interpretative ingenuity of the exegetical creative mind. For the religious act is essentially a *mitzvah*, a moral deed in response to God's actual biblical command. The symbolic aspect of man's response is only incidental; he worships symbolically no more than he eats and sleeps symbolically. Religion is not simply one of the dialects of man's symbolic language, because religion also sanctifies besides signifying, it expresses more what God wills than what man experiences. Man is not just Cassirer's symbol maker, he is by definition created to *become* a symbol, representing and imitating the holiness of God. Understandably anxious to extricate the believer from an epistemological fastidiousness and despair over hermeneutics, the convolutions of literary criticism, the biblical myths and symbols devised by the human mind of the prophet speaking and the exegete hearing, Heschel argues for a literalistic simple directness that for many believers generates more problems than it resolves. For Jahweh is portrayed as sulking, petty, and vindictive in the literal text. Heschel is convinced that since I love not a symbol of another human being but the person himself, so in reading the Bible I can achieve a nonsymbolic or metasymbolic, direct, immediate contact with God.

KARL BARTH. The name most frequently associated with contemporary biblical positivism is the complex figure of Karl Barth, always fluctuating and evolving dynamically beyond the frozen positions of most neo-orthodox Barthians. It is exhilarating to follow his successive animated exchanges with Harnack, Bultmann, Tillich, Gogarten, and Brunner; and especially to analyze his changes of mind in three articles written for *The Christian Century* in 1938, 1948, and 1958, each summarizing his thought during the preceding decade (Brunner, 1946; Smart, 1967; Barth, 1966; and James Robinson, 1964, pp. 1–77, and 1968, pp. 142–54, 205–20).

Barth's methodology in explicating Paul's Epistle to the Romans can be placed somewhere between that of Adolf Harnack and Rudolf Bultmann. Harnack expects the exegete to get intellectual control of the object, to establish the objective content of the Gospel by a detached rigorous method. Yet Bultmann demands that it be fully reenacted in a new context and demythologized so that it communicates with the present era. Barth defends the flexible type of spiritual creative exegesis characteristic of Luther and of Paul's own interpretation of Old Testament passages. It is a committed personal exegesis, permeated by one's own theology, fully responsive to yet critical of the present milieu. Previous Liberal exegetes had stripped from Paul's thought its allegedly unpalatable accidental features, whereas Barth seeks to recapture the original situation of the text and then translate it into the present. The vital question for Barth is always the extent to which a biblical exegete's own personal theology becomes operative, with the danger that it might intrude as a secondary source of revelation and authority alongside the Word of God.

Barth in his heated exchange with Brunner (1946) slaps down any point of contact between God and man, especially the doctrine of analogy as formulated by a Scholastic like Przywara, suggesting that the divine and human can be apprehended under a single conceptualization of being. A purely nonbiblical natural theology is a dangerous man-made religion, an idolatry of arrogant self-sufficiency, presuming to treat God, grace, and history "as if one had them pocketed, as if one had the knowledge of them below one instead of always behind and in front" (p. 77). Bultmann's fallacy is to make theology too homocentric, as though the Bible were simply a religious myth of man's salvation. In a rebuttal during the early twenties to Tillich's plea for a theology of culture uncovering the logos and Holy Spirit even in the literature, arts, civilization of heathen and Jews, Barth censures Tillich for this evasion of "the scandalous historicity and factuality of revelation," which occurs in the Bible alone. Tillich insists the Christian must say a qualified yes and no to the world, not simply a Barthian no, in "a very undialectic supernaturalism," referring of course to Barth's resolute Kierkegaardian leap of faith, requiring a sectarian, dualistic teleological suspension of the natural and rational man. Barth detects in Tillich a naive assumption that judgment and grace already reign everywhere, which is nothing more than a theology of cheap universalism, worthy of no better than "The God of Schleiermacher and Hegel" (1968, p. 142). Barth's attack here against Schleiermacher's cultural theology and romantic Liberalism brings to mind a perceptive psychological critique by Henry Wieman and Bernard Meland (1936, pp. 77–98), which at that time associated Barth, Tillich, and the Niebuhrs all in a single "neosupernaturalist" clique, viewed from an anti-Fundamentalist process-theology perspective. The childhood of Barth and Tillich, for example, was dominated by traditional supernaturalism, which became a compromised Protestant Liberalism in young adulthood, but eventually reverted in middle age to the pristine stage, denying the aberrant phase with all the punitive scapegoating of a zealous convert.

Barth's odyssey beyond this biblical positivism is a familiar narrative. It can be studied in successive volumes of his *Church Dogmatics* (1969), especially from the second volume up to his 1956 essay on "The Humanity of God," if you painstakingly hunt down topics like grace, Christ, man as an image of God, and Barth's progressively conciliatory attitude toward Catholicism and the major world religions. The effect of his earlier dialectical theology was to encourage a new biblical emphasis, and to render negligible or even suspect the questions raised by contemporary human sciences, by any attempt at a theology of acculturation or correlation, or a philosophy of world religions. Barth can joke in the 1938 version of "How I Changed My Mind" about others' caricatures of his earlier neoorthodox posture, affirming an "abstract, transcendent God . . . separated from state and society by an abyss," and epitomized in the distorted aphorism, "God is all, man is nothing!" Barth becomes gradually both "very much more churchly and *very* much more worldly."

Why did Barth change? He could finally no longer center his attention only on the Bible, insulated from an autonomous Nazi state ethos supported by Luther's tidy theology of two separate kingdoms, but had to *confess* against Hitler, and accept exile, becoming a prophetic theologian of contemporary political and cultural realities. Also, Barth had opened himself to the religious-literary phenomenon and a more inclusive religious humanism. He was now ready to occupy himself "more than formerly with universal *Geistesgeschichte;* on two journeys to Italy to let classical antiquity speak to me as it had never done before; to gain a new relationship with Goethe, among others; to read countless novels, a good many of them from those first-rate producers of the English detective novel; to become a very bad but very passionate horseman, and so on" (1966, pp. 44–48).

12

HUMANIST SEMIOTIC RELIGIOUS THOUGHT

In the last chapter I tried to isolate the autotelist instant in two apparently disparate movements evolving rapidly toward a surprising convergence, which I shall now analyze in this present chapter as a humanist semiotics. A self-confident simplistic reductionism, almost caricatured in the two positions I have sketched, gradually disappears as the language phenomenon proves itself so subtle and intricate a problem, whether present in the biblical Word, a systematic theological treatise, or the grammar of preaching, liturgy, private prayer, and other forms of personal religious experience. Although adhering basically to the rhetoric and phenomenology categories useful in chapter 6 to classify Anglo-American and French semiotic criticism, I shall subdivide rhetoric into the more generic British analytic tradition and the German hermeneutic movement. Both the German biblical hermeneutic and the British religious language positions are parallel to the Anglo-Saxon rhetoricians' meticulous textual scrutiny and anxiety to recover the authentic religious tradition and context. It was claimed before that the French phenomenological or structuralist critics derive their methodology explicitly from Sartre, Merleau-Ponty, Levi-Strauss, and Heidegger. Reserving Sartre for a later section on political theology, I shall focus here on the phenomenological style of these latter three figures, notably Heidegger, who has such a pronounced influence on the New Hermeneutic.

RELIGIOUS RHETORIC

The demolishing positivism of Ayer and Carnap has provoked some brilliant counterattacks. The most obvious response is to turn their own theoretically exacting verification method against the shoddy argumentation supporting the method. You have perhaps noticed their constant prescriptive use of language in the passages I have quoted—words like "better" or "worse," "more meaningful," "more significant," in the very act of rejecting value judgments. Willard Quine's "Two

Dogmas of Empiricism" (1969, pp. 398–497) demonstrates that according to their own canons, the reduction of all significance to the immediately verifiable by empirical methods is a belief, a philosophical presupposition not strictly scientific. In *The Edges of Language* (1972) Paul Van Buren takes up an apparently clever position against Flew's parable. He substitutes a sophisticated religious analyst for the doctrinal literalist character in the tale, who tells our skeptic that the believer uses the word "God" because he cares so much about where we come from and where we are going and the beauty of the garden. Yet here Van Buren scarcely gets much further than Hare's noncognitive *blik*. The most effective rebuttal of all is M. B. Foster's essay on "'We' in Modern Philosophy" (1957, pp. 194–220), which selects passages from Ayer, Hare, and G. E. Moore, containing muted assertions such as "we call," or "we do not know," suggesting a community of usage or viewpoint. Foster categorizes the different ways such assumptions allegedly held in common by some or all persons creep into the analytic philosophers' rhetoric. He calls their characteristic vision a transition from spiritualistic metaphysics to humanism, "not susceptible of empirical verification or falsification in the ordinary sense." This is actually a humanist metaphysics or a humanist myth, or a theological anthropology in the Humean sense of a natural religion that can include professed atheists. In this same vein Sten Stenson has analyzed the mode of prophecy, apologetics, and dogma, which can be found in every separate language domain, not merely in religious language. Prophecy is creative inspiration and originality, apologetics is an effort at correlation with everyday language or special fields, dogma is an expansion of discourse within an established community. Deriving most of his illustrations from the field of physics, Stenson cogently shows the ubiquitous presence of implicit theological, scientific, jurisprudential, political, and artistic dogmas (1969, pp. 193–225).

A leading positivist of the Vienna Circle, Friedrich Waismann in his essay "How I See Philosophy" (1959, pp. 345–80) gives plausible justification for the nonsense of metaphysics as something other than strict formal logic or Carnap's pure lyrical attitude. He cites examples from Plato, Spinoza, and even Wittgenstein to show that philosophy essentially effects a gestalt change in one's whole mental attitude. It is truly cognitive, a new way of seeing or breaking through to a deeper realization, despite the possible imprecision of its language or misuse of formal logic in the arguments it offers. Waismann's approach to metaphysical and theological world views is echoed in all the more flexible types of language analysis. James Martin (1966) describes metaphysical language as an "articulation of general visions of experience" (pp. 101–29, 181f.), and Frank Dilley asserts that "the various metaphysical theories are each rooted in some basic judgment about reality, a fundamental faith in whichever of the competing metaphysical possibilities is to be trusted" (1964, p. 71). For the careful language analyst, each element of his faith system is tentative, modified as inquiry precedes, until the system eventually exhibits a coherent empirical fit, possessing qualities of adequacy, scope, generality, and authenticity. Each thinker has "antecedent metaphysical assumptions which determine in part how reality is seen, what methods are thought to yield cognitive results, and what kinds of symbols and modes of symbolic reference are deemed necessary . . . ." It is noteworthy that M. B. Foster, Waismann, Martin, and Dilley are trying to describe nothing other than the religious dynamic of a figure's corpus.

If the prescriptive assumptions of Carnap and the early Ayer are trimmed down more accurately to descriptive canons only, then we do not have better or worse, but only differing language contexts, none of which requires a priori empirical verification. There exists first the universe of ordinary language, and then its extended specialized usage in science, religion, and other relationally autonomous domains. David Crystal's *Linguistics, Language, and Religion* insists that the sole criterion must be relative linguistic appropriateness. The question is only this: how can any specific language be verified, tested, and justified? And "if meaning is ultimately determined by use, and use resides in the users, then the beliefs of the users are obviously going to be an important part of the total context which must be considered before language can be assessed" (1965, p. 176). The later Wittgenstein encourages this attention to language when it is functioning, not when it is idling—thus he sanctions a conversion from verificational analysis to functional analysis (Ferré, 1961, p. 58). Edward MacKinnon requires an adequate clarification of the meaning and use of religious or any other language, with criteria more solid than a few protocol sentences by the logician about the cat on the mat, or "what an Oxbridge don might possibly mean were he to utter a belief-like statement, or a fideistic linguistic performative" (1971, p. 131). So much of the express linguistic analysis by Flew, Hare, Ryle, Wisdom, and others seems to be addicted to this glib slipshod manner, with a handful of the same stale proverbs, parables, or amusing anecdotes, analyzed in an ever more subtle, dazzling legerdemain. Instead, the function of religious language must be studied by more disciplined empirical methods within a specific religious community or church, not by detaching antiseptic sentences from their living context.

The popular book *Religious Language: An Empirical Placing of*

Theological Phrases (1967) by Ian Ramsey reconstructs a vital religious context that I think would be available to most Christian churches. He gives a few simple rules implicitly operative in most religious discourse. We stretch various models beyond their literal empirical origins and give them appropriately strange qualifications; also, we make the word "God" the subject of significant tautologies. For example, in the traditional five proofs for God's existence, we do not logically prove, but characterize God as First Cause or Infinitely Good or the source of Eternal Purpose merely to evoke five types of religious disclosure. The words first, infinitely, and eternal are qualifiers or signals of odd usage; the words cause, good, and purpose are the ordinary language models twisted into a new linguistic context. In using the qualified language model of Eternal Purpose, for instance, I religiously confess that by reflecting indefinitely on my experience of everyday purpose, I can eventually point to something beyond purpose language altogether, worthy of discerning commitment. Other deliberate signs of logical impropriety in religious syntax are the presence of capital letters, hyphenated words, or quotation marks to indicate how ordinary language must be restructured and forced into new contexts. Ramsey views Christian orthodoxy as the ability to let alternative models of dogma qualify and balance one another, whereas heresy pushes one model woodenly to extremes. In Christology, for example, both human and divine analogies must be delicately counterpoised to focus on the crucial hyphen in God-Man (MacKinnon, 1971, pp. 129–84; Hepburn, 1966, pp. 24f.).

Frederick Ferré's essay on "Science and the Death of 'God'" goes a step beyond Ramsey and MacKinnon by demanding an active revolutionary critique of religious language. We must admit the cognitive defects in our theological systems, and distinguish more carefully between dogmas with strong belief claims and those permitting tentative assent and radical revisibility. Frequently there is too quick an appeal to paradox and mystery. The anodyne of certitude is valued more than truth. The intricacy of religious language and the nest of potential misunderstandings it generates should give us a tolerance for nontheistic possibility in the contemporary consciousness. The theist's anthropomorphic models and warmly all-encompassing imagery may hinder some temperaments from reaching the essential religious values themselves. There is a valuable therapeutic agnosticism present in the greatest explicit theists and nontheists—the "posture of watchful waiting, of reverent openness to the data of life, of ambiguity-tolerance before the new, the disturbing, the unclassified, the potentially fuller and richer" (1968, p. 156). This puralistic religious perspective is analyzed sharply in William Christian's terse *Oppositions of Religious Doctrines* (1972). I may observe structural similarities between your religious beliefs and mine, and behind our manifest doctrinal differences we might presume there lie fundamental hidden beliefs on which we actually agree. But must we endorse the dissimilarities, too, because they implicitly contain the similarities, or to what extent are these covert moral and intellectual agreements necessary for mutual affection and respect? From both a psychological and analytical linguistic approach, this study explores the religious variants of hidden opposition and agreement, genuine and suspect tolerance in human relationships.

I think such analyses of the complex transaction between religious beliefs confront the critic's poetry and belief dilemma more forcefully and productively than the simplistic approach adopted by Richards, Eliot, and the Anglo-American rhetorician critics. Among religious language analysts there is no dearth of theory on textual interpretation and judgment, which would expand the rationale and techniques of any informed literary critic. Jules Moreau's *Language and Religious Language* (1961) appeals desperately for an interdisciplinary science of communication to link isolated overlapping specialists such as linguists, literary critics, psychologists, educators, theologians, social scientists. His own comprehensive theory is based on the familiar Sapir-Whorf hypothesis that the structure and general limits of a speaker's vocabulary define the way that person or his community organize their experience of the world. He derives separate logical systems for history, science, and religion from hints in Wittgenstein's *Tractatus Logico-Philosophicus,* and his key term is "translation" or Kierkegaard's repetition. David Crystal (1965, pp. 101f.) explicitly attributes his theory of meaning to the influence of I. A. Richards's triadic conception in *The Meaning of Meaning*—Crystal's four variables are signs, context, connotation as private meaning, and denotation as public meaning. In John Macquarrie's approach to the interpretation of myth and analogy in religious language, I recognize the triadic personal communication structure central to the philosophy of Peirce and Royce—the translator, the person translated, the person to whom he is translated (1966, p. 114). Every language universe must take account of these three aspects.

In his laconic skeletal *Method in Theology* (1972), Bernard Lonergan upholds the separation of spheres of meaning, each with differing language contexts. He maps out progressive stages of meaning in man's evolving consciousness—from undifferentiated common sense, to theory, and finally to a more interiorized self-critical meta-theory. He applies this triadic scheme to the evolution of philosophy and of conciliar and systematic theology, suggesting at least one parallel in the history of literature, between the prephilosophical Homeric epic and the post-philosophical Virgilean epic, more self-consciously literary. One of the most germinative and extensive treatments of religious language is Gilkey's massive *Naming the Whirlwind* (1969a), attempting a radical critique and reformulation of religious language that seriously reckons with factors like autonomy, mutability, and historical relativity in the contemporary consciousness, which clash with most traditional religious categories.

One of the most lucid nonjudicial aesthetic theories growing out of the analytical movement is Nelson Goodman's *Languages of Art* (1968), offering a strong corrective to noncognitive biases against the languages of art and theology. His canons of appropriate symbolization in any work of art involve the critic's discrimination of its power and freshness, how it works at grasping, exploring, and informing the world; how it analyzes, orders, organizes; how it participates in the creation, manipulation, retention, and transformation of knowledge. A surprising reversal of Goodman's emphasis on the cognitive import of art is tested out in Ronald Hepburn's essay on "Poetry and Religious Belief" (1959, pp. 85–166). Carnap reduced theology to poetry, and Arnold exalted poetry to the status of religion—consequently both figures implicitly equate the tasks of the theologian and literary critic. Although he disagrees with both positions, Hepburn decides to learn what he can discover by approaching Christian religious language experimentally as a sheer linguistic *blik,* and the language of poetry as a religious world view. Quoting Cleanth Brooks and I. A. Richards on the paradoxical inclusiveness of great poetry, he recognizes that poetry can provide experimental grounds for realizing a truth better, framing new patterns of experience, reorganizing a field of vision, finding more coherence and integration. Although these are also characteristics of religious experience, Hepburn eventually demonstrates how truth, inspiration, and imagination in religion actually do function differently than in an aesthetic experience. There are some excellent examples of the romantics' use of poetic language to evoke the illusion of numinosity and apparent cosmic wholeness, in an aura of sublime visionary strangeness and exhilaration. Hepburn cites parallel strategies in biblical descriptions of Creation or the Kingdom of God. Julián Marías's "Philosophic Truth and the Metaphoric System" (1967, pp. 40–53) delineates ways that both philosophy and literature use metaphor as a strategy to name and discover truth. The very literary form in which most philosophy is expressed is indispensably tied to its meaning, especially in Wittgenstein's aphorisms, the idealists' *Geistesgeschichte,* the pre-Socratics' myths. The genres of fiction and myth are a mode of knowledge and interpretation, offering a detour through imagination to get at realities otherwise inaccessible.

RELIGIOUS HERMENEUTICS

The Marías paper just cited was originally delivered at the Third Consultation of Hermeneutics at Drew University in 1966, introducing religious and literary perspectives on language and meaning. The first session in 1962 was devoted to Bultmann's historical-ontological approach; the next in 1964 to the Heidegger-Ott position. Although it is difficult to separate the techniques and scope of hermeneutic theologians from those of most religious language analysts I have already discussed, they have made some unique contributions to the critic's self-understanding. The essential focus of this group is not religious language in general, but the language of the Judaeo-Christian Bible and the problem of its Kierkegaardian repetition today.

RUDOLF BULTMANN. Modern hermeneutic, or the art of interpretation, is dominated by the figure of Rudolf Bultmann. It might prove instructive to insert him as an intruding presence into the Barthian theological situation I have already depicted. In his introduction to Adolf Harnack's *What Is Christianity?* (1957b, pp. x–xiii) Bultmann accuses Harnack of a facile reconciliation between the Christian Gospel's problematic and Harnack's own Goethian world view. Harnack misses the transcendental eschatological paradox in Christianity, the tensions of its hovering between-the-times perspective, which Bultmann credits Kierkegaard and Barth for asserting. Harnack tried to discover the present validity of the Christian past event, yet, although he was an historian, "he never portrayed the *essence itself* as a historical phenomenon." Ironically, we discover these identical complaints uttered by Barth and others against the demythologizing program of Bultmann himself. Bultmann allegedly dilutes the Gospel proclamation into stereotyped existentialist themes, discards the divinity of Christ and the early Church's paradoxical eschatology along with the first century mythical world view, and offers only timeless generalities stripped of their historical particularity. I have mentioned before that Barth charges him with substituting anthropology for theology. In the course of an outstanding systematic rebuttal to his critics in the famous *Kerygma and Myth,* Bultmann distinguishes his position from Feuerbach's, "I *am* trying to substitute anthropology for theology, for I am interpreting theological affirmations as assertions about human life. What I mean is that the God of the Christian revelation is the answer to the vital questions, the existential questions" (1961, pp. 107–8).

The principal motive behind Bultmann's theology is to *translate* the culturally conditioned world view and language of the New Testament so that it becomes meaningful to contemporary man. "Can we recover the truth of the kerygma for men who do not think in mythological terms without forfeiting its character as kerygma?" (p. 15). To rephrase part of Bultmann's question in my own myth language used throughout this present book, I would ask how we can *re*-mythologize the New Testament message accurately from cosmological myths into current existentialist, anthropological, psychological myths. Bultmann remythologizes the Gospel to achieve precisely what Harnack purportedly avoided, to throw into sharper relief "the paradoxical or scandalous character of its claims, so that they become as clear for modern man as they were in apostolic times" (p. 122). The hermeneutic that Bultmann advocates is what he calls existential, a method that *Jesus and the Word* explains concisely: "When we encounter the words of Jesus in history, *we* do not judge *them* by a philosophical system with reference to their rational validity; *they* meet *us* with the question of how we are to interpret our own existence. That we be ourselves deeply disturbed by the problem of our own life is therefore the indispensable condition of our inquiry" (1958, p. 11). Yet there actually is a philosophic system at work in Bultmann's exegesis—or more correctly, at least a presystematic theology. For these are a few of the existentialist presuppositions through which he filters the text: the thought and teaching of Jesus "are understood in the light of the concrete situation of a man living in time; as his interpretation of his own existence in the midst of change, uncertainty, decision; as the expression of a possibility of comprehending this life; as the effort to gain clear insight into the contingencies and necessities of his own existence."

The best examples of Bultmann's applied criticism are the two volumes of his *Theology of the New Testament* (1951–55), or the second half of his principal essay in the *Kerygma and Myth* (1961) debate, which interprets Christ's death, for example, as a call to authentic human existence. This is addressed to every man, whom God will embrace and sustain even in man's fallen, self-assertive condition. Bultmann asks that I be an authentically religious interpreter, beginning from a prior unthematized relationship between myself and a God revealing Himself through the biblical text, between my own questioned existence and Jesus's own questioned existence. Employing this encounter and shared life-situation as a touchstone, I attempt to assess and winnow the culturely conditioned biblical language that impedes communication. We can associate this hermeneutic assumption of existential preunderstanding with Tillich's method of correlation between the Gospel and man's present situation, and with Heinrich Ott's *hermeneutical arch.* Ott interjects a theology of existence, the crucial existentialist questions asked by contemporary man, at a midpoint in the arch stretching from a biblical text to its embodiment in the present context of religious preaching.

POST-BULTMANNIANS. Two specific problems raised by Bultmann influence subsequent discussions in the so-called New Hermeneutic. I must confess the debates often seem repetitive and verbose, but they have generated significant insight (Funk, 1966; Palmer, 1969; James Robinson, 1959; Robinson and Cobb, 1963 and 1964). Bultmann's first problem is an apparent deemphasis on the actual historical person of Jesus. What interests him is God's interaction in man's history, not Jesus's earthly career. He applies to Christology the distinction first used by Martin Kähler—*Historie* and *Geschichte,* the dichotomy between factual historicity of the past and its interpreted eschatological significance. Yet this leads to such misunderstanding among his critics that Bultmann must immediately deny he intends to "run away from *Historie* and take refuge in *Geschichte.* . . . I still deny that historical research can ever encounter any traces of the epiphany of God in Christ; all it can do is to confront us with the Jesus of history. Only the Church's proclamation can bring us face to face with *Kyrios Christos*" (1961, pp. 117–18). We can watch Bultmann attempting here to evade the same dilemma Rahv and others smoked out in the transhistorical myth critics. Besides assigning the early Church an incredibly creative, almost fictive, role in formulating the Christian kerygma, Bultmann seems to locate the central word-event not in Jesus's actual death or deep faith but in the Church's own religious experience.

The second problem inherited from Bultmann is inseparable from the first. How can a Christian today really repeat and appropriate the past event of Christ's redemption? This religious recollection of the past, Bultmann suggests as a tentative solution to his dilemma, "does not present us with facts of the past in their bare actuality . . . but, as a sacramental event, it re-presents the events of the past in such a way that it renews them, and thus becomes a personal encounter for me" (p. 115).

The task of the post-Bultmannians—Conzelman, Bornkam, Ebeling, Fuchs, Käsemann—has been to clarify a presupposition never explicitly denied by Bultmann, that the Church's Christ bears an essential continuity with Jesus's actual life and message (Harvey, 1966, pp. 174f.). When Jesus taught or preached, according to the theory of Ebeling and Fuchs especially, His conduct and words witness to each other, so that the faith which the Church says He demands of us today was a faith

He surely achieved in His own historical existence. The interpreter is called upon to *repeat* the same word-event that Jesus Himself enacted —to be changed into what Jesus was as man authentically preaches the self-transforming words He preached. Bultmann called this word-event a sacrament, and its sacral overtones should be more evident now in this explanation by Ebeling and Fuchs. Gerhard Ebeling's "Word of God and Hermeneutic" (1964, pp. 107–109) compares the existentialist interpretation of a biblical passage with a judge's use of the received text as an illuminating and guiding precedent for the present creative decision. If disinterested in articulating present decisions, he will make a poor historian also. The Bible is intended to be preserved, read, handed on, but especially *proclaimed.* I must transform the text into God's spoken word-event in the present. Wolfhart Pannenberg's "Hermeneutics and Universal History" (1967, pp. 122–52) presents his own variations on H. G. Gadamer's occurrence-of-transmission theory. We are already formed by history and language before we come to a moment of self-understanding. In a methodological approach to the New Testament the interpreter must "first of all be clear about the difference between his own spiritual and intellectual situation, the horizon of 'modern man' in which he shares, and the horizon of the New Testament authors . . ." (p. 139). He tries to achieve a comprehensive horizon of understanding, embracing all these world views, and to restore the word of a transmitted text to its unspoken horizon of meaning, its original context. The transmitted text is to be related "not simply to a currently available horizon of the subject matter, but to the present age's future horizon, and thereby to the questionableness of the current understanding of the subject matter" (p. 149). This hermeneutic of Gadamer and Pannenberg helps to account for the claim, judgment, and disclosive power a sacred text is designed to reveal in its present challenge to the era and the person of the interpreter.

The application of hermeneutical theory to actual biblical exegesis today has not yet produced results worthy of such gandiose promise. After all the scrutiny into sources and parallels and the genesis of a particular biblical text, its final redaction is seldom treated as a relatively sophisticated integral literary document. There has been interest in the originating situation of a Gospel pericope within Jesus's actual preaching or the situation of collective oral preaching within the early Church where the pericope takes shape, but insufficient attention to the religious dynamic in the final redaction that gives the text coherent literary meaning. The more threatened types of biblical positivism have understandably resisted the creative and sophisticated styles of literary criticism. The Liberal Higher Critics of the last century and their contemporary disciples, on the other hand, still apply to Scripture the earlier philological techniques of studies in the classics, searching for the actual historical figure of Homer or Socrates, sleuthing for strands of folk history and the evolving oral tradition, recording elaborate word-counts and historical parallels. Yet we recognize that Job in its final form is a type of dramatic dialogue; there are the Samuel-Kings epic, and the letters, sayings, apocalyptic romances, and other distinctive biblical literary forms that Amos Wilder discusses so perceptively in his *Language of the Gospel* (1964).

Another example of intelligent redaction-criticism is Daniel Via's *The Parables: Their Literary and Existential Dimension* (1967), surpassing the earlier concern of Jeremias and others about a taxonomy of the parables and the role played by allegory in their form-history. Via focuses rather on their tragic or comic structure, and characteristic imagery. He gives an inventive interpretation of the perplexing unjust steward parable, for example, as a picaresque narrative. James Barr's provocative work (1961) on biblical semantics attacks the biblical dictionary approach of scholars like Kittel, who by atomizing obvious ideas on the surface of the text in the Lovejoy manner, miss the more subtle and massive linguistic complexes. Barr thinks Fuchs and Ebeling have discovered no more definitive word-event in Scripture than in any other literary document. An especially effective polemic emerges against biblical theologians who maximize the differences between dynamic-concrete-synthetic Hebraic thought and static-analytic-deductive Greek thought, a favorite dichotomy in the literary criticism of Auerbach and Driver. William Beardslee's *Literary Criticism of the New Testament* (1970) surveys the optimistic prospect yet jejune achievements of applied redaction-criticism, with an analysis of parable, history, and apocalypse genres to illustrate Beardslee's own suggested religious-literary approach.

RELIGIOUS PHENOMENOLOGY

By phenomenology I mean C. S. Peirce's phaneroscopy, or the general methodology associated with Husserl especially and with later figures in his tradition. Each phenomenologist employs his own specific techniques of describing the content and structure of the phenomenon itself, while trying to minimize or at least clarify the influence of presuppositions and previous stock interpretations. There is an attempt to explore around the periphery of the phenomenon in all its relationships, and to reconstruct a new context in which it can disclose itself with as little distortion as possible. The pertinent figures I shall discuss are

Merleau-Ponty, Levi-Strauss, and notably Martin Heidegger, whose phenomenological method, themes, and foundational studies in metaphysics are acknowledged by Bultmann, Rahner, Macquarrie, Ott, and disciples of the new hermeneutic as their major sourcebook.

MARTIN HEIDEGGER. It is customary to divide Heidegger's corpus into an early and late phase (Borgmann, 1968; Robinson and Cobb, 1963). What Heidegger himself calls an intellectual reversal occurs in the decade between 1930 and 1940, which is explained variously by commentators as a dramatic advance beyond the scope and method of his monumental *Being and Time* (1962), or an escape into intended obscurity and mysticism. Besides introducing his own phenomenological analysis of man, history, and time, Heidegger's *Being and Time* is a critique of traditional approaches to these themes, and a search into the foundations of metaphysics and of other sciences. After World War II Heidegger turns aside from his earlier promise to establish a basic ontology, and focuses instead on man's prior experience of being. This primordial encounter with being he discovers in Hölderlin and the poets, and in the myths and spirituality of the pre-Socratics, employing terms like *logos, moira,* and *aletheia* before the more abstract metaphysical phase of later Greek thought. The grasping, manipulating, plundering attributes of contemporary technological control blunt man's sense of Wordsworthian sensitivity and wonder, thus deafening him to the contemplative self-disclosure of being.

I prefer to follow an interpretation stressing the continuity of Heidegger's thought and method, such as that proposed by John Macquarrie (1966, pp. 84f., and 1967, pp. 147–67). It combines calculative thinking, interpersonal and Kierkegaardian repetitive thinking, with Heidegger's later mode of primordial or essential thinking. In this multiple hermeneutic, for example, the more exacting methodology in *Being and Time* influenced Bultmann's emphasis on clarifying and organizing the presuppositions brought to a text for an existentialist interpretation, whereas Heidegger's later "What Is Metaphysics?" requires a more passive contemplative waiting, listening, responding to the address of being. In both works, an active and creative appropriation is expected of the text, but with less insistence later upon plans and rules, for "the language itself acts as a norm and sets limits to the exegesis; yet these limits are wide ones, and clearly much depends on the sensitivity and perceptiveness of the exegete" (1967, p. 164). Macquarrie cites three examples of Heidegger's applied literary criticism from *Being and Time, Introduction to Metaphysics,* and *Unterwegs,* showing an alleged progression toward a more meditative hermeneutic. In his explication of the classical Latin fable by Hyginus, Heidegger gives a simple paraphrase of it as a preontological description of man's self-understanding. There is purported repetitive thinking in Heidegger's approach to a chorus from Sophocles's *Antigone*: he paraphrases the meaning, then passes successively through various sections of the text to discover how they embody the theme, and finally takes his stand at the center of the text, tries to restore life to the original thought in a new situation, and judges how it answers for the interpreter himself the question of who man is. The third text is a poem by Stefan George, which Heidegger interprets by characteristic praying and brooding over the text. He immediately intuits the theme and carries on a dialogue with the poet as an oracle of being.

Two primary specimens of Heidegger's mature literary criticism are "Remembrance of the Poet" and "Hölderlin and the Essence of Poetry" in Heidegger's *Existence and Being* (1949), with a fine 200 page introduction by Werner Brock. It is evident that Heidegger expounds the poems seriously, although without the exhaustive attention to detail characteristic of proficient formalist critics. Heidegger calls his first essay on Hölderlin's "Homecoming," a dialogue in which Heidegger intends his own commentary to vanish "together with its explanations in the face of the pure existence of the poem." This reverent care toward the text keeps him from wandering too far away from it, although his method is mostly a philological discussion of some phrase or a speculative digression occasioned by topics arising in the text. The poet and the philosopher are both guardians of being, their task is the naming of what is holy, waiting silently in an era when the gods remain afar, trusting eventually to be granted the right word that gives being its expression. Truth is uncovering, letting-be, re-velation, un-veiling, and it cannot be worded and grasped by analysis, but only by "bringing near the Near, while keeping it at a distance," respecting the mystery of being. In *Poetry, Language, Thought* (1971), a collection of Heidegger's random pieces on aesthetics, linguistics, and some of his own verse, there is a passage from "The Thinker as Poet" that distills much of his later thought:

> We are too late for the gods and too
> early for Being. Being's poem,
> just begun, is man.

Despite Heidegger's outrage at the translation of his thought into religious equivalents, there are undeniable parallels between letting-be and Macquarrie's "divine self-disclosure," between the devout primordial interpretation of a poem and an appropriate biblical hermeneutic, between Heindegger's sacramental activity of naming and the post-Bultmannians' word-event. In fact, I think Heidegger has written a phenomenological experiential theology, articulated in the evocative desacralized vocabulary of German idealistic philosophy and the romantic poets. One of the most systematic and faithful adaptations of Heidegger's thought to a biblical hermeneutic is the work of Heinrich Ott. In his brief essay on "Language and Understanding," he crystallizes the complex hermeneutic problem in a metaphor drawn from Lessing, the *aporia,* a multifaceted Greek word referring to what hinders the flow or journey, and to a puzzle or exigency. There is a problematic gap between judgments of historical probability and the certainty of faith, between the claims of the past and what is meaningfully present. From Heidegger's reflections upon language, Ott assembles his own hermeneutic of *trans-lation.* Language is a transcendental event overtaking man, allowing him to participate in this event, addressing and challenging him to discover himself through his own language. The interpretation of a text "does not proceed simply between two points, ourselves and the text being apprehended. Rather it constitutes a triangle: by means of the text we perceive the object which addresses the text as well as ourselves, and only in so doing do we genuinely come to understand the text as such." We must re-actualize "the relation of the past thinker to the object confronting him, an object which must be capable of becoming ours as well" (1967, pp. 143–44). Bultmann himself has raised interesting objections to the applied literary criticism of Ott and Heidegger. Not interpersonal enough, both men focus on the poet's vocation and fuss about language, but they evade poetic themes of love, duty, guilt, and forgiveness (James Robinson, 1963, p. 66).

Essential to the phenomenological method is the presupposition of a *Lebenswelt, Mitwelt, Umwelt,* or prior situation of unthematized experience, which Bultmann calls an existential preunderstanding or which Ott and others describe as an a priori transcendental language event. John Wild in "Man and His Life-World" (1959, pp. 90–109) describes the core of Heidegger's *Being and Time* and Maurice Merleau-Ponty's *Phenomenology of Perception* as an intensive investigation of this *Lebenswelt* phenomenon. It is a vague region of immediate experience which thinkers attempt to describe in strained hyphenated phrases or by spatial and temporal models, like the field of thermodynamics and gestalt theory, horizon, Zen preverbal experience, Heidegger's *in-der-Welt-sein* or Merleau-Ponty's *l'etre au monde.* We have noticed this phenomenon in words like vision, intentionality, horizon, *Weltanschauung,* world view, and religious dynamic, recurring constantly among literary critics and theologians. The Dewey-Whitehead process and transactional paradigm behind my own theory of literary criticism correlates neatly with Wild's delineation of this life-world: "Man is a moving system of intentions which pervade the things and agencies with which he interacts and give them meaning" (p. 95). This world belongs to the very being of man, precedes philosophic reflection, "possesses an overarching structure which is neither purely subjective nor purely objective, and can be described" (p. 92). Thus, philosophy or theology ought to aim at describing and understanding this phenomenon, no longer fretting about the subject-object dichotomy, or trying to construct inclusive, coherent intellectual systems.

MAURICE MERLEAU-PONTY. Merleau-Ponty's thought can be represented best in five of his essays from *Sense and Non-Sense* (1964a) and *Signs* (1964b) (Rabil, 1967, and Kaelin, 1962). His explicit religious position is developed in "Faith and Good Faith" (1964a, pp. 172–81) and "Christianity and Philosophy" (1964b, pp. 140–46), his attitude of Sartrean political criticism in "The Philosopher and Sociology" (1964b, pp. 98–113), his theoretical and applied literary criticism in "Metaphysics and the Novel" (1964a, pp. 26–40) and "The Film and the New Psychology" (1964a, pp. 48–62). The literary symbol is saturated in a single intentionality behind every detail, just as the rules of the game are present in every stroke of a tennis match. A novel is a unique world, demanding a limitless body of reflective criticism; its task is to help others recover the primary experience embodied there. Metaphysics used to be treated as a detached conceptual reflection on life, far removed from literature, whereas today in phenomenology and existentialism the intents of philosophy and literature are inseparable, both articulating an experience of the world that precedes any thought about it. And life *is* latent metaphysics, for man's questioning is present, "as Pascal thought, in the heart's slightest movement. . . . Man is metaphysical in his very being, in his loves, in his hates, in his individual and collective history . . . . Philosophical expression assumes the same ambiguities as literary expression, if the world is such that it cannot be expressed except in 'stories' and, as it were, pointed at" (1964a, p. 28). The movie maker and philosopher both share a similar perspective—consciousness is not separated from the world but poured out into the world, life is not a mosaic of atomized images but a total temporal gestalt. In "Metaphysics and the Novel" Merleau-Ponty applies this experiential method to a competent analysis of underlying currents of fidelity and respect behind the individual separate acts of immorality immediately apparent in Simone de Beauvoir's *L'Invitée*. He also shows how the corpus of Stendhal, Balzac, and Proust can be summarized tentatively, each a matrix of two or three major philosophical themes, the function of which is not to instruct but to raise critical questions about life.

Merleau-Ponty employs an interesting distinction between an interior and exterior God, corresponding simply to what Rahner calls transcendental and predicamental revelation, the inner summons of being and the outer historical Gospel preaching. An extrinsic faith imposed by the church or political party is dead unless it matches a person's true inner religious dynamic: "Obedience to God does not . . . consist in yielding to an alien and obscure will but consists in doing what we truly want, since God is more ourselves than we" (1964a, p. 172). Gradually disengaging himself from a committed Sartrean political literary criticism, Merleau-Ponty also abandoned Roman Catholicism, then Marxism, and eventually any possible fixed religious or ideological institutions. His view of traditional theology is colored by the Scholastic natural-supernatural dichotomy and the Gilson-Maritain distinction between systematic Christian wisdom-philosophy versus a church theology confining itself mostly to supernatural revealed truth. "If philosophy is a self-sufficing activity which begins and ends with conceptual understanding, and faith is assent to things not seen which are given for belief through revealed texts, the difference between them is too great for there to be conflict." In his own style of a comprehensive life-world, of course, there is no dualism, for "philosophical questioning involves its own vital options, and in a sense it maintains itself within a religious affirmation" (1964b, p. 146).

In the Merleau-Ponty tradition, there are innumerable phenomenological studies on such familiar topics as lived space and time, imagination, body-love, language, and hope. (Lawrence and O'Connor, 1967). In "Aesthetic Experience and the Aesthetic Object" (1967), Roman Ingarden analyzes the way a reader actively constructs the aesthetic object out of his own more immediate experience of the wider aesthetic phenomenon. Maurice Natanson's *Literature, Philosophy, and the Social Sciences* conjectures how we reinterpret the fictive characters' own interpretations in a novel, subscribe to or deny their faith, experience the "as-if" horizon interior to the literary work. There is a simultaneous extrospective and introspective aspect to my interpreting, for by attending to the new horizon given me I find an epiphany of the experiential foundations of my own life-world. His essays on Camus and Thomas Wolfe, and especially "Existentialist Categories in Contemporary Literature" (1962, pp. 116–30) treat the literary themes encountered as instrumental problems for inquiry into human doubt, choice, authenticity. The concept of horizon is also developed by Lonergan (1972, p. 235f.) to account for the conflicting world views met in different professions, divergent philosophies, and separate phases in one's own development. Horizon is the pivotal term in Michael Novak's succinct essay on "Philosophy and Fiction" (1969, pp. 209–24). Whereas science emphasizes a restricted public objective horizon, and Socratic philosophy demands an articulation of one's own horizon in comparison with others', the work of fiction has a different function. It presents an image to live through, an action to adopt vicariously. It "invites us to enter into a new horizon. It re-creates the standpoint and furnishes the pointers by which we live-through a way of conceiving our lives" (p. 211).

CLAUDE LEVI-STRAUSS. Levi-Strauss has been invoked alongside Merleau-Ponty since the fifties as an important source for the active imaginative style in French phenomenological literary criticism. Like their critical role, his structural anthropology is conceived as an uncovering of concealed meaning in a text, myth, or custom, "to grasp beyond the conscious and always shifting images which men hold, the complete range of unconscious possibilities." *The Savage Mind* (1966) is based on Levi-Strauss's presumption that the kind of logic in so-called primitive thought is as rigorous as that of modern science, not the crude prelogical thought popularized by Levi-Bruhl, Cassirer, and earlier anthropologists. In his *Structural Anthropology* he describes his search for the implicit psychological attitudes and logical structures underneath what is consciously recorded on stone or paper. A myth is "an intermediate entity between a statistical aggregate of molecules and the molecular structure itself" (1969, p. 229). The context of this definition is a fundamental analogy that Levi-Strauss draws between myth-criticism and functional linguistics: look for the unconscious substructure, not the words themselves but the relations between the words, the logical system. He cuts up the myth into constituent units like phonemes and morphemes, then classifies them in columns to establish their frequency, and finally tries to arrange them in various novel groupings to permit diachronic and synchronic readings that reveal latent patterns and themes. Levi-Strauss gives a sample of this exhaustive and at times brilliant technique in his explication of the Oedipus tale and also of a few Zuñi myths (1963, pp. 206–31).

Edmund Leach in his "Genesis as Myth" (1967, pp. 1–14) has applied Levi-Strauss's method of structural atomization to the biblical Creation myth, split into parallel narrations of the cosmic creation, Adam and Eve, and Cain and Abel. Analogies with other Near-Eastern myths and many apparent repetitions, inversions, and variations in the conjectured structure highlight sexual resonances in the material. Wayne Shumaker's "Fictive Plot: Its Genesis and Some Recurrent Motifs" (1960, pp. 107–54) suggests even more intricate possibilities in this method. He takes chapter 39 of Dickens's *Great Expectations,* jumbles all the episodes into a stream-of-consciousness flow, and then supplies his own connectives, like "but," "if," or "because" between the incidents to catch new patterns in Dickens's individual consciousness or in the collective unconscious. Certain affective impulses in Dickens's creative imagination—gentility in Pip, warmheartedness in Gargery—establish appropriate polarities within a magnetic field of plot fragments. Then Shumaker generalizes from this chapter to the organization of the entire novel. In my opinion, these intoxicating cerebral techniques, if used with insight and originality, could be one among many productive styles of interpretation, but I can imagine nothing more lethal than to program them into an unimaginative systematic scholar.

13

ORTHO-CULTURAL RELIGIOUS THOUGHT

IN *Christ and Culture* H. Richard Niebuhr defines culture as the artificial environment which man superimposes on the given natural. As the total process of human activity, it comprises "language, habits, ideas, beliefs, customs, social organization, inherited artifacts, technical processes, and values" (1956, p. 32). The rest of Niebuhr's book develops five differing responses throughout Christian history to human culture, from the dour "Christ against culture," which I characterized above as an exaggerated biblical autotelism, to a "cultural Christianity" in which the distinctive Christian prophetic impulse dies of inanition.

In this chapter, parallel to chapter 7 on ortho-cultural literary criticism, I shall include theologians whose methodology corresponds to the critical analysis of a literary work in all its relatedness to the social and intellectual context. Their focus is not the religious factor alone, but its congruence, correspondence, incorporation, conjunction, transaction with the progressively more humanized *world,* a crucial biblical category with both negative and positive implications. In my division of theologians here, the first group attempts to explore and clarify religious congruence in inclusive concepts that are largely transhistorical. The second group stresses more the historical, evolving, communal, radically revisable dimensions of this congruence. These theologians correspond to the more activist *ortho* ideological critics of chapter 7, and will include religious sociologists, Marxist philosophers, and finally three politically oriented existentialists.

THEOLOGY OF CORRELATION

The term "correlation" is Tillich's, meaning a reconstructed coherence between question and answer, between man and God. Tillich initially rejects any exclusively naturalistic method elevating man to the status of both the one questioning and answering, where everything would be said *by* man, yet nothing *to* man. The basic question for the Christian, for example, is human existence itself, a question posed by man's "creative self-interpretation in all realms of culture. Philosophy contributes, but so do poetry, drama, the novel, therapeutic psychology, and sociology. The theologian organizes these materials in relation to the answer given by the Christian message." As a Christian, he believes that the substance of his answer will always contain the "*logos* of being, manifest in Jesus as the Christ." He believes that God is the answer to every fundamental question—He is the infinite power of being confronting my experienced threat of nonbeing, for example, or divine courage and providence corresponding to my anxiety (1967, I, pp. 62–66). In a manner similar to Tillich's, Lonergan describes theology as the mediation "between a cultural matrix and the significance and role of a religion in that matrix" (1972, p. xi). A culture is viewed empirically as a set of meanings and values informing a way of life, and both culture and theology may remain relatively embalmed for ages, or be in a process of slow advance or rapid dissolution.

In *Feast of Fools* Harvey Cox develops Tillich's method into a vital theology of juxtaposition, which I find an attractive improvement. The theologian becomes a controversial jester-like prophetic figure, often exploiting discontinuities and collisions between present, past, and future, recognizing religion should often be out of step with present cultural realities, seeking not merely to address existing social structures but to undermine them. Tillich began by articulating the questions he believed implicit in culture and then proceeded to show how the symbols of faith correlate with these questions. "In my view," says Cox, "the relation between faith and culture is a more complex one. Faith does not always answer the questions posed by human existence; it sometimes raises questions of its own. And the cultures into which human existence organizes itself sometimes give answers, however provisional and partial, to the questions raised by faith" (1969, p. 131). Furthermore, every aspect of culture manifests itself to us from the very beginning with an intrinsic religious dynamic of its own. The theologian of culture, then, "cannot shift back and forth from his role as cultural analyst to his role as theological exegete as smoothly as Tillich could, or thought he could" (p. 176). His theological viewpoint will color everything he does, and his methods will involve a variety of techniques, historical and psychological and phenomenological.

We have already witnessed many phenomenologists and language analysts searching for an implicit life-world and vision, but such a concern ought to be even more characteristic of the correlational theologian. Arnold Toynbee has more recently been approaching nationalism, communism, and individualism as substitute religions, post-Christian ideologies that fill a spiritual vacuum. He expects to uncover a religious dynamic in every cultural phenomenon, because "in my belief, every human being has a personal religion, and every human community has a collective religion, whether the person or community is aware of this or not" (1969, p. 322). The very words "ideology" and "culture" are controversial notions in this discussion (Kroeber and Kluckholm, 1952). Nigel Harris's *Beliefs in Society: The Problem of Ideology* neutralizes the usually pejorative term ideology, and lets it stand for the language about purposes of a social group, a committed act of faith, the link between our perception of reality and the purposes we seek to realize (1968, pp. 1–26). Harris recognizes that our ideology is generally not established prior to experience but evolves during our exploration of specific problems in the world. In discerning an author's ideology, too, the ideas must not be abstracted from the living personal situation, for the actual drive, motives, psychological matrix that function behind an ideology and at times shape it as a rationalization, must be apprehended along with the conceptualized ideology. In contrast to Harris's approach, Patrick Corbett (1965) proposes a demolition of all ideologies. Obviously the word here is confined to partisan certitudes and loyalties, polemics and proselytism, which Corbett himself detects in fallacious versions of Catholicism, Marxism, and democratic idealism.

What especially interests Anders Nygren in "The Role of the Self-Evident in History" (1948, pp. 235–41) are the assumptions *not* tested by any parties in controversy because they seem so unproblematic, yet they are for that reason most important of all, the axiomatic shibboleths behind anything a period expressly discusses. As illustrations of these self-evident presuppositions, he suggests the Hellenic postulate of two separate worlds of idea and sense, eternal and temporal, or the homocentric perspective behind the threatened censorship against Galileo. Herbert Richardson (1967) calls these assumptions an "intellectus" or felt basis of discourse, and exemplifies their function in the way that models of God as changeless sovereign or personal guide actually influence the problematic of entire epochs. Thomas Kuhn's *Structure of Scientific Revolutions* (1970) is an incomparable analysis of the role played by these unconscious propositions in the scientific community before, during, and after a paradigm revolution. Scientific textbook histories, and the scientist's inherited proclivities and techniques, are organized by a world view basically conservative, shielding the everyday research scientist from the chaotic insecurity of a revolutionary gestalt shift in perspectives.

At the root of all value systems are what Stephen Toulmin in *An Examination of the Place of Reason in Ethics* (1968, pp. 204–21) calls limiting questions, expressions of basic wonder or ontological searching, not for a literal exact knowledge, but for cosmic reassurance. "Why must they die so young," or "why ought I to do what is right?" When such questions are asked, ethical and strictly logical reasoning beyond this point does not satisfy the questioner, who is asking fundamentally religious questions which pertain to the underlying axioms of his world view. Another truly fascinating study by Toulmin is "Contemporary Scientific Mythology" (1957, pp. 13–76), in which he shows how a modern scientific theory such as entropy or evolution functions as a myth of creation, apocalypse, the justification of morality. "An anxious fear of the remote and unknown past, and of the remote and even more unknown future: these lead us to look for eschatological morals even where there is no hope of finding them—in physical cosmology" (p. 65). How can these contemporary myths be spotted, when they pervade so deeply the perspective of the questioner himself? Toulmin answers that first we must expect such myths today will be mechanthromorphic rather than anthropomorphic in form. Second, that we must test a specific scientific theory to see what sorts of questions it attempts to answer—if these are ethical or theological, the theory has already taken on a mythical double-life.

In *Visions of Culture* (1966) Karl Weintraub traces in six historians of civilization including Voltaire, Huizinga, and Ortega y Gasset their search for a "spirit underlying all the expressions of life," a collective individuality. Burkhardt, following the tradition of Herder and Goethe, saw culture as the manifestation of a *Geist;* Huizinga emphasizes the para-rational play instinct; Ortega finds *creentias* or unquestioned beliefs prerationally surrounding us and through which we encounter ourselves. Associated with this approach are terms like *Stimmung,* cultural mood, milieu, ambience, and temper, the wide linguistic and historical implications of which have been resourcefully explored by Leo Spitzer (1963). Stephen Pepper's *World Hypotheses* (1966) focuses upon the central root-metaphors of metaphysical systems and discovers four basic alternative ways of organizing evidence, "four different approximations to the nature of the world," which he terms formism, mechanism, contextualism, and organicism. No single approach is completely corroborated by its evidence, none is a comprehensive description of the world. In his aesthetic studies, Pepper attempts to contrive a synthesis of these four approaches to art criticism, concentrating especially on Dewey's perspective (1949 and 1965).

We would expect the aesthetic theory and applied literary criticism of cultural theologians to be cosmic and generic in scope. Let me attempt to suggest the achievement of nine major theologians of culture, with no pretense at synopsizing the larger systematic themes and methodology of each theological corpus.

PAUL TILLICH. In *On the Boundary: An Autobiographical Sketch* (1966) Paul Tillich describes how he developed the fundamental categories of form and substance, creative ecstasy, and revelatory breakthrough. All these concepts employed in his philosophy of religion and culture stem from an appreciation of literature and painting, notably his experience of a Botticelli painting in Berlin, "almost a revelation." He read widely in Hofmannsthal, George, Werfel, remarking about Rilke's later poetry, that "its profound psychoanalytical realism, mystical richness, and a poetic form charged with metaphysical content made this poetry a vehicle for insights that I could elaborate only abstractly through the concepts of my philosophy of religion." *The Religious Situation* (1932, pp. 53–70) comprises probably his most extensive treatment of art, alongside discussions about science, politics, and ethics. Unfortunately he expressly omits literature from his essay, except for a few silly pontifical observations about Zola and Ibsen, for example, who somehow lack inner self-transcendence. The actual religious situation of a period is an underlying final source of meaning, an unconscious faith that is lived before it is ever articulated. "Whenever a period speaks most effectively and clearly of itself it speaks no longer of itself but of something else, of a reality which lies beneath all time and above all existential forms." In cubism and expressionism, Tillich finds not the separate transcendent world of the ancients but "the transcendental reference in things to that which lies beyond them," an almost mystical transparency, religious in style rather than subject matter. This is almost the sole recurrent insight in Tillich's practical criticism, which he delights to illustrate by the shocking discovery that a spiritualized realism is better actualized in some contemporary office buildings than in a pretentious neo-Gothic church building.

In "Religion and the Visual Arts" (1955) Tillich calls Picasso's *Guernica* the most characteristic "Protestant" painting because it captures the fragmentary character of the era "without any cover," the human situation in its despair and estrangement. What Tillich means by a religious style, which he finds in Van Gogh's *Starry Night* or a Cezanne still life, for example, is an art that "puts the religious question radically, and has the power, the courage, to face the situation out of which this question comes." An El Greco and Grünewald crucifixion or Rouault's *Christ Mocked by Soldiers* he considers superior expressions of ultimate concern in both style and subject, a level of achievement difficult to match today, since the explicitly religious is so often stereotyped. Tillich's questioning of a work of art seems equivalent to the best literary critics' quest for the metaphysic: What does this picture express in terms of an ultimate interpretation of human existence? Unfortunately his answer too often neutralizes itself in the language of metaphysical platitude, so that his critique of Jan Steen's *World Upside Down* could apply to almost any great painting: it expresses the power of being "in terms of an unrestricted vitality in which the self-affirmation of life becomes almost ecstatic." John Dixon (1963) and others chide Tillich for forcing Platonist theological categories upon the art object, and for his incapacity to discover anything other than anxiety, brokenness, and the void.

KARL RAHNER AND HANS URS VON BALTHASAR. Karl Rahner's few scattered pieces on aesthetics bear a close kinship with Tillich's theory. I have already discussed how Rahner blurs the strict perimeters of Christianity to embrace the unconscious theist, anonymous Christian, and crypto-theologian. God is not a reality alongside others but is always present indirectly as the "transcendental horizon or 'space' within which a determined object is encountered," or again, as an "unclassified horizon of the knowing and acting intentionality of man and not as an 'object' represented by an idea within this horizon" (1969, p. 237). Accordingly, we can reason that an art object is religiously transparent only when it is most itself, when its subject matter is most human. In "Poetry and the Christian" (1966, pp. 357–67) Rahner expects every human word to be approached as a possible revelatory situation. For "in every word, the gracious incarnation of God's own abiding Word and so of God Himself can take place." Presuming that "great poetry only exists where man radically faces what he is," the critic must strain to listen, then, "for this incarnational possibility in the human world" (p. 363).

Just as Luther felt productive biblical exegesis depended on flourishing literary studies, Rahner believes "the capacity and the practice of perceiving the poetic word is a presupposition of hearing the word of God." But Rahner is trapped by his enthusiastic rhetoric into doubts that anyone could remain unreceptive to poetry and be a Christian. Such an absurd implication is finally trimmed down to a moderate assertion: "poetry is one way of training oneself to hear the word of life" (pp. 363–64). The essay "Priest and Poet" (1967, pp. 294–320) adapts Heidegger's comparison between the poet and philosopher as namers and guardians of holy being, to the ministerial priest's function as preacher of the primordial word. Rahner's hermeneutic emphasizes that demythologizing in the pulpit is no simplistic translation into a single contemporary language. "Demythologization and the Sermon" (1968, pp. 20–38) requires that the preacher *hear* and make imaginative use of the overlapping languages of common parlance, educated academic talk, poetry, and sacred language. The apparently archaic tendencies in religious speech ought not to be suppressed peremptorily. For "something like the 'archetypes' of Jung may persist in modern man and may be brought to life in sacred language" (p. 37).

Hans Urs Von Balthasar's *Herrlichkeit: Eine Theologische Ästhetik* (1961–69) offers four of a six-volume projected systematic theology of revelation, approaching God through the symbols of glory and beauty. There are extensive essays on Goethe, Hölderlin, G. M. Hopkins, the mystics, the early Fathers, all viewed as significant cultural prototypes representing successive historical phases. We move through vignettes on *Don Quixote,* Dostoevsky's *Idiot,* Rouault's clown, to the explication of a Hopkins lyric which attends to its imagery, diction, themes, supported by research into the poet's correspondence and notebooks. Urs Von Balthasar's work could accurately be termed a Christian anthropology, which he describes in *A Theological Anthropology* (1967) as an exploration into the relationship between the first and second Adam. Man is the "image and likeness of a figure of fulfillment who is still to come and, therefore, [man] cannot be fully interpreted by himself. He is still intelligible only in the final figure of the dying and resurrecting Son of God." Perhaps Urs Von Balthasar's most brilliant pages consist of an applied remythologizing that moves from cosmological models to new categories of interiority and depth. There are studies of the liturgical, credal, and mystical implications in such themes as the Descent into Hell and "Being Lost" (1958, pp. 119–41), purgatory and eschatology (1964a, pp. 147–75). "Revelation and the Beautiful" (1964b, pp. 121–64), an accessible introduction to the thesis of *Herrlichkeit,* vindicates the poets of romantic idealism for preserving the authentic religious impulse in a period when most church theology was lost in arid rationalism.

JACQUES MARITAIN AND ROMANO GUARDINI. The name of Jacques Maritain has arisen before as one of the many acknowledged influences behind the formalist bias in Anglo-American rhetorical criticism. His line "It is a deadly error to expect poetry to provide the supersubstantial nourishment of man" has proved a favorite aphorism of Eliot against Arnold and the New Humanists. *Art and Scholasticism* (1943) is preoccupied with this theme—artistic experience and creativity as a distinct talent, separate from man's other connatural activities of mysticism, moral judgment, metaphysical questioning. Religion teaches art to keep its own place and refrain from arrogance. *The Responsibility of the Artist* (1960) struggles for a mediating position between those familiar extremes of art for art's sake, and *l'art engagé.* This latter book and especially *Creative Intuition in Art and Poetry* (1953) reinforce the semblance theory of Susanne Langer, requiring that the poet's "passions, ideas, or beliefs: religious, philosophical, metaphysical" must be truly "internalized in the creative source, integrated in the poetic intuition, and therefore transmuted . . ." (1960, p. 71). Maritain fears the religious conversion of any minor artist, for his newly discovered moral ideas may "prey upon his art as substitutes for insufficiently deep experience and creative intuition" (1960, p. 98). There is little detailed practical literary or art criticism in Maritain, but he chooses his illustrations with taste, mostly from modern poetry and abstractionist art, which can be sampled in the fine plates selected for *Creative Intuition.* A characteristic theme is the parallel between artistic creativity and God's creative act, an analogy which prompts Maritain to view the novelist's fictive characters, for example, as virtual aspects or possible developments emerging from the novelist's unconscious life.

Romano Guardini's books on Plato, Augustine, Dante, Dostoevsky, and Rilke show an outstanding intuitive practical criticism joined with theoretical presuppositions that are often somewhat homiletic and crude. In *Rilke's Duino Elegies,* for example, Guardini defends his own style of judicial philosophical criticism impatiently against relativists and autotelists. A poetic work is "more than mere 'expression'—it is a *declaration* and the truth of a declaration is necessarily verifiable. This means that it must not only be sincere and authentic but must also grasp the nature of Being. If a poet says 'It is so,' he has committed himself to a declaration and . . . he is also answerable for the truth of his declaration . . ." (1961, p. 15). Yet the line by line explications of Rilke that follow this clumsy manifesto are superb; in fact I know of no more thorough or imaginative readings of these elegies. Guardini consults Rilke's letters to illuminate his eccentric symbolism, he gives variant critical readings and multiple interpretations of intricate passages, he constantly interlocks the elegies into an organic sequence. But I find the performance marred by brusque scolding and preaching. For example, in the "Fifth Elegy," the imagery of acrobatics captures the strength and drama of love but perhaps misses its personal depth. This insight leads Guardini to complain about this "same attitude to values as we have noted several times before and it is both false and disastrous" (p. 159). We hear repeatedly that Rilke seems incapable of an authentic interpersonal relationship and thus he sentimentally exalts impersonal love, or that his angel is a deficient surrogate for a misunderstood Christian God.

Similarly, in the two fine Dostoevsky essays, "The Legend of the Grand Inquisitor" (1952, pp. 58–86) and "Dostoevsky's Idiot, a Symbol of Christ" (1956, pp. 359–82), Guardini both confirms and surprises our negative expectations. He wastes effort defending Germans against their cold, narrow, pedantic stereotype in the novels, and vindicating historical Caesaro-Papism against its masterly caricature in the Grand Inquisitor figure. In the midst of these energetic rebuttals, Guardini's anxiety to appear unruffled leads to an abrupt fatuous evasion: "we hold Dostoevsky in too great esteem to believe that this amazing psychologist could have given us an obvious piece of polemics, even if he wanted to." Guardini would overlook Dostoevsky's evident militant biases against Germans, Poles, Jews, and Roman Catholics, among others. The second Guardini essay, on the contrary, unexpectedly supports Dostoevsky's choice of human impracticality, disease, and insanity as an apt composite symbol of the "adorable transgression of the frontiers of humanity" in Christ, whereas some other Christian literary critics generally carp about the alleged Manichean dualism implied in Myshkin's extremity. Guardini reads the final scenes of this novel as a religious affirmation that no character could be redeemed by Myshkin. Nothing of the divine is mimicked, there are no sudden conversions, no deus ex machina. In *Brothers Karamazov* Guardini's interpretation of the Inquisitor Legend as a symbol of Ivan's approaching schizophrenia is certainly accurate: the weak Christ and powerful Inquisitor of the Legend are both facets of Ivan's own complex personality, and Ivan dramatizes them in such a way that he subconsciously justifies suppressing the imperatives of his conscience and delivering himself to the Satan-Inquisitor of his later hallucinations.

In Guardini I believe the doctrinaire theologian occasionally tramples upon the sensitive religious critic. Perhaps his theory of myth, liturgy, and sacred images, especially in *The Spirit of the Liturgy* (1937) and *Sacred Signs* (1955), gives the plausible grounds for his best critical practice, despite the lapses already indicated. The sacred liturgy is joyful play before God, like David dancing before the ark, relishing a world of divine realities. And an artist gives form to the hidden life of man, not for instruction and good advice, but merely for the joy of expression. Thus, there is a zone of relative autonomy for play, liturgy, and art, freed from didacticism and the zealous scrutiny of a poet's verifiable declarations.

GABRIEL MARCEL AND MIGUEL DE UNAMUNO. Gabriel Marcel, in an essay on "My Dramatic Works as Viewed by the Philosopher" (1967, pp. 93–118) remarks that his plays "portray real existence more powerfully than any of my philosophical writing ever could." His commitment to literature has long been manifest, even as early as his doctoral dissertation on Coleridge. Marcel's emphasis on the privileged affectivity and cognitive potential of literature and myth, a mode superior to conceptual discourse, characterizes also the work of the following three existentialist theologians I shall discuss. Marcel recognizes that his plays challenge people more than do his philosophical essays. Generalizing too rashly from his statements on hope, people attribute to him a facile optimism belied by the tensions and complexities of despair he can preserve more sharply in the plays. Much of the content of Marcel's literary work stems from actual incidents of fear and restlessness in his own life. *Homo Viator* (1951, pp. 213–70) contains two essays on Rilke, whom Marcel calls a witness to the Spiritual, not just observing and commenting but someone participating, nourishing, and confessing. Rilke's philosophy is existential, or experiential, apprehending reality as a network of protective or hostile influences. Although not developed logically, Rilke's thought shows consistently throughout his corpus a "progressive transformation of vision" (p. 215). Marcel quotes lengthy passages from the "Elegies," and especially the letters, to sound out Rilke's principal motifs. He is fastidious about the distortions caused by paraphrase, so that his task as critic is mostly reduced to quotation, questioning, evoking a mood, contributing insights from Marcel's own philosophy to the exposition of Rilke's themes.

Miguel de Unamuno is convinced in his *Essays and Soliloquies* that impersonal philosophical systems possess less consistency and vitality than those closer to poetry where the inward biography of the author openly pervades all his thought. It is not our philosophy that makes us optimists or pessimists, but the fundamental optimistic experience or the tragic sense of life, stemming from a "physiological or perhaps psychological origin, as much the one as the other, that makes our ideas" (1925, pp. 196–97). Unamuno's first principle is to *live,* then philosophize; his second is to treat man as an end, never as a means. Philosophy occurs as deeply in Goethe as in Hegel, and especially in Spain it exists not so much in a *Critique of Pure Reason* as in actual people, a *Lebensansicht* diffused in literature, action, and mysticism. Like Paul, Augustine, and Luther, Unamuno realizes he philosophizes best rhetorically, with pen in hand, not thinking of himself but of others, writing in passionate antitheses. His words press themselves upon the reader, with the immediate vibrancy of actual speech.

Unamuno's mission as a writer is "to war against all those who resign themselves, whether to Catholicism or to rationalism or to agnosticism; it is to make them all live lives of inquietude and passionate desire" (p. 117). He wants to confront men individually and "frontally, and if possible split them in two. It is the best service I can do them" (p. 167). His religion itself is a violent quarrel with God, whose existence cannot be proved nor disproved. Man should determine to do good, even for no other motive than to protest the radical injustice of the cosmos, if there should eventually prove to be no afterlife. Unamuno's novels, too, employ the same belligerent confrontatory vocabulary. The author's fictive characters are set loose upon the page in search of a reader to give them life and to re-create each person's own values in the process.

In the 1914 foreword to *Our Lord Don Quixote* (1967), Unamuno undertakes the free creative interpretation he expects of his own readers. Leaving to historians the worry about what Cervantes sought to express and actually did express, Unamuno lifts the book out of its own epoch and nation for a "mystical interpretation," or an assertion of whatever the text suggests to the reader. "I consider myself more Quixotist than Cervantist, and . . . I attempt to free Don Quixote from Cervantes himself . . . ." Unamuno's style of criticism is to paraphrase a scene from the book, then freely allegorize and rhapsodize, addressing himself to Spain, to the world, or to his own soul. The essay on Ibsen and Kierkegaard in *Perplexities and Paradoxes* (1945, pp. 51–57) meanders between the theme of a specific play, Ibsen's life, and the impact of his corpus, concluding that Ibsen succeeded in transcending the Kierkegaardian initial aesthetic phase. Denouncing autotelist critics as repugnant aestheticians with "that pestiferous professional indifference toward the basic religious and ethical meaning" of Ibsen's dramas, Unamuno vigorously affirms that although an author may not express any religious doctrine didactically, still if "he has not seen the reality which lies behind a philosophy or a religion, he has seen nothing which deserves to be perpetuated" (p. 52).

MARTIN BUBER. An impressive example of Martin Buber's literary creativity is the narration of twenty stories about Hasidic origins in *Legend of the Baal-Shem*: "I bear in me the blood and the spirit of those who created it, and out of my blood and spirit it has become new" (1955, p. x). His applied literary criticism can be sampled in Buber's collected studies *On the Bible* (1968), his aesthetic theory in the essay "Arts and the Man" (1958, pp. 41–52), along with Louis Hammer's "Relevance of Buber's Thought to Aesthetics" (1967), to which Buber has written his own "Replies to My Critics" (1967). Rejecting dualism of all types, legalism and institutionalism, Buber stresses unhindered human intersubjectivity, the direct personal relationship between God and man, and the prophetic oracular role of poet and theologian. His religious beliefs can be stated succinctly: "I have not been able to accept either the Bible or Hasidism as a whole; in one and in the other I had to . . . distinguish between that which had become evident to me out of my experience as truth and that which had not become evident to me in this manner" (1967, p. 744). In his literary criticism Buber characteristically focuses on the personal bond established between the author and reader, delineated in categories of dialogue, encounter, and presence. The critic ought not to evaluate so much as *create* favorable conditions for a meeting between the work and its potential audience. Art is a means of communication between persons, not reducible to knowledge or emotion. In a literary work I simultaneously discover and create a new aspect of reality, which would not have become visible unless my eyes had searched for it. "It is not something that existed in itself outside these eyes; it is a reality of revelation, the product of a meeting" (1958, p. 45). This hermeneutic resembles Eliade's paradoxical axiom that the scale creates the phenomenon, which I shall develop later.

In his biblical exegesis, Buber seems to situate himself at the exciting periphery of recognized scholarship. I think his responses to Glatzer's and Muilenburg's detailed critiques of his scriptural interpretation show competent etymology and textual scrutiny (1967, pp. 726–31). Buber's ideal is to read "the Bible with an appreciation of its poetic form, but also with an intuitive grasp of the suprapoetic element that transcends all form" (1968, p. 234). In his translation of the Hebrew Bible into a very rough German, he and Franz Rosenzweig attempted to reproduce nuances, emphases, and word placements in order to get back as closely as possible to the spoken personal word. Buber's theology tends to be devoutly conservative, professing belief in a very early realization of monotheism in Israel, and in the literal historicity of major Exodus events. It is helpful to read Buber in the dissentient context of Ronald Hepburn's exposure of limitations and potential distortions concealed in the simple I-Thou encounter language then applied to religious experience (1966, pp. 24f.).

KARL JASPERS. Jaspers's aesthetic is obscurely diffused throughout his intricate philosophical theory, which is itself an impressive construct enriched with spatial and visual metaphors. For example, the shifting but ever-present limit to my experience is my horizon; the sacred background behind all horizons is the encompassing or holy being itself. The implications of this theory can be followed in *Philosophy* (1969), *Tragedy Is Not Enough* (1952), and *Truth and Symbol* (1959), the latter two of which are fragments from his lengthy *Von der Wahrheit*. We can read any object or event as a *chiffre,* cipher, or symbol in an ascending quest for knowledge mounting into the indefinite horizon. We manage to approach God "only through the world, only with its phenomena and the historicity of our life. . . . We should always hold ourselves open for the cipher-script whose communication we cannot force by intention and plan. Everything which is, must become a cipher" (1959, pp. 73–74). God is not a cipher but reality, accessible only through this cipher-script of the world. And an analysis of ciphers in their relationship to being is what Jaspers means by philosophy, more liberated and sociologically formless than a theology, which binds itself "to a distinct, historic form of religious community and to its documents which have been canonized as revelations" (1969, p. 296).

Two conditions are indispensable to the genuine philosopher and religious believer in their search. First, no cipher is to be absolutized in the endless ascent to the hidden encompassing; for all objectivity must be grasped in its gliding relativity, pointing always beyond as foreground, question, and task (1959, pp. 69–73). Since "there is no complete truth, our movement toward it is itself the only form in which truth can achieve completion in existence, here and now . . . This is the vision of a great and noble life: to endure ambiguity in the movement of truth and to make light shine through it; to stand fast in uncertainty; to prove capable of unlimited love and hope" (1952, pp. 1–5). The second condition is that a "hearing of the symbols is the first precedent and incomprehensible experience out of which philosophical thinking arises and toward which it strives" (1959, p. 65).

These concepts of an endless religious search and the iconic character of reality support an aesthetic that is responsive to contemporary issues of doubt and secularity. Jaspers's approach to tragic experience, for example, is a direct corollary to the principal themes of his philosophy. A tragic experience occurs when a person confronts an authentic boundary situation of suffering, death, severe contingency. He experiences tragedy if he senses and suffers beyond his ability to act; if his limits of awareness should coincide with the limits of his power to act, then there could be no tragedy. "Myths, images, and stories of tragic inspiration are quite capable of containing truth without losing their uncommitted, hovering character. If preserved in its purity, the original vision of the tragic already contains the essence of philosophy: movement, question, open-mindedness, emotion, wonder, truthfulness, lack of illusion" (1952, p. 103). The tragic experience also contains within itself its own release, not through doctrine and revelation but through a vision of order, justice, love, and a trusting acceptance of the boundary situation itself, never completely understood. In other words, the philosopher approaches Shakespearean tragedy, for example, first ready to listen, and open to experience an identity of style between his own metaphysical questioning and the "open, jagged fractures of [Shakespeare's] work, in what it leaves unresolved, in the tenseness of his characters, and in their straining, unspoken and unconscious, toward the chance of being saved" (1952, p. 39). He learns from Shakespeare to retain potentially the hovering, searching suspension peculiar to an authentic tragic experience, without clamoring for premature conceptual solutions. An art that has become so expressive a cipher of being is called metaphysical art.

In his typology of Greek, Shakespearean, and modern genres of tragedy, Jaspers singles out Oedipus, Hamlet, and Lessing's Nathan the Wise as prototypes attempting to transcend human limits of knowledge. Jaspers's applied criticism is cursory but accurate and sensitive. Like Marcel and Heidegger, he preserves a stance of devout listening to the work, which he scrupulously hesitates to paraphrase. Great literature offers "no more than directions for interpretation to pursue. Where rational interpretation is possible, poetry becomes superfluous" (1952, p. 43). What the reader seeks in a poem is its *Weltanschauung,* a stock term which Jaspers labors to revitalize as the way things are evaluated, the attitudes and range of values, lived in a restless tension of belief and unbelief (1969, pp. 250–55).

THEOLOGY OF POLITICAL ESCHATOLOGY

SOCIOLOGISTS OF RELIGION. The conditions for an authentic human culture must be created, not presumed. And in the Marxist tradition especially, cultural theology is itself praxis. Johannes Metz (1969) and Harvey Cox (1967) have both advocated a public theology, not only demythologized but deprivatized, beyond the closed circuit of existentialist personal experience, assessing and at the same time seeking to transform political institutions. It must focus on the polis and help man to become a fully post-town and post-tribal adult agent (Cox, 1965, p. 255). A responsible literary criticism in this spirit must be as profoundly sociopolitical as it is aesthetic, what Cox calls a genuine *Kulturpolitik.* Cox's own work shows a discriminating use of spirited brief political literary critiques, in the Dwight MacDonald and Susan Sontag style of creative social commentary on films, pop art, public taste (1969, pp. 166f.).

Robert Bellah's "Confessions of a Former Establishment Fundamentalist" (1971, pp. 229–33) gives one explanation for the recent upsurge of investigations into the religious phenomenon by sociologists in the Weber, Durkheim, and Talcott Parsons tradition. By an establishment fundamentalism, Bellah means he used to dispose of religious beliefs in the classroom from an unconscious stance of rationalistic dogmatism, attributing to his scientific and historical concepts a higher ontological status than the religious realm he was analyzing. "What I was doing, I thought, was a science; what the poor people I studied were doing was religion, and my science understood their religion." Eventually Bellah realized he was offering an alternative religious view of his own, a burden of illicit implication, a peculiarly abstract conceptual perspective on the complex experiential issues of religion. Today in teaching the sociology of religion he recognizes his greatest resource is himself, mind and spirit and body. His task is not merely to analyze and criticize but also to evoke a group experience of the unconscious religious depths, a method that deliberately blurs the distinction between a religious experience itself and the teaching about religion.

Bellah's *Beyond Belief* essays present basically a *Lebensphilosophie*, upholding piety, religiousness, religious experience rather than institutional crystallized belief. Bellah narrates his own transition from the self-assured commitments of Harvard to the immediacy and openness of Berkeley, from the systems of Christianity and Marxism to his present loyalty toward religious truth beyond yet partially embodied in all combined systems. The secularity of today he interprets as an interiorization of religious authority, a decline in external control systems of religion. Religion, the "symbolic form through which man comes to terms with the antinomies of his being, has not declined . . ." (1970, p. 227). He finds religious community today in the Peace Corps or Black Power movements at their best, and wherever two or more people achieve an international moral solidarity transcending their partisan loyalties. The contemporary equivalent of the conventional nonbeliever is someone who does not experience the "dimension of innerness, who accepts the literalness of everyday as the sole reality." An adept literary critic, Bellah centers his essay on "Transcendence in Contemporary Piety" (pp. 196–207) on Wallace Stevens whom he calls the greatest theological poet of this century, and "Stevensian Piety." Based on poetic lines and obiter dicta from Stevens, Bellah's theme is a secular religiousness, which locates in everyday realities themselves both an experience of deficiency or a sacred boundary situation evoked by anxiety and despair, and an experience of fulfillment or sacral well-being and wonder.

The two books by Peter Berger that suggest the most likely parallels to Bellah's approach are *The Precarious Vision* (1961b) and *A Rumor of Angels* (1969). The former presents fragmentary exercises, fantasy tales and case studies and brief essays, to induce an experience of precariousness, the prototypical modern mood. Then Berger asks the ethical implications of this perspective, and demonstrates how the Christian way responds to such a situation. The second book seeks out "signals of transcendence within the empirically given human situation," man's propensity for order, play, and hope as modest contemporary equivalents of the traditional proofs for sacrality. Instead of a univocal contemporary mood of secularity, Berger finds a plurality of community structures, each with its own plausible world view, one of which is Christian faith. *The Noise of Solemn Assemblies* (1961a), like much of *Precarious Vision,* is a sharp neoorthodox polemic against the social adjustment and mental health shibboleths peddled by a cultural religion. Berger's later books become gradually more correlational and inclusively religious. *The Social Construction of Reality* (1967) by Berger and Thomas Luckmann gives a fruitful social emphasis to the phenomenologists' *Lebenswelt* perspective discussed before. Each person attempts to legitimate his experiences by locating them "within a cosmological and anthropological frame of reference," a general mythological *Weltanschauung* that orders and sanctions his values. These symbolic universes are shared. They function as "sheltering canopies over the institutional order as well as over individual biography," by which we conceive ourselves as part of a social history with a common past and anticipated destiny. We each project a world into which we externalize ourselves, and our common political order is essentially a projected myth of shared power and justice.

Religious sociologists like Cox, Bellah, and Berger, then, have been developing a flexible encompassing methodology to explore the deeper political significance of communal religious experience. The broader aesthetic and theological implications of this political communitarian theme can be discovered in R. G. Collingwood and Jurgen Möltmann. Collingwood's familiar collaboration theory, notably in his *Principles of Art* (1960) and *Faith and Reason* (1968), emphasizes an implicit community of experience and technique among artists, and the intelligent sympathetic reconstruction required of his public. Articulating the most secret aspirations of the community as their prophetic spokesman, an artist does not so much choose a subject as let the subject choose him, responding to the public's collaboration from the very inception of his work. It is instructive to observe how Bultmann's *History and Eschatology* (1957a) reconciles with his own individualistic philosophy of history Collingwood's theory of historiography as an act of self-understanding by the community mind. Collingwood, he says, believes "every *now,* every moment, in its historical relatedness of course, has within itself a full meaning of responsibility, of decision. . . . [For] Collingwood every present moment is an eschatological moment, and . . . history and eschatology are identified" (pp. 135–43). It is this tendency to identify eschatology with a transhistorical present instant of decision that prompts Jurgen Möltmann to argue against Bultmann for an eschatology that preserves the evolving future-oriented dynamic within each historical moment. Even though Bultmann's theory of the *eschaton* or final sacral event is a strained "already-not-yet" dialectic, affirming that Christ both has come and will come, Möltmann demands more explicit emphasis on the "not yet" expectancy.

Möltmann's *Theology of Hope* (1967) and *Religion, Revolution, and the Future* (1969) develop exclusively, almost obsessively, the future-oriented world view of many New Testament writers, awaiting the Second Advent and New Creation that has not yet been accomplished. He links this viewpoint with Old Testament messianic expectations, the philosophical millenarianism of Joachim di Fiore, and many historical theories from the developing God of Goethe and Herder to the present. A balanced context for Möltmann's thought can be assembled from Frank Manuel's survey (1965) of the intricate variations on two basic approaches to history, as either novelty creating and variant, or eternally recurrent; and from John Baillie's famous study (1950) of the myth of progressive evolution, associating it with biblical viewpoints, modern developmental theories, and biological organicist models. Reinhold Niebuhr's characteristic warning against a buoyant futurism is that the free society functions best in a cultural and religious atmosphere encouraging neither too pessimistic nor optimistic a view of the human future. "Both moral sentimentality in politics and moral pessimism encourage totalitarian regimes" (1944, p. viii). The first encourages fascism because it trusts political power too much to restrain it, the second because it prefers the strongest countermeasures against conflict and moral chaos.

Möltmann's essay "Toward a Political Hermeneutic of the Gospel" (1969, pp. 83–107) is a brilliant Marxist reinterpretation of religious experience. Once the religious symbol is accepted as somehow a projected negation or sublimation of the actual human misery in a particular society, then this symbol can only be properly demythologized in one way. It must be reinterpreted to speak not of another world but to protest actual present afflictions in this world and the revolutionary means to redress them. Möltmann argues: "Religion therefore originates in the concrete experience of the difference between existence and essence. . . . The 'protestation against real affliction' is the unmythological kernel of religion" (pp. 94–95). Bultmann's existentialist hermeneutic tends to remythologize from the biblical perspective to a horizon simply of present human self-understanding. Möltmann's practical or material hermeneutic translates to a horizon of the present personal, social, and political lack of freedom, what Pannenberg has called a horizon of concern. Since the Bible promises and proclaims a new era of freedom, the responsible interpreter today must turn it into a program of poltical liberation.

POST-MARXIST THEOLOGIANS. I have remarked before that Marx and Trotsky enuntiated a far more sophisticated view of art and literature than the stereotype of smiling Socialist factory workers we associate with recent Soviet propagandist art. An anthology on Karl Marx and Frederick Engels, *Literature and Art,* will prove surprising to many readers. In "The English Middle Class," Marx praises Dickens, Thackeray, and Charlotte Brontë for their satire on the affectations and tyranny in the British middle class. These novelists have "revealed more political and social truths than all the professional politicians, publicists, and moralists put together . . ." (1947, p. 133). Marx lists his favorite literary classics, ranging through Aeschylus, Dante, Shakespeare, Goethe, Fielding, Scott, and Balzac. Abhoring prescribed public taste and gray official colors, he expects each work to achieve its own freedom of form. He asks Ferdinand Lassalle in a critique of his play *Franz von Sickingen* not to propagandize but to "Shakespearize," to devise better characterization and more plausible dialogue, for "at present I consider Schillerism, making individuals the mere mouthpieces of the spirit of the times, your main fault" (p. 48). Art can be authentically appreciated by neither the worried poverty-stricken person nor the rich burgher vulgarized in a capitalistic utilitarian economy, but only by a humanized leisure class. Leon Trotsky's *Literature and Revolution* (1924) expects to discover a preconceived artistic idea in each work of literature that reflects personal and social feelings, but he realizes that verbal form will often transform the content in the creative process and push it into unforeseen paths. A work of art can be assessed as art only according to its own literary canons, although Marxism can explain what class struggles led to a change in artistic expectations and why. Art is a "function of social man indissolubly tied to his life and environment" (cf. Demetz).

The Marxist Roger Garaudy in his remarkable book *From Anathema to Dialogue* presents his own reinterpretation of the Christian faith largely in terms of Möltmann's future-oriented critique and Teilhard de Chardin's evolutionary panentheism. The contrast between this type of Christianity and his own Marxist existentialism is sharp but not insurmountable. Man has a never-satisfied exigency for totality and absoluteness. "We can live this exigency, act it out, but not name, conceive, expect it; nor hypostatize it under the name of transcendence. It is always deferred, growing, like man himself" (1966, pp. 94–95). Garaudy interprets religion as transposing into answer, promise, and presence something which pertains only to the order of question. And Marxist demythologization requires a Feuerbachian reduction of the myth back into the original human aspiration that brought it forth. Garaudy has apparently not yet familiarized himself with the process theologians' models of sacrality, for his basic assumption is that if we name this immanent self-transcendence in man, "the name will not be that of God, for it is impossible to conceive of a God who is always in process of making himself, in process of being born. The most beautiful and the most exalted name which can be given to this exigency is the name of man." For man by definition is precisely "he who is not. This exigency in man is, I think, the flesh of your God" (pp. 94–95). Both Christians and Marxists live this passionate exigency for the same absolute, but "yours is presence while ours is absence."

The Marxist Ernst Bloch's *Man on His Own* (1970a), his *A Philosophy of the Future* (1970b), and Möltmann's "Hope and Confidence: A Conversation with Ernst Bloch" (1969, pp. 148–76) give a more systematic foundation for Garaudy's position and suggest intriguing aesthetic implications. God is the longed-for future, the not-yet-worked-out depths in man and the world. God is not just a conceptual projection but an actual transcendental vacuum that draws man onward toward a real objective possibility. Bloch remythologizes the Christian messianic and apocalyptic myths into an ethos of militant optimism and revolutionary social activity, and stresses the Old Testament promises that we shall be like God, yet a God that is never Baal, Marduk, Ptah, Jupiter, but always the unnamed Good without representation. Bloch's essays "Christian Social Utopias" (1970a, pp. 118–41) and "Indications of Utopian Content" (1970b, pp. 84–141) are studies of Augustine, More, Campanella, and major utopian archetypes of the labyrinth, dragon quest, servant-savior, exodus. Every great work of literature has an augmented utopian horizon, so that it "belongs only ideologically, not creatively, to the age in which it is socially rooted" (1970b, p. 94). It has a cultural surplus that persists as a heritage for later times when the original social situation decays. The work contains within itself this utopian momentum, a poetic anticipation, or the "pre-semblance of what, objectively, is still latent in the world" (p. 96). In Bloch's theory, then, the work of literature is not quiescently rooted in its manifest historicity and social matrix, but it prophetically drives the present human situation toward a new political future.

POLITICAL EXISTENTIALISTS. All these political aesthetic issues raised by Marx, Garaudy, Möltmann, and Bloch come into dramatic focus in the controversy between Sartre and Camus, summarized in Germaine Brée's *Camus and Sartre: Crisis and Commitment* (1972). From 1930 to

1970 the three passionate political issues in France were the Spanish Civil War, the German occupation, and the Algerian War. Often linked together as articulate antifascists on the Left, near to but never simply identified with French Communism, both Sartre and Camus gradually developed conflicting political styles characteristic of their personalities. In their writing, Sartre seems more passionately revolutionary, a radically utopian activist, whereas Camus is more hesitant and pluralistic, questioning any myth of social progress that involves violent bloodshed, trying only to enunciate his own deep moral revulsion. Sartre is accused of detachment from actual politics and, instead, of constructing an intellectual system dressed up in revolutionary rhetoric to fortify himself with illusions that he can dominate a disordered world from his armchair. Brée describes Camus's *The Rebel: An Essay on Man in Revolt* (1956) as "the demythicizing of Marxist eschatology." Camus tells the myth of Prometheus, rebelling against the pain and suffering of the world, firing man's enthusiasm and leading people into the desert. Yet this messiah gradually transforms himself into an authoritarian caesar, requiring the challenge now of yet another Prometheus, in a continuous succession of rebellions by the rebel against his own unconsciously emergent totalitarian impulses. The *Rebel* is undoubtedly Camus's most ambitious work of literary criticism and philosophy, tracing various archetypes and ideologies of rebellion through a broad history of literature and political thought. All crystallized religious and political dogmas attempting to rationalize or explain evil must be discarded, for they trap man in the complacent illusion that evil has been eradicated in principle if not in fact. Man must never stop his Promethean rebellion against the plague of suffering and moral evil in its unrelievable absurdity.

"People can think only in images," Albert Camus once wrote in his *Notebooks*. "If you want to be a philosopher, write novels" (1963, p. 10). His review of Sartre's *Nausea* in *Lyrical and Critical Essays* develops this dictum one important step further. "In a good novel the philosophy has disappeared into the images. But the philosophy need only spill over into the characters and actions for it to stick out like a sore thumb, the plot to lose its authenticity, and the novel its life" (1968, pp. 199–202). An appropriate semblancing of philosophy, what Camus in this review calls a "secret fusion of experience and thought, of life and reflection on the meaning of life," is thus one basic component in Camus's theory of criticism. It is debatable whether his own philosophical fiction achieves this ideal integration. Another characteristic principle in Camus's criticism is his advocacy of a mediate position between aestheticism and a fascination with the political Gorgon. Artistic creation, "instead of removing us from the drama of our time, is one of the means we are given of bringing it closer" (p. 353).

Camus thinks *Man's Fate* by Malraux ideally semblanced, but not Sartre's *Nausea.* The latter is essentially a philosophical essay on anxiety, and it conveys an experience only of dull human wretchedness, lacking the profundity of genuine tragedy. Silone's *Bread and Wine* is the rare achievement of a timely revolutionary theme that succeeds as propaganda only because it has become great art, with terse natural dialogue, short sentence structure, convincing characterization. Camus's applied criticism is generally an occasional jejune review or preface, consisting of a quick plot summary, followed by a comment on sentence structure, minimally the critic's dutiful nod in the direction of style and technique. Then he makes a few remarks on the theme, often with an aphorism that is the best feature of the essay. Of Sartre he says, for example, "The realization that life is absurd cannot be an end, but only a beginning." Or on Silone's critique of Italian Catholicism, he says, "the grandeur of a faith can be measured by the doubts it inspires." Again, in contrasting Kafka and Melville, he judges that Kafka's spiritual experience exceeded his ability to express it, but that in Melville both were commensurate. "In Kafka, the reality that he describes is created by the symbol, the fact stems from the image, whereas in Melville the symbol emerges from the reality, the image is born of what is seen" (p. 293).

Jean-Paul Sartre's *What Is Literature?* is an incomparably brilliant book, his vibrant manifesto for a criticism and literature of praxis. Beginning with the disparity between man's possibility and facticity, Sartre defines the public for whom a novelist must ideally write and the social assumptions from which he writes as those of a potential classless society. He must project his work to address this audience, composed of "a collectivity which constantly corrects, judges, and metamorphoses itself . . ." (1949, p. 159). Until this political utopia is achieved, there will remain a conflict between a writer's virtual and actual public, a dichotomy between word and action, his aesthetic private myth and society's accepted clichés. He does not search for a subject, but the problematic situation solicits him to express the situation to himself and others in order to change it. Just as "physics submits to mathematicians new problems which require them to produce a new symbolism, in like manner the always new requirements of the social and metaphysical engage the artist in finding a new language and new techniques" (pp. 26–27). This active intentionality pervades the initial material, its final artistic embodiment in the novel, and reaches out to draw upon the critical reader's directed creation. Raskolnikov's hatred is transformed into my own hatred "solicited and wheedled out of me by signs." Each word is a path of transcendence, shaping and naming my feelings, a hypothetical imperative asking for my free collaboration in the production of this work. "The imagination of the spectator has not only a regulating function, but a constitutive one. It does not play; it is called to recompose the beautiful object beyond the traces left by the artist" (p. 47). Like Ernst Bloch's theory of the utopian momentum in all great art, Sartre's aesthetic perceives the work as a summons for man to create the ideal universe it discloses.

The act of literary criticism, then, is essentially *political*. The critic must help fashion a society capable of appropriate response to such a literature, so that the work can "reveal itself in all its depth to the examination, the admiration, and the indignation of the reader; and the generous love is a promise to maintain, and the generous indignation is a promise to change, and the admiration is a promise to imitate. . . ." Although Sartre does not simplistically identify literature and morality, he is convinced "at the heart of the aesthetic imperative we discern the moral imperative" (p. 62). The latter part of *What Is Literature?* conjectures about the relationships between writers and their public in various historical periods. For example, in French classicism, the writer apparently accepts the ideology of an elite class that is convinced of its superior taste, and each work is a bow of courtesy between writer and reader in complicity. The actual society becomes the only virtual society projected during such a period.

Most of Sartre's commentators focus on fluctuations throughout his career in the synthesis between individuality and solidarity, existentialism and Marxism (G. Novack, 1966; Bauer, 1969; Kaelin, 1962; and Lessing, 1968, pp. 158–83). In addition to his outstanding book on Genet cited before, Sartre's applied criticism can be examined in *Literary and Philosophical Essays* (1955). His explication of Camus's *The Stranger* (pp. 24–41), employing themes from *The Myth of Sisyphus* as a commentary on the novel, associates Camus with Hemingway and Kafka. Like Hemingway, Camus has created a style that is neo-classical, sober, giving an impression of isolated neutral sensations appropriate to his theme of innocent detachment. Kafka writes of an impossible transcendence, a world full of signs no one can read, whereas Camus asserts the absence of all transcendence. In a spirited polemic against Mauriac, Sartre demonstrates how the novelist violates the purported freedom of his main character by slipping in and out of her consciousness omnisciently, expressing sympathy, disapproval, and predetermining everything she plans to do (pp. 7–23). His essay "On *The Sound and the Fury:* Time in the Work of Faulkner" (pp. 79–87) enunciates a sound principle: "A fictional technique always relates back to the novelist's metaphysics. The critic's task is to define the latter before evaluating the former." Unfortunately the metaphysic Sartre distills is too selectively drawn from Quentin's consciousness alone in *Sound and Fury* and from portions of *Sartoris* and *Light in August*. When it is claimed that Faulkner's metaphysic distorts time, representing man as time-bound, closed off to the future, Sartre overlooks a range of other Dilsey-like *bliks* in Faulkner, and the wide varieties and polarities of Faulkner's comprehensive world view.

As much a political existentialist philosopher as Sartre and Camus, Nicholas Berdyaev proves himself also a capable applied literary critic in his popular book on Dostoevsky (1969). Like Sartre's study of Genet, Unamuno's on Don Quixote, or Northrop Frye's on Blake, the book examines Dostoevsky's literary corpus and biography in detail, but the novelist's metaphysic becomes identified unmistakably with Berdyaev's own. Ivan-Raskolnikov-Stavrogin in Dostoevsky's world represent Berdyaev's principle of violent irrational *meonic* freedom, Alyosha-Myshkin-Sonya the immanent panentheist God of the Russian soil. These two principles, along with his messianic eschatology, constitute the three fundamental emphases in Berdyaev's existentialist theology.

In *The Meaning of the Creative Act* the passionate recusant searching of Dostoevsky, Nietzsche, Ibsen, Baudelaire, and others becomes a Dionysian religious art which Berdyaev links with a "Third Age of the Spirit" or an "Epoch of Creativity" in Joachim di Fiore's familiar historical typology. He calls this an eschatological or theurgic art, an art of divine-human creativeness, man working with God to build the future messianic era (1955, p. 247). Apollonian or canonic art is serene academic Goethianism in settled bourgeois forms. Sartre and Bloch have demanded a similar future-oriented revolutionary art that foreshadows and helps create the ideal political future. In Berdyaev's pronounced religious philosophy, however, it is God and the coming Christ who stand horizontally at the end of history, not a God spatially vertical and beyond me. The world moves toward something far more than Bloch's metaphysical vacuum and the Marxist perfect future society. "Art is religious in the depths of the very artistic creative act," he says, and "the symbol is a bridge thrown across the gulf from the creative act to hidden, final reality" (pp. 248, 239). The religious dynamic in a work is anticipatory, proleptic, then, orienting the work less toward a present center of meaning than toward the future revelation of final meaning.

The outlines of Berdyaev's panentheism can be studied in *The Destiny of Man* (1937) and especially in the invaluable *Christian Existen-*

tialism: A Berdyaev Anthology (1965). Perhaps the keystone of his approach is the statement, "man is the child of God and of non-being [or] *meonic freedom*" (1937, p. 60). This means that any study of man is a distortion unless it is a religious anthropology. Man by definition is a being who transcends himself, with a tendency toward mystery and the infinite. "The transcendent comes to man from within, from the depths. God is deeper within me than I myself . . ." (1965, p. 238). Authentic religious revelation is not something finished, static, handed to a person by church theologians from the outside, but the life and mind of Christ "given in spiritual experience, an event which takes place within the person to whom divine things are opened" (1965, p. 234). Since Berdyaev reconciles the divine and human so closely, he apparently feels compelled to adopt emphatic measures to escape pantheism. But pantheism is less a heresy about God than about man's freedom. Berdyaev protests that transforming man into an emanation of God is equivalent to some teachings of Dostoevsky's Zossima and Russian Orthodox mystics that declare God all in all, the only true being, dominating everything. Therefore, "to avoid both monism and pantheism we must recognize man's freedom . . . uncreated and not determined by God; man's capacity for creativeness" (1965, pp. 227–28). Berdyaev constructs the myth of an *Urgrund*, a blind chaotic force of nonbeing or *me-onic* passionate freedom, into which God breathes His spirit to create man as a dynamically polarized human being.

Berdyaev's concept of radical freedom expressly guarantees man's unrepeatable individuality and independence, at the cost of this rather eccentric dualism between being and nonbeing. Berdyaev thinks that the mark of each philosopher's individual personality can be found on any philosophy of importance, especially in Augustine, Pascal, and Kierkegaard. This personal experiential quality is evident "in the choice of problems, . . . in the pervading intuition, in the direction of attention, in the man's general spiritual experience . . . The whole living man philosophizes" (1965, pp. 127–28). Yet to counterbalance this individualistic emphasis, Berdyaev reaffirms the traditional Russian concept of *Sobornost*, religious solidarity, or "the church as communion rather than the church as society" (1965, p. 225). Our life "and our myth-making cannot be separated from that of earlier generations . . . It is all one unending, continuous, creative life, . . . [with] the whole world-historical process as divine revelation, as the intimate mutual action and reaction between humanity and divinity" (1965, pp. 243–44).

14

PSYCHO-MYTHIC RELIGIOUS THOUGHT

We have observed the attempts of most ortho-cultural theologians in chapter 13 to remythologize theos as the innermost entelechy of culture and of all that is most genuinely human in human experience. As the analyst of this human religious experience turns his tools back upon himself as experiencer, searching intensively how in himself or in the world the correlative human-divine dynamic is being repressed, distorted, or authentically actualized, we have a theology progressively *in-depth,* all I have described before in chapter 8 as the *psycho-mythic* dimension.

In this present chapter, we can first distinguish a psycho-social anthropological group, exploring this nominal undifferentiated phenomenon of religious experience. A mature adult's religious experience is not that of a neurotic, nor is a child's experience that of an elderly adult. Similarly, the communal religious experience that occurs within a deteriorating society is unlike that within a politically vital society, nor is that within an overtly religious society like that within one more or less secularized. I have termed the dimensions of experience investigated by this group archetypal in Jung's protean sense—the most intensive and extensive resonances of religious experience as it has been lived and symbolized throughout the history of human civilization.

My second psycho-mythic group is distinguishable from the ortho-cultural theologians of chapter 13 only in the extent to which they remythologize the Christian or broad religious center of meaning *within* human culture. Their repudiation of the sacred-profane or natural-supernatural dichotomy and unfeasible models of transcendence here becomes far more decisive. Their search for a radical new myth of panenchristism or panentheism is more daring and controversial. Included in this second group are theologians of post-Barthian prophetic secularity, theologians of Dewey-Whitehead immanentist empiricism, and some popular theologians of common experience.

THEOLOGY OF ARCHETYPAL EXPERIENCE

In offering a functional description of genuine religious experience, I have implied before that a given profession of belief can express mature authentic faith or can disguise the most shallow and neurotic attitudes. The religious dimension cannot be scrutinized in isolation, but only in its total human functional context, whether it furthers man's development or paralyzes it. Tillich's *Dynamics of Faith* distinguishes between an integrating faith and one that is idolatrous or disintegrating. The first type centers the personality "upon something of ultimate meaning," uniting and giving creative eros to moral life, artistic achievement, scientific knowledge, and political organization. In idolatrous faith, "the centering point is something which is more or less on to the periphery" (1965, p. 11). Preliminary and transitory values are invested with ultimacy and an integrating power they do not possess. Unconscious drives are repressed or explode chaotically, the center is lost, the personality disrupted (p. 106).

Erich Fromm has analyzed the personality and societal structures behind these same two conflicting styles of religion, which he calls humanistic and authoritarian. God in the first type is the image of man's higher self, what he in his idealized maturity can be, whereas in the second God is the symbol of power that alienates and dehumanizes man. Society or individual needs dispose man toward submissive fear or responsible freedom, symbolized in the type of government or religion to which he is attracted. "The real fall of man is his alienation from himself, his submission to power, his turning against himself even though under the guise of his worship of God" (1967, p. 51). Abraham Maslow has developed Max Weber's charismatic-institutional dichotomy, a distinction between the religious experience of a prophet, "who has discovered his truth about the world, the cosmos, ethics, God, and his own identity from within, from his own personal experience," and that of the organizer or legalist, simply "loyal to the structure of the organization" (1964, p. 21). This distinction is parallel to Merleau-Ponty's concept of an interior and exterior God, and especially to Gordon Allport's famous distinction between intrinsic and extrinsic religion (1954). The extrinsic religious experience is used by the nominal churchgoer for safety, social standing, endorsement of his own values, thus consolidating his self-interest and all forms of prejudice.

SIGMUND FREUD. I have already outlined Freud's rejection of antihumanist religion, and have also illustrated the undisciplined cerebral and capricious extremes of some criticism that calls itself Freudian. Yet Freud's own literary criticism is remarkably sensitive and imaginative.

He need only apply his many resourceful canons of interpretation from *Interpretation of Dreams* (1969) to other human constructs as well. "The Theme of the Three Caskets" matches his best dream analyses. These caskets in the *Merchant of Venice* are compared to the three daughters in *King Lear,* Cinderella and her two sisters, the three goddesses from which Paris must choose, and the three Fates. The gold and silver boxes are flashy, whereas the lead is prosaic. Like the lead box, Cordelia is silent, Cinderella conceals herself. Freud associates dumbness and silence with death, and believes that choosing the last alternative is equivalent to choosing apparent death. But the story transforms the Goddess of Death into the Goddess of Love—a reaction formation, by which man's imagination replaces the gift that reality denies him by a wishful opposite. "Contradictions . . . offer no serious difficulty to the work of analytic interpretation," says Freud, who would be appalled to recognize how this paradox has been abused by some Freudian analysts and critics. Freud illustrates his principle of interpretation by citing the myths that identify Aphrodite with the underworld, fertility with death, and the many creator-destroyer goddesses of the East. This insight prompts an interesting symbolic reading of Lear's death scene, a frieze in which an old man is being absorbed into Mother Earth, the condition of the dead Cordelia whose body he carries.

In "The Claims of Psychoanalysis to Scientific Interest" Freud indicates the ways in which his psychoanalytic method can be applied to the other human sciences. We can conjecture about the affective units motivating any strikingly individual thinker and his apparently detached logic in a given philosophical system, and detect weak spots or highlight otherwise neglected areas of significance. Yet Freud warns of the genetic fallacy, from which he himself was never immune, "the fact that a theory is psychologically determined does not in the least invalidate its scientific truth" (1957, p. 79). His hermeneutic principle is to presume that the complexes and emotive traits peculiar to dreams and symptoms are analogously at the root of morality, religion, justice, philosophy, myth, and art. The thesis of *Civilization and Its Discontents* (1962) can be summarized by Freud's remark in "Claims of Psychoanalysis" that the "whole course of the history of civilization is no more than an account of the various methods adopted by mankind for 'binding' their unsatisfied wishes . . ." (p. 186). Neuroses are individual attempts to seek symbolic compensation; myths, religion, and morality are social solutions to essentially the same problems.

In this wider cultural context, perhaps Freud's fundamental aesthetic will seem less simplistic. He defines art as "an activity intended to allay ungratified wishes—in the first place in the creative artist himself and subsequently in his audience or spectators. The motive forces of artists are the same conflicts which drive other people into neurosis and have encouraged society to construct its institutions" (1957, p. 187). We have already seen how a critic of Norman Holland's stature could imaginatively modify this approach to analyze the dynamics of audience catharsis, stock response, or suspension of disbelief. Freud also recognizes the validity of Langer's semblance canon: an author's personal wishful fantasies "only become a work of art when they have undergone a transformation which softens what is offensive in them, conceals their personal origin and, by obeying the laws of beauty, bribes other people with a bonus of pleasure" (p. 187).

The least reputable legacy stemming from Freud is a type of pseudo-anthropology that accepts as canonical and literal his fantastic myths about a primal horde, patricide, totem banquets, from which all religious and cultural institutions allegedly derive. Also, Freud is caught in an unquestioning Comtean typology of evolving stages, from religion to metaphysics to the positive sciences, finally synthesized in his own metapsychology. The historicity and verifiability of these theories are scarcely defensible today. Yet such myths can still function as heuristic constructs for the later social scientist, as useful as the nonfactual "State of Nature" and "Social Contract" myths of Hobbes and Rousseau for modern political scientists. Like so many other nineteenth-century cultural philosophers, Freud was misled by the remarkable analogies between ontogenesis and phylogenesis, individual development and the evolution of civilizations, dream-neurosis and cultural artifact, microcosm and macrocosm. Ernst Cassirer's volume on myth in his architectonic *Philosophy of Symbolic Forms* (1955) seems dated today in its phenomenology of the primitive mind, with the generalizations about animism, magic, and prescientific affectivity. Levi-Strauss and most structural anthropologists today presume a hidden logical structure in every society, and impugn arrogant assumptions implying that societies less complex than our own are somehow equivalent to a childish undifferentiated consciousness (Kirk, 1970, pp. 252–86).

Norman Brown and Herbert Marcuse are two of the most influential contemporary neo-Freudians developing the cultural implications of psychoanalysis. Brown's *Life against Death* seeks to expand Freud's ideas into a wider theory of human nature, culture, and history, tracing the many affinities in poetry, politics, and philosophy. For example, by enlarging the Nirvana, repetition-compulsion, and masochism phases of Freud's death-instinct, Brown tries to interpret all the aggressions and artifacts of human life essentially as a flight from death.

Repudiating the authority and repressions of an Apollonian scholasticism, his essay on "Art and Eros" (1959, pp. 55–67) describes a new Dionysian consciousness demanding an art that is uninhibited dream, play, and neurosis. "The Protestant Era" (pp. 202–33) is a spirited apology for the use of demonic mythology by Luther and Tillich in their theology. Satan represents a dramatic evangelical protest against an otherwise smug acculturated religion. In his introduction to *Life against Death* Brown describes its format as mad and eccentric, yet his remarks seem more appropriate to describe *Love's Body* (1966), a capricious nonlinear book which, by a generous distribution of the equal sign, implies dialectically that love is resurrection is death is everything.

Herbert Marcuse's *Eros and Civilization: A Philosophical Inquiry into Freud* also seeks a nonrepressive culture, liberated from the utilitarian and puritan ethos. In "The Images of Orpheus and Narcissus" (1955, pp. 159–71) and "The Aesthetic Dimension" (pp. 172–96), he develops a theory of art as play and irresponsible fancy. Orpheus stands for the poet, creator, liberator, and the homosexual; Narcissus for the ecstatic contemplator of beauty, and the autoerotic. Marcuse supports these rebellions against conventional procreative sexuality as possibly a deeper uninhibited realization of the erotic drive in man, productive of a new Marxist messianic aesthetic. Another book celebrating and analyzing the new sensibility patterns in recent subcults is *The Varieties of Psychedelic Experience* (1966) by R. E. L. Masters and Jean Houston. Their concluding chapter is an unexpectedly stern indictment of the drug user's arrogant self-indulgence mistaking heightened empathy and sensory awareness for a genuine religious experience. They define religious in such a way that it must imply an empirically testable dramatic and positive self-transformation in orientation and behavior. Their study offers sound phenomenological analyses of empathic communion, ego loss, and body dissolution, which are experiences common to both psychedelic and mystical states. Also they present a survey of the religious imagery uncovered in their case studies, including symbols drawn from light, galaxies, architecture, and more recognizable literary sources. Fasting and other ascetical practices in the traditional mystic probably cause chemical reactions similar to LSD and other drugs—both are simply preliminaries to the actual religious vision. The type of reading and training beforehand will predetermine the style and imagery of a particular psychedelic experience, which the authors suspect is too often colored by expectations derived from Aldous Huxley, Alan Watts, and Eastern gurus.

CARL JUNG. Jung's theory of archetypes has affected almost all schools of modern literary criticism. *The Spirit in Man, Art, and Literature* collates his major essays on this topic, of which "The Relation of Analytical Psychology to Poetry" (1966, pp. 65–83) and "Psychology and Literature" (pp. 84–105) are the most coherent and accessible. A psychologist will speak more appropriately of the artistic creative process rather than the work of art itself, just as he must focus on "the emotions and symbols which constitute the phenomenology of religion, but which do not touch upon its essential nature." Jung is careful, in other words, to center on the anthropology in a theology, not on its metaphysics. As expected, just as Freud's metapsychology is denounced as a disguised theology, so Freud's aesthetic is parodied as an interest not in symbols themselves but in their reduction to infantile sexual fantasies. "A work of art is not a disease," says Jung in ridicule of Freud. Most important to Jung's theory is a distinction between an *introverted* or carefully intended finished work of art, and an *extraverted* visionary work that takes possession of an author, willfully completing itself, assuming its own form and effect from the depths of his creative unconscious. Illustrations of this second type are Nietzsche's *Zarathustra,* part 2 of Goethe's *Faust,* Dante, Wagner's operas, Blake, Boehme, with strange intuitive language, pregnant and evocative imagery. If we define a symbol as "the intimation of a meaning beyond the level of our present powers of comprehension," then these latter works that stimulate and challenge us deeply are more symbolic, suggesting a source "not in the personal unconscious of the poet, but in a sphere of unconscious mythology whose primordial images are the common heritage of mankind."

By archetypes Jung means these perennial mnemonic images or a priori patterns. Goethe at the end of *Faust* spoke not as an individual but for the race. He responded socially to the needs of his age, elucidating its spirit, creating forms to compensate for its particular bias and psychic malaise. An archetype instinctively and unconsciously reappears whenever certain characteristic human situations recur in an individual attuned to his society and its expectations. Such are the outlines of Jung's significant aesthetic theory, yet his applied literary and art criticism is a very different matter. Lacking Freud's carefully reasoned and minute analysis, it is incredibly digressive and garrulous, evasive and disjointed. At best it produces random insights, imaginative leads for deeper research. In "*Ulysses:* A Monologue", for example, Jung confesses his inability to read Joyce's book as an "extraverted" archetypal work. "I cannot find the key," he says, but attempts to explain its popularity as a reaction to the hideous sentimentality of prevailing taste. With nothingness at its core, *Ulysses* resembles the mind of a schizophrenic in its rambling solipsism and atomized sense impressions and uncontrolled neologisms (1966, pp. 109–34).

Jung's *Answer to Job* is not detached exegesis but the free-floating subjective reactions of a commenting chorus on this great tragedy. Jung will tell "what I feel when I read certain books of the Bible" and "I shall express my affect fearlessly and ruthlessly." He interprets *Job* fancifully as an unconscious revelation of God's dual nature, which was defeated morally in the argument with Job, so that afterward God becomes a humanized Father. The answer to Job is God's later incarnation, the humanization of God, who proved in his suffering on the cross that with the quarrel between Job and God "the encounter with the creature changes the creator" (1965, p. 108).

I suppose the most characteristic and in some ways the best practical criticism in Jung is in his evocative typological studies on folk literature. My favorites are "The Psychology of the Trickster-Figure" (1959, pp. 255–74) and "The Phenomenology of the Spirit in Fairy Tales" (1958, pp. 61–112) on mandala, wise old man, and mother archetypes. The early Christian classic *Shepherd of Hermas* yields a startling array of church, woman, and tower symbols (Philipson, 1963, pp. 75–87). In interpreting dreams as imaginative constructs, certainly few critics can surpass Jung in his tenacity, erudition, and daring intuitive commentary. The merits of Freud's *Interpretation of Dreams* are its minute empirical detail, its categories, and the shrewd reduction of so many dreams to their atomized origins in incidents and attitudes of everyday situations. Jung's essay on "The Transcendent Function" (1973, pp. 280–83) offers a superb illustration of the contrast between the Freudian analytic and Jungian constructive interpretation of an identical dream. Jung is less concerned with the historical antecedents and sexual sediment remaining from earlier experience, more with the dream's function, purpose, its symbolic role as a not yet consciously realized cry for help. "Individual Dream Symbolism in Relation to Alchemy" (pp. 323–455) is proof of a staggering persistence and inventiveness in pursuing this thesis. Jung interprets the collated 400 dreams and fantasies of a single patient, covering a period of nearly ten months. This style of commentary is a marriage of Northrup Frye and William Empson, moving from a symbolic hat in one dream, for example, to proverbs about the head, the meaning of crowns, hoods, and hats in various ceremonials, Athanasius Pernath's hat in the novel *Golem,* halos, sun-discs, and finally, of course, mandalas.

The heirs of Jung are the multitude of modern historians and phenomenologists of comparative religion, the anthropologists, and literary folklorists. They have often produced junkheaps of data and pretentious syntheses, and the strained cultural parallels have been insufficiently investigated. But at its strongest the search for religious patterns and archetypes is a profound discovery of the contemporary in the archaic and the archaic in the contemporary, as exacting a scrutiny of our own culture as of other peoples and eras. Myth, symbol, and archetype are such elastic categories that they invite the wide interdisciplinary collaboration of many scholars (cf. Murray, 1960; May, 1961; Slote, 1963; and Middleton, 1967). Joachim Wach's *Comparative Study of Religions* (1961) offers some of the most lucid methodological guides to this bulky material, suggesting various styles of symbolism, action, and fellowship in world religions (cf. Campbell, 1968; Geertz; Van der Leeuw, 1936a). James Frazer's *Golden Bough* (1964) still bears a widespread influence, mostly because of its effective narrative style and the coherent literary theme throughout. John Vickery describes the work as a romance, with suspense and irony, that begins in a quest into the meaning of the "King of the Wood" ritual and gradually evolves toward the central experience of crucifixion and resurrection (1963, pp. 174–79). Gaster's *Myth, Legend, and Custom in the Old Testament* (1969), subtitled "A Comparative Study with Chapters from Sir James G. Frazer's *'Folklore in the Old Testament,'*" rearranges and expands the original material so that by reading the Bible sequentially, one can easily consult Frazer's parallel myths. For example, the Tower of Babel story suggests many myths of language confusion, an obscure line in Job 15:29 about man's shadow perhaps takes on meaning when interpreted alongside folktales about the disappearance of one's shadow as a token of death. In other words, it may not be essential to discover the exact Canaanite myth reinterpreted historically by the Old Testament writer, for more generic folk paradigms might provide insights of equivalent value.

Specific aspects of religious experience in different cultures can be explored more deeply in a controlled comparison of the ways a single theme is treated in different religions, or in an intensified investigation into a single religion other than one's own. A stimulating anthology by R. C. Chalmers and John Irving, *The Meaning of Life in Five Great Religions* (1965), introduces scholars of Islam, Hinduism, Buddhism, Judaism, and Christianity to explain how their specific beliefs help man to face honestly and creatively the same inescapable realities of suffering and death. Titus Burkhardt's *Sacred Art in East and West* (1967) correlates particular artistic traditions with the spiritualities characteristic of five world religions. The design of a Hindu temple, for example, is regulated by an intricate symbolic cosmology. In Islamic art, rug patterns or tent furnishings or the stucco stalactites in arches are associated with Muslim iconoclasm and their belief in the world's fragile contingency. An example of more concentrated thematic study within another religion is "The Nuer Concept of Spirit in Its Relation to the Social Order" by E. E. Evans-Pritchard. These people experience God as *Kwoth* but in a very diffuse manner, refracting the divine presence into separate spirits that are then ranked in an elaborate hierarchy, parallel to the graded levels of social activity and custom in their society (1967, pp. 109–26). Similarly, Miguel León-Portilla's *Aztec Thought and Culture* questions the relationship between their dualistic language and religion. Their language uses twofold metaphors—e.g., "water and hill" is a town, "skirt and blouse" is a seductive woman. Perhaps the Nuhatto deity could only be experienced as polytheistic and dualistic within such a linguistic universe. One wonders if "the dual god was the cause—or effect—of this view of divinity, man, and the universe" (1963, p. 103).

MIRCEA ELIADE AND PAUL RICOEUR. Two outstanding names invoked repeatedly in any contemporary theology of religious symbols and archetypes are Mircea Eliade and Paul Ricoeur. Besides his essays on the history of religions, Mircea Eliade has published literary criticism, memoirs, a diary, novels, short stories, and a play, most of them still untranslated from the Roumanian. An illuminating perspective on his vision and method can be recovered from lengthy journal extracts by Eliade on his own corpus (Kitagawa and Long, 1969, pp. 343–406). Eliade recognizes that the central theme of all his mature work, especially the later novellas, is the hiddenness of miracle. The fantastic and sacral reality lie camouflaged beneath the banal, and thus the sacred cannot be distinguished from the profane. His fiction is dominated by an ironic interplay between the imaginative and prosaic, between everyday characters in familiar settings and fantastic plots. Eliade admits his fictional style lacks polish, appearing incomplete and written at ferocious speed, a montage of philosophical dialogues and meditations and overt narrative. In *Caete de Dor* #9 (written in December, 1955) he observes, "I am incapable of being at the same time in two spiritual universes: that of literature and that of science . . . As soon as 'I make literature,' I find again another universe; I call it oneiric, for it has another temporal structure, and above all because my relations with the characters are of an imaginary and not a critical nature." Later he tells how for ten years he "renounced writing novels (the only literary genre that was suitable to my talent). I have done it in order to inculcate a new comprehension of *homo religiosus.*" In *Caete de Dor* #7 (written in July, 1953) Eliade recounts the preoccupation in his alchemy and oriental metallurgic studies with "the *metaphysical values* present in these traditional techniques and not the eventual scientific discoveries." He was interested only in the spiritual world of myths and symbols at the center of all these scientific materials published by ethnologists, folklorists, and sociologists. Such a world "ought to be known and understood in order to be able to comprehend the situation of man in the Cosmos. For, as one knows, this situation constitutes already a metaphysic."

In reading Eliade's popular *Sacred and the Profane* (1959) or *Patterns in Comparative Religion* (1963), we are astonished at the extensive range and quantity of illustrative detail, an atmosphere of hasty and unfinished composition often blamed on the translator, but with an impressive literary acumen in selecting and presenting the numberless myths. The novelist is clearly present despite the flat impersonal language of these scientific studies, and his characteristic theme is the sacrality of ordinary life. Especially helpful are the vivid centering of archetypal materials around images of water, fire, sun, sky, stones, vegetation. In *The Quest: History and Meaning in Religion* (1969), Eliade's perceptive literary criticism can be sampled. He traces the rite de passage archetype through authors like Jules Verne, Cooper, Melville, Faulkner, and especially in Goethe's remarks on his earlier Sturm und Drang phase. The myths of human origins and destiny, paradise and utopia, are illustrated in Hawthorne, Thoreau, Whitman, the New World dreams of Europeans, and an archaic Brazilian group's search for El Dorado. *Shamanism* (1964) explores the symbolic techniques and mental universe of the shaman, whose trancelike activities include mimicry, dancing, singing to enact and evoke a group's religious beliefs. Eliade and others have conjectured about the origins of drama, poetry, and the other arts in this shamanistic ritual and myth-making. In all these books Eliade's hermeneutic can be summarized in his motto, "the scale creates the phenomenon." Or if you approach documents, artifacts, and myths as expressly religious phenomena, you will discover the actual religious universe concealed behind them (1969, pp. 5–7).

Paul Ricoeur's *Fallible Man* (1965) and *Symbolism of Evil* (1967), though quite dense and obscure in texture, grapple with themes and a hermeneutic of major significance. The first stage of the hermeneutic sketched in his latter book is that our age does not need demythologizing but a restoration of religious myth and symbol. Our language has become too barren, precise, and technical. We have forgotten the hierophanies and sacred symbols. "It is in this very age of discourse that we want to recharge our language, that we want to start again from the fullness of language" (1967, p. 349). The second step in Ricoeur's argument is that our intent is not to brush aside the narrative structure of a myth to reach the primordial religious experience behind that myth. We must recognize that "narrative form is neither secondary nor accidental, but primitive and essential" (p. 170). For the original experience is a *drama,* and the narrative framework is indispensable to conjure up the tensions and time scheme in that experience. "By its triple function of concrete universality, temporal orientation, and finally ontological exploration, the myth has a way of *revealing* things that is not reducible to any translation from a language in cipher to a clear language" (p. 163). I call attention here to Ricoeur's emphasis on the narrative and temporality factors in every religious myth, in opposition to Auerbach's restriction of these universal attributes to the specific Judaeo-Christian myths.

Ricoeur's third step is his assertion that the symbol gives rise to the thought. He asks for a philosophy instructed by myths, a creative interpretation of religious experience that is faithful "to the gift of meaning from the symbol" (p. 348). This involves a phenomenology of *re-feeling* the symbols, criticizing, and revivifying them. Then finally, starting from these symbols a philosophy must analyze the rationality of its foundations, develop existential concepts, "not only structures of reflection but structures of existence," and "make its presuppositions explicit, state them as beliefs, wager on the beliefs, and try to make the wager pay off in understanding" (p. 357).

Fallible Man is an exploration into the basis of man's fragility, symbolized in the Nietzschean image of a geological fault in human nature. Man's reality is distended tragically between possibility and facticity, essence and existence, so that his consequent precariousness and contingency offer the point of least resistance for the insertion of evil into the world. A weak link in the real, his fragility is a dizzy proclivity to fall, a capacity for evil. The myth of creation and innocence is a logical corollary to any myth of the fall, for the idealized primordial *elsewhere* and *formerly* manifest themselves in the fallen situation as the norm exposing it as now fallen. *Symbolism of Evil* treats the biblical myth of Original Sin as not a beginning but a refined speculative construct at the end of a cycle of living experience. Such an experience can be recovered only by meditating on more basic inarticulate confessions of human evil, the archetypal symbols of deviation, wandering, exile, captivity, and the myths of chaos, blinding, mixture, and fall. Ricoeur's fascinating mythological data is gathered principally from the Bible, Greek epic and orphic traditions, and ancient Semitic religions.

THEOLOGY OF PANENTHEIST EXPERIENCE

I have suggested that the transition from an ortho-cultural theology to a more explicit panentheism can be stated in three significant steps. First, there is a more vigorous rejection of the traditional supranaturalist paradigm, its heightened dualism of secular and sacred, body and soul, earth and heaven. In the same moment as this rejection, a theologian tends to take more seriously the contemporary experience of secularity, affirming the raw facticity of human experience, devoid of any relationship to a religious or metaphysical source of meaning that is other than itself.

Second, there now follows a new attitude that we might call prophetic and celebratory. Because a faulty paradigm of traditional transcendence has collapsed, the modern secular experience is viewed not as a retrogression but actually as a bracing maturation in religious consciousness. Barth in the first volume of *Church Dogmatics* (1969) impeaches a human religion approaching God only on its own terms, a religion turned in upon itself, an idolatrous block to hearing God's authentic word. In many ways the traditional supranaturalist models had enlisted such a distorted religious response. Bonhoeffer can speak with incredible optimism in *Letters and Papers from Prison* of a profound this-worldliness, "the beyond is not what is infinitely remote, but what is nearest at hand," "we should not run man down in his worldliness, but confront him with God at his strongest point," and his most misunderstood paradox, "In the presence of God and with God we live without God" (1967, pp. 188–99). The biblical iconoclasm of the Prophets can be interpreted, too, as a gradual desacralization of the earth, liberating its actuality from magic and pagan myth, so that it can be approached as more genuinely itself.

The third and final step in this logical succession of attitudes views such a prophetic acceptance of naked secularity as sheer prelude to the recovery and remythologization of authentic transcendence. God can now be relocated *in the midst of* the secular experience, as ground or depth of being—an earnest reaffirmation of the sacred not so much despite, as because of and inseparable from the worldly and human. I select the "Death of God" theologians of prophetic secularity to represent the second step outlined above. But theological reconstructions in the third step are panentheist, neoempirical developments of Tillich's ecstatic naturalism or Rahner's transcendental Heideggerianism already discussed. This final step is represented by the theologians of radical immanence in the Dewey-Whitehead tradition, and implicitly by a random group preoccupied with the original datum of human experience, whom I have labeled theologians of experience.

THEOLOGIANS OF PROPHETIC SECULARITY. John A. T. Robinson's *Exploration into God* presents a superior introduction to the issues and divisive stances in this entire discussion. The first party supports a religionless Christian secularity, represented by Bonhoeffer, R. G. Smith, Hamilton,

Van Buren, Harvey Cox. The second group views the entire universe as sacred—its exponents are Tillich, Berdyaev, Buber, Hartshorne, Cobb, Ogden, Jung, Alan Watts. The conflicting shibboleths are nothing-is-religious and the penultimate, versus everything-is-religious and the ultimate, a dichotomy which Robinson hopes to reconcile in a theology that locates God within what is most central to human life, that depersonifies the divine without depersonalizing it. His own definition of panentheism is based exactly on the *Oxford Dictionary of the Christian Church,* "the belief that the Being of God includes and penetrates the whole universe, so that every part of it exists in Him, but (as against pantheism) that His Being is more than, and is not exhausted by, the universe" (1967, pp. 74–96).

The Altizer-Hamilton "Death of God" and Robinson's own "Honest to God" controversies of the sixties seem in retrospect overblown and dated. Perhaps the most substantial treatment of the theology of radical secularity can be found in Langdon Gilkey's brilliant analysis of contingency, relativity, transience, and autonomy as four components of the secularity phenomenon (1969a, pp. 31–71). Also, the varieties of secularism and secularity are developed richly in Ronald G. Smith's *Secular Christianity* (1966, pp. 135–204).

Johannes Metz's *Theology of the World* (1969) attacks what he terms an inadequate incarnational optimism that believes the world immediately divinized by God's incarnation, whereas Metz reads Christianity as a setting free of the world, dispelling myth and magic. He does not identify the actual process of modern secularization with this normative Christian dedivinization, for the former is often falsified ideologically as a naive utopianism or a resigned skepticism. Metz locates hierophanies not in the world, which must be affirmed in its own reality, but in man's activity to humanize it. The world loses its numinosity, but instead there arises an "'*anthropocentric*' place in which the numinous is experienced: no longer the comprehensive openness of the pre-given world, but the freedom that acts on this world . . . ."

A more eccentric mythologized version of Metz's argument occurs in Thomas Altizer's *Gospel of Christian Atheism* (1966a) and *New Apocalypse: The Radical Christian Vision of William Blake* (1967b). For the world fully to come of age in Bonhoeffer's sense, the transcendent supranatural God must annihiliate Himself, ceasing "to exist in His original mode as transcendent or disincarnate Spirit, . . . gradually regressing to a formless state of an abstract and empty nothingness" (1966a, pp. 69–101). As Jesus Christ proceeds to His death, God in Him completes a movement from transcendence to immanence, and now by the Resurrection is present in the actual moment before us. In his second book Altizer does little close textual explication of the poetry, but attempts to reenact Blake's vision of the fall, redemption, and apocalypse, as the expression of "a prophetic seer, a visionary whose work records a new epiphany of the Spirit." Altizer ranks Blake alongside Nietzsche as a prophetic Christian atheist, especially in his identification of Jesus's satanic body of holiness with humanity and the total cosmos. William Hamilton's essay "Banished from the Land of Unity" (1966, pp. 53–86) identifies Ivan's effectively semblanced atheism in *Brothers Karamazov* with the actual disbelief and revolutionary nihilism in Dostoevsky's mind that escaped the sanctimonious czarist censors. The pale figures of Zossima, Alyosha, and the silent Christ in the Inquisitor Legend are clumsily semblanced rebuttals to Ivan's unanswerable disbelief. The Russian sacramental earth mysticism of Alyosha and Zossima, their sense of solidarity in guilt and forgiveness, the hope professed at Ilusha's final resurrection in the last pages of the novel—Hamilton finds all these unconvincing immanentist responses to the death of the nineteenth-century traditional transcendent God.

Two books by Gabriel Vahanian, *Wait without Idols* (1964) and *The Death of God* (1967), represent a more traditional Barthian critique against inauthentic styles of both immanence and transcendence. Modern "post-Christian" literature is eulogized for its prophetic iconoclasm against the insufficiencies that mark a decadent Christian tradition, including church theologians with their cultural ineptitude. With what is perhaps excessive latitude, Vahanian approaches all literature after Augustine in the West as Christian in the sense that it "presupposes a cultural context informed and shaped by Christianity," even when it contradicts or deviates from Christianity (1964, pp. v–xiv). His principal thesis is that the death of God might mean a death of those pagan idols that somehow survive in our Christian conception of God as a mere cultural accessory. Stripped of this subtle deification of ourselves and the world, perhaps we can actually reach God as the wholly Other. Vahanian tends to center his literary criticism on part of a single work, next establish the general cultural context, and then move rapidly to his limited repertoire of post-Barthian themes. There are creditable essays on Hawthorne, Melville, Dostoevsky, Auden, Faulkner, Greene, and Bernanos. For example, Kafka "succeeded in translating into immanentist terms the value of a transcendental universe now discredited." Or Vahanian argues for his own theology of "the charismatic compenetration or interdependence of faith and secularity," which retains the true secularity of the secular, rather than the later Eliot's "sacramentarian dualism of sacred and secular" (1964, p. 124).

THEOLOGIANS OF RADICAL IMMANENCE. The Panentheist theologians, more architectonic and metaphysical than the theologians of secularity, are therefore less accessible to the casual reader. In *American Philosophies of Religion* (1936, pp. 211–308) Henry Wieman and Bernard Meland label themselves empirical theists, alongside categories of evolutionary theists, religious humanists, and the cosmic theist Whitehead, all under a heading described as "Rooted in the Tradition of Naturalism" (J. Martin, 1970; D. D. Williams, 1961, pp. 443–96). The matrix of this theology is Peirce, James, Dewey, and the American tradition of radical empiricism, Bergson's theory of an intuitive unstructured flow of experience, and the more abstruse process philosophy of Alexander and Whitehead. When the movement crested three decades ago, the names associated with an explicit theology were Hartshorne, Hocking, Brightman, and a Chicago group including Wieman, Meland, E. S. Ames, Shailer Matthews, and G. B. Smith. Each theologian apparently understands experience and empirical method in his own way, but all converge in emphasizing the affective, volitional, valuational components in experience, and a carefully regulated method imitating the working procedures effective in the positive sciences, with a free imaginative construction of hypotheses. Bernard Meland summarizes this method as a "guiding vision of experience, tentatively embraced, and subject to subsequent verification and correction as further data of experience make themselves known . . ." (1969, p. 54). Stressing the experiential aspect of Tillich's correlational method, Langdon Gilkey asks an empirical theology to thematize the range of our ordinary experience where the basic hierophanies occur. Our religious symbols are meaningful for us "only when these symbols are united to the experiences in our actual contemporary life which they symbolize, when they are conceived and understood as answers to the questions the ordinary life we lead raises . . ." (1969b, p. 365).

The most pronounced apologist of panentheist theology has been Charles Hartshorne, whose position is summarized briefly in the essays on "Panentheism, Transcendental Relativity, and the Trinity" (1941, pp. 347–52), and "Abstract and Concrete Approaches to Deity and the Divine Historicity" (1941, pp. 126–37). All is in but not of God; God is distinct from all but embraces everything as an inclusive agent acting on its parts. Hartshorne explains to my own satisfaction how temporality as it is humanly experienced can be purified of deficiencies to become a transcendental analogue, and therefore as applicable to theos as are the classical attributes of immutability and eternity. In an anthology *Philosophers Speak of God* (1963) Hartshorne and William Reese have a section on panentheism, demonstrating its universal prevalence in quotations from Schelling, Fechner, Peirce, Whitehead,

Berdyaev, Schweitzer, Buber, Radhakrishnan, and the Muslim Iqbal.

Schubert Ogden in *The Reality of God* has credited Hartshorne and Whitehead for the basis of his own theology, especially Whitehead's reformed subjectivist principle. Ogden simply means that the paradigm of reality in classical theism was the perception of tables and chairs. From this experience it derived the categories of substance and essence, and then applied these concepts analogously to God. Ogden's new paradigm begins with the experiencing self as relational, social, in a temporal process, and from this experience derives categories of internal relations to others and of intrinsic temporality, which are attributed analogously to God. God must then be conceived as the supremely relative self, at the root of all human experience, genuinely temporal, social, self-creating, the absolute ground of all real relationships (1966, pp. 1–70).

John Cobb's *Christian Natural Theology* (1965) and *The Structure of Christian Existence* (1967b) develop a position similar to Ogden's, centering on the Holy Spirit as a "self-transcending Self," an entelechy immanent to men's evolving experience. The second book locates this experience of the Spirit in a progressively unfolding historical context, from a period tendentiously called primitive, to what Jaspers calls the "axial" transition from mythos to logos, to Buddhist-Homeric-Socratic, to Hebraic prophetic, to the finality of spiritual existence in Christianity. In *The Spirit and the Forms of Love* Daniel Day Williams presupposes that God's Spirit in history is the empirical correlate to the activity of man's loving, and thus Williams's metaphysical inquiry searches for the structures of being which make this phenomenon intelligible. His method is first a phenomenological analysis of love, revealing the components of individuality, freedom, and suffering. Second, he argues that whatever is present in human existence must somehow be present in Being itself. For example, "we discover that love presupposes beings who can both give and receive in relation to one another, and that therefore God must have ways of receiving and responding to what happens in the world. We discover that suffering in its ontological sense of 'being acted upon' is a requirement of all love, and thus a new way is opened to reflection on the suffering of God" (1968, p. 10). Finally, Williams applies his categories derived from this love experience to a remythologization of the incarnation, atonement, and other traditional Christian dogmas.

Gregory Baum's *Man Becoming* (1970) expands the thesis outlined in his "Divine Transcendence" essay (1971) describing God as the "more than human in human life. God's immanence refers to his presence in and through human life, and his transcendence qualifies that this presence is never one of identity." God is operative in the *becoming* of man and his world, yet "without ever being bounded by this process, without being caught up in it, or in any way necessitated by it" (p. 128). Christ is redefined essentially as the final person each of us hopes to become and the transcendental dynamism by which we grow toward that destiny. Baum's empirical basis for theological reflection is the experience of the unexpected, gratuitous, and marvelous, analyzed in categories of immanent grace and Holy Spirit. Unfortunately, a disproportionate segment of Baum's book is devoted to defending panentheism as a theological position consonant with the natural-supernatural duality in Catholic doctrinal tradition—he invokes Blondel's rejection of extrinsicism, for example, and other hackneyed precedents.

The theology of Pierre Teilhard de Chardin interweaves all these strands of process theology into a single visionary metaphysic—Cobb's evolving historical stages of experience, Ogden's and Hartshorne's God of relativity, Williams's and Baum's focus on the sacrality of empirical love, wonder, and the centrality of Christ. I have introduced the *panenchristism* of Teilhard and Rahner before in expounding my own theological position, but a few lines of poetry from *Hymn of the Universe* (1965b) can typify the major themes of his *Phenomenon of Man* (1961) and *Divine Milieu* (1965a). The first is from the "Hymn to Matter": ". . . hand of God, the flesh of Christ: it is you, matter, that I bless . . . I acclaim you as the divine *milieu,* charged with creative power, as the ocean stirred by the Spirit, as the clay moulded and infused with life by the incarnate Word" (1965b, pp. 68–71). The second is a prayer addressed to Christ: "I love you as the source, the activity and life-giving ambience, the term and consummation, of the world, even of the natural world, and its process of becoming. . . . I love You for the extensions of Your body and soul to the farthest corners of creation through grace, through life, and through matter" (p. 76).

The panentheism of Alan Watts is an important stage in his popular odyssey from Anglican theology, to meta-Catholic syncretism, and finally to his own version of an apophatic mysticism and Hindu pantheism. In *Behold the Spirit* (1947), Watts attempts to get behind the sacramental, ecclesial, historical forms of Christianity to reach an essential "Christian state of consciousness, a nonduality" consonant with Western mysticism, in which God and the universe are coterminous. Anxious to avoid both pantheistic monism and theistic dualism, he tries to conceptualize an experience of the Holy Spirit nearer to us than we to ourselves, worthy of Eckhart's insight, "When a man goes out of himself to find or fetch God, he is wrong." *The Supreme Identity* further decries the tendency to project religion as discontinuous with our own depths, and to conceive the beatific vision as gazing on God as an object. God must be transposed back into man's subjective life, as the source and ground of consciousness; holiness means plunging into that life, not retreating from it. "Man as finite, as a creature of reason, feeling and awe, revolves about the central Self, and is subordinate to that Self as to God" (1950, p. 184).

Myth and Ritual in Christianity is a revolutionary remythologization of Christianity, emphasizing its most anti-Protestant syncretistic High Church components. Here Watts establishes a heightened sacralized polarity as distant as conceivable from Barth and the theologians of radical secularity. His Christianity becomes scarcely any longer recognizable. Satan becomes a dialectical aspect of the divine; Mary is divinized; in Jesus, God becomes not *a* man but becomes mankind, individuality and time and historicity are illusion and *maya.* Watts's task is to reinterpret the Christian myth "along the general lines of the *phlosophia perennis,* in order to bring out the truly catholic or universal character of the symbols" (1968, p. 23). Ironically, this philosophia perennis is precisely what Bultmann and other demythologizers would have called the irrelevant human sacralized framework out of which they were attempting to transpose the Gospel. Here is a core of cosmic oneness, interiority, atemporality common to most world religions and the vocabulary of all mystics. The content of this philosophy Watts derives expressly from the writings of Jung and Ananda Coomaraswamy. Like Ricoeur, Watts pursues genuine religious experience back to originative situations behind the myths and symbols themselves.

THEOLOGIANS OF EXPERIENCE. The avowed interest of panentheist theologians in human experience and the empirical method attracts them necessarily to a theoretical and applied aesthetic, but generally their actual approach to works of art and literature has been abstract, cursory, and macrocosmic. Alfred North Whitehead devotes a few chapters to aesthetics in *Adventures of Ideas* (1961), but especially in an essay on "The Romantic Reaction" in *Science and the Modern World* (1926). His intellectual history style of criticism is based on the principle that "in each period, there is a general form of the forms of thought; and, like the air we breathe, such a form is so translucent, and so pervading, and so seemingly necessary, that only by extreme effort can [the critic] become aware of it" (1961, p. 14). He cites lines from the poetry of Milton, Pope, Wordsworth, and Tennyson to illustrate varying attitudes toward science and nature. Wordsworth more than other poets preserves the aesthetic attributes of nature, viewing the world as exhibiting "entwined prehensive unities." Then Whitehead builds a philosophy of nature consisting of six components—change, value, eternal objects, endurance, organism, interfusion—that he allegedly learned from Shelley, and especially from Wordsworth's *Excursion.* Kenneth Marshall's essay on "Wieman's Philosophy of Art" (1963, pp. 222–35), and Henry Wieman's own reply (pp. 236–43) present an aesthetic that approaches art as a propaedeutic to adoration and mature sensitivity. Wieman repudiates Tillich's canonization of *Guernica* as Protestant art. It is only an art of despair, unless it in turn leads "to art which points the way of redemption. But the latter is only religious" (p. 237). Bernard Meland, too, relates the aesthetic experience to man's capacity for religious awe. Not a strict scientific empiricism, his theological method is based on an appreciative awareness and wonder reaching behind the vulgarizing materialism of our epoch. In *Modern Man's Worship* Meland thinks religion is best understood when it is taken "with the arts to be an appreciative response to reality; when its concepts are viewed as aesthetic forms, not science; its words, poetry, not prose; its chief end appreciation and devotion, not inquiry, industry, or control" (1934, p. xiv). So often in these empiricist traditions, religion survives primarily as an emotive lyrical phenomenon, as in the positivism of I. A. Richards and Carnap.

The formal treatise and other genres of disciplined academic prose are surely resistant media to evoke and synthesize this basic data of human experience. A few of Marshall McLuhan's books prove relevant here, with their theory of visual, nonlinear explorations (McLuhan, 1969, and Rosenthal, 1968). Perhaps *experience* must eventually be broached through training in human sensitivity, psychosynthesis, expressive body language, and especially in the fragile Zen *centering* and *koan* exercises toward preconceptual awareness.

Theologians of experience like Sam Keen, Michael Novak, Rosemary Haughton and others try to evoke this preconceptual awareness through their experimental creative literary style. Thus, I think they are minor but legitimate heirs to the original aim and promise of the Dewey-Whitehead tradition. One fine example of this analysis of religious experience through both medium and content is the nonbook *To a Dancing God* by Sam Keen, a loose collage of personal anecdotes, brief informal essays, sketches for possible courses to teach, exercises to perform, some original poems, the paraphrase of a Kazantzakis novel or a Zen parable—and all without footnotes. The "I" in this book is not modern man or the voice of philosophy, hiding behind a front of invulnerable authority or anonymity, but Keen himself, sharing everyday experiences. He calls for a visceral theology, searching for the

Incarnation in our own body-spirit, not back in history—for a theology of what moves and touches us in the present, the proximate rather than ultimate, quotidian and human rather than the ecclesiastical, the sacred rather than God. The task of this theology is "the continual exploration of the changing ways in which the graceful and the inviolable appear in human experience. . . . When theology abandons the claim to revelation and ceases to speak with institutional authority it becomes a species of philosophy; and when philosophy uncovers principles or structures which are the preconditions of human wholeness it discovers the sacred" (1970, p. 157).

An example of Keen's method is a narration of his actual return home upon his father's death, and a later psychoanalytic return "home" to his past. This theme of exile and homecoming then becomes a metaphor for sin and grace, living a fully human at home existence in the vibrant present. His *Apology for Wonder* is a more systematized development of these themes, again a manifesto for a new and deepened empiricism, an "immediacy, a new immersion in the primal simplicities of the world which are given in sense and feeling" (1969, p. 210). He offers a superb description of what I have called the functional religious dynamic and functional theology. Explicit God-talk is less important than an implicit sense of religious wonder. "Whether the language that gives us our primary orientation to what we consider the ultimate context of human existence is political, mythological, poetic, philosophical, or theological is not so important as the manner in which the language functions. Any contextual language must be judged by its ability to nurture those attitudes which are essential to authentic life: openness, availability, epistemological humility in the face of the mystery of being, and the ability to admire and be grateful" (p. 212).

In the spirit of Keen's nonbook above, David Miller's *Gods and Games* (1969) is a whimsical relaxed essay on game motifs in mathematics, psychology, the theology of Heidegger, Huizinga, Hugo Rahner, and literature such as Hesse's *Magister Ludi* and Genet's *Balcony*. Michael Novak's *Ascent of the Mountain, Flight of the Dove: An Invitation to Religious Studies* (1971) is another nonlinear book, with abrupt perspectival shifts, written from successive standpoints in a quest up the religious mountain, in which readers are invited to share. "I have tried to write in my own voice," says Novak, and there follows a sloppy collection of fragments that at times almost seem to ape or parody Keen, with moments of insight, but in a disappointedly uneven and casual manner that seems willed and self-consciously tricky. *The Experience of Nothingness* (1970) is Novak's more convincing apology for myth, fantasy, and an appreciation for the preconscious level of religious experience. One successful passage in the *Ascent* book, an essay on "Religion as Autobiography" (1971, pp. 44–49), receives more thorough development and illustration in *Experience.* In any one of his actions a person implicitly declares his cosmology, politics, identity, and religious faith. "The story a man is acting out determines his actions more than the verbally stated rule he is following. . . . To study what a given pragmatist takes to be effective, real, and relevant is to discover the story he is acting out, the identity he imagines himself to possess, the contours of the world as he pictures it" (1970, p. 23). Even the apparently nonmythical, nonideological, realistic thinker is acting out his own myth.

In *The Transformation of Man* Rosemary Haughton chooses "not to begin with general ideas and illustrate them by examples, but to begin with particular examples of human behavior and to try to discover in them the elements of the human situation as we are aware of it, now, in our particular culture" (1967, p. 12). She creates imaginative stories of a quarrel between children, a sexual love affair, a family trying to establish communication, and in each she invents intricate psychological details of the motivation behind conflicts and decisions. Then Haughton theorizes on her stories in a vocabulary of descriptive ethics and existentialist psychology, gradually introducing biblical and traditional theological concepts such as law or reconciliation, and working their definitions out of the previous story details, or now developing her thesis by new fictive variations on the original material. Her theory is that an *experienced* conflict, resolution, and human transformation, for example, are the best analogues for transcendent realities.

The Theology of Experience argues that people must hear and trust their own experience as an authentic source of religious insight. Haughton's illustrations are very creative. An event is experienced that seems to contradict your previously unchallenged religious concept of God's will and plan, and you gradually open yourself to an expanded notion. In their postexilic theology, for example, the Jews learned from the human experiences during their captivity that Yahweh's kingdom had room for foreigners. In the parables and sayings of Jesus, He often appeals to what you would humanly expect a father or judge to do or how a sensible man would behave whose animal is in distress on the Sabbath. Haughton takes the ordinary experience of community, family, service, sexuality, and unravels some religious implications in the various interpretations possible. "A person may not even know the meaning of the word theology, but there is scarecly a conscious act which does not express a theological position of some kind, and even unconscious motivations often grow from the theological views of our forefathers" (1972, pp. 31–32). In her essay on "The Intuitive Experience of Sexuality" (pp. 121–54) Haughton selects many poetic passages describing the experience of sexual love, with imagery and attitudes parallel to the language of prophets and mystics on the reality of conversion, prayer, and mystical experience. There is the same paradoxical longing for fusion with the other person, yet also a maturing self-discovery and passionate autonomy.

15

CONCLUSION: A THEOLOGY OF THE RELIGIOUS-LITERARY EXPERIENCE

JUNG ONCE observed that slavish adherence to a favorite thesis is often evidence of repressed doubt. Once genuinely convinced of its value, we should be ready to view the theory as an unthreatened personal viewpoint, inviting every reasonable audit and challenge.

In the preceding chapters, I have sorted an extensive gathering of critics and religious thinkers into four categories to emphasize insightful similarities in method, premises, and values. There is the autotelist style of disciplined textual formalism, logical positivism, and biblical fundamentalism (chapters 5 and 11). Second, a more inclusive humanist semiotic focus on rhetoric, phenomenology, and hermeneutics (6 and 12). Then the ortho-cultural perspective ranges broadly over the human situation in its history, politics, and eschatology (7 and 13). Finally, the psycho-mythic style searches into the chthonic depths of our full human myth, the personal and collective psyche (8 and 14).

My thesis in literary criticism has been the following: each genuine incremental attempt to transcend the literary text itself leads to a deeper penetration into its functional religious dynamic. A corresponding thesis in religious thought might be the following: every genuine incremental attempt to transcend the literalness and humanness of the religious symbol opens man up more profoundly to the sacred as distinct but inseparable from the human depths.

These categories and theses, and especially the many random assessments throughout this book, can be best adopted as tentative scaffolding, a serviceable catalyst toward deeper personal insight and synthesis. Such theories never deserve uncritical allegiance or simplistic rigidity of application. I have insisted repeatedly on the debatability of including or classifying specific literary or religious figures. Even though the fourfold categories themselves suggest a hierarchical progression toward wider comprehensiveness, I have demonstrated how individual achievement often transcends the limits of conscious self-definition, and that failures especially within the psycho-mythic mode of criticism and theology are as grandiose as potential success.

My fourfold classification should prove a useful heuristic guide to bridge intimidating distances between fields of knowledge. I have presented an epistemology of theologizing and criticizing: the integral human consciousness, experiencing poetically-religiously, can function in four modes of increasing inclusiveness. We observe the human mind doing some remarkably similar things when it thematizes aspects of this integral experience in an act of literary criticism or religious thought.

It is symptomatic that the last figures studied in the previous chapter should be creative myth makers, and also advocates of nonbooks and of preverbal religious experience. For they direct attention back to the primary religious-literary experience itself, at the heart of all the many styles of participatory criticism and theology discussed in this book. This original hyphenated experience can prompt a rich, dynamic, comprehensive transaction between literary critics and theologians, or it can isolate them sharply into the most constricted autonomous specialties. How professional and fruitful are studies in literature and religion? As this book has patently demonstrated, it depends on *which* criticism and *which* theology are correlated. It depends on each person's own gift of aesthetic perceptiveness, spiritual consciousness, and his implied or conscious choice of perspectives.

A shrewd remark of Simon Lesser was previously cited, noting that critics do not use or misuse psychology, they proficiently avail themselves of the empirical knowledge accumulated by psychologists for half a century, or else they rely on their own implicit commonsense psychology. Similarly, critics are either theologians decisively committed to exploit the almost limitless resources outlined in the last five chapters, or they are implicit commonsense theologians—with individual experiences and definite unquestioned assumptions, a few stock biblical images and phrases, and fragments from childhood memories, religious pop journalism, and desultory reading in the human sciences. We have noticed the almost ubiquitous authority of Matthew Arnold among the best literary critics, his encouragement of responsible theologizing and of a venturesome search for the religious dynamic. Also humanist semiotic critics and many explicit religious critics have fixated on the deficient statement by I. A. Richards of the poetry and belief problem, the biased polemic by Hulme and Eliot against the romantics, and Eliot's delimiting emphasis on Original Sin and the idealized Christian dogmas invoked to buttress his vision of a medieval utopia. Yet such limited inbred theological horizons need a bracing exposure to more immediate ethical and ideological issues, a wider religious perspective on symbol, myth, sacrament, human language, and history. They need a more intelligent clarification and articulation of their own religious suppositions. They should turn to Ricoeur and Berdyaev on the profound experience of human evil instead of carting out a few stale aphorisms from Eliot and Auden on Original Sin. They must learn a more informed use of Sartre and Freud than merely as sources for cursory labels like bad faith and the death instinct. They should search into Jaspers, Urs Von Balthasar, and other theologians of correlation instead of their recurrent unimaginative recourse to the authority of Arnold, whose adequate but essentially lightweight philosophical talents scarcely merit such unreflective obeisance.

There is no critic who could not profit, then, from a sustained challenging interchange with theologians. And I am convinced the transaction would prove mutually productive. The many resourceful theological sytles we have examined focus either on the Judaeo-Christian Bible and other sacred literatures, or on the more widespread theos revelation in human experience and all cultural symbols, including literature and the arts. The critical quest, hermeneutic, and literary assessment proper to biblical exegetes are basically identical with those of Daiches and Howe as they read Faulkner and Dostoevsky. Ricoeur's recovery of the primary symbolic religious experience is equivalent to the psycho-mythic translation by Holland and Northrop Frye. The articulation of fundamental horizons by Merleau-Ponty, Lonergan, Ott, and Jaspers *is* the literary critic's resourceful search for the metaphysic of a work or corpus. The theologian's customary global metaphysical perspective needs exposure to the literary critic's detailed textual scrutiny, his creative perceptiveness and technique.

Perhaps the professional vice of both theologians and literary critics is precisely the inability to listen, to open themselves fully to each new religious-aesthetic experience encountered. They have trained themselves so long to generate answers that they scarcly recognize the actual questions being asked. When I as critic approach a Faulkner novel, for example, I am struck by the cry of loss and despair resounding through its pages. After careful textual analysis, my first impulse is to trim this material so that it can fit into easy familiar categories. One critic is programmed to respond with sin and redemption, another reaction-formation and mandala archetypes, and another ironic texture and semblanced feeling. Yet an authentic work of art essentially does not so much need my judgment as first stand in judgment over me. It demands an opening and reversal of consciousness. The text challenges me with this sharp question: How does my religious faith now look in the light of this heightened realization of what it is like to be dead or alive, or dead in the midst of life? Once I have listened to, appropriated, and experienced this question as a genuine religious and aesthetic human being, only then can I venture to name it and try to assess it (cf. Jenkins, 1965). Only then, too, can I also criticize, reshape, and remythologize my categories and personal theology, to account for the human realities given artistic expression in Faulkner and other literature. The authentic religious-literary critic must aspire to this stance of questioning openness—unflinchingly self-critical, ready to experience reality *in-depth,* undismayed at the risk of fallible value judgments.

BIBLIOGRAPHY

AARON, DANIEL

1961. *Writers on the Left: Episodes in American Literary Communism.* New York.

ABRAMS, MEYER H.

1958a. (editor) *Literature and Belief.* New York.

1958b. *The Mirror and the Lamp: Romantic Theory and the Critical Tradition.* New York.

1971. *Natural Supernaturalism: Tradition and Revolution in Romantic Literature.* New York.

ADERETH, MAXWELL

1968. *Commitment in Modern French Literature: Politics and Society in Peguy, Aragon, and Sartre.* New York.

AIKEN, HENRY

1967. "The Aesthetic Relevance of Belief" in *Aesthetic Inquiry: Essays on Art Criticism and the Philosophy of Art,* edited by Monroe Beardsley and Herbert Schueller. Encino, Calif.

ALLEN, DON CAMERON

1964. *Doubt's Boundless Sea: Skepticism and Faith in the Renaissance.* Baltimore.

ALLPORT, GORDON

1950. *The Individual and His Religion: A Psychological Interpretation.* New York.

1954. *The Nature of Prejudice.* Reading, Md.

ALTIZER, THOMAS

1966a. *The Gospel of Christian Atheism.* Philadelphia.

1966b. (and William Hamilton) *Radical Theology and the Death of God.* New York.

1967a. (editor) *Toward a New Christianity: Readings in the Death of God Theology.* New York.

1967b. *The New Apocalypse: The Radical Christian Vision of William Blake.* East Lansing, Mich.

AUDEN, W. H.
1950. *The Enchaféd Flood: The Romantic Iconography of the Sea.* New York.
1956. *Making, Knowing, and Judging.* London.
1962. *Dyer's Hand and Other Essays.* New York.

AUERBACH, ERICH
1957. *Mimesis: The Representation of Reality in Western Literature,* translated by W. R. Trask. Princeton, N. J.
1961. *Dante: Poet of the Secular World,* translated by Ralph Manheim. Chicago.
1965. *Literary Language and Its Public in Late Latin Antiquity and in the Middle Ages,* translated by Ralph Manheim. New York.

AYER, ALFRED J.
1952. *Language, Truth, and Logic.* 2nd ed. New York.
1959. (editor) *Logical Positivism.* New York.

BACHELARD, GASTON
1964a. *The Poetics of Space,* translated by Maria Jolas. Boston.
1964b. *The Psychoanalysis of Fire,* translated by Alan Ross. Boston.

BAHLKE, GEORGE
1970. *The Later Auden.* New Brunswick, N. J.

BAILLIE, JOHN
1950. *The Belief in Progress.* New York.

BALTHASAR, HANS URS VON
1958. *Science, Religion, and Christianity,* translated by Hilda Graef. Paramus, N. J.
1961–69. *Herrlichkeit: Eine Theologische Ästhetik,* 4 vols. Einsiedeln.
1964a. *Word and Redemption,* translated by A. V. Littledale and Alexander Dru. New York.
1964b. *Word and Revelation,* translated by A. V. Littledale and Alexander Dru. New York.
1967. *A Theological Anthropology.* New York.

BARCIA, JOSÉ
1967. (and M. A. Zeitlin, editors) *Unamuno: Creator and Creation.* Berkeley, Calif.

BARR, JAMES
1961. *The Semantics of Biblical Language.* New York.

BARRETT, WILLIAM
1952. "Existentialism as a Symptom of Man's Contemporary Crisis" in *Spiritual Problems in Contemporary Literature,* edited by Stanley Hopper. New York.
1956. (editor) *Zen Buddhism: Selected Writings of D. T. Suzuki.* New York.

BARTH, KARL
1963. *Evangelical Theology: An Introduction,* translated by Grover Foley. New York.
1966. *How I Changed My Mind,* edited by John Godsey. Richmond, Va.

1968. *Epistle to the Romans,* translated by Edwyn Hoskyns. 6th ed. New York.
1969. *Church Dogmatics,* translated by G. T. Thomson. 13 vols. Naperville, Ill.

BATSON, BEATRICE
1968. *A Reader's Guide to Religious Literature.* Chicago.

BATTENHOUSE, ROY
1969. *Shakespearean Tragedy, Its Art and Its Christian Premises.* Bloomington, Ind.

BAUER, GEORGE
1969. *Sartre and the Artist.* Chicago.

BAUM, GREGORY, O.S.A.
1970. *Man Becoming: God in Secular Language.* New York.
1971. "Divine Transcendence" in *The God Experience: Essays in Hope,* edited by Joseph Whelan, S. J. Paramus, N. J.

BEARDSLEE, WILLIAM
1970. *Literary Criticism of the New Testament.* Philadelphia.

BELLAH, ROBERT
1970. *Beyond Belief: Essays on Religion in a Post-Traditional World.* New York.
1971. "Confessions of a Former Establishment Fundamentalist," *Theology Today* 28 (July).

BENTLEY, ERIC
1948. (editor) *The Importance of Scrutiny: Selections from Scrutiny, A Quarterly Review, 1932–1948.* East Aurora, Ill.

BENZIGER, JAMES
1964. *Images of Eternity: Studies in the Poetry of Religious Vision from Wordsworth to T. S. Eliot.* Carbondale, Ill.

BERDYAEV, NICHOLAS
1937. *The Destiny of Man,* translated by Natalie Duddington. New York.
1955. *The Meaning of the Creative Act,* translated by Donald Lowrie. New York.
1965. *Christian Existentialism: A Berdyaev Anthology,* translated and edited by Donald Lowrie. London.
1969. *Dostoevsky,* translated by Donald Attwater. New York.

BERGER, PETER
1961a. *The Noise of Solemn Assemblies: Christian Commitment and the Religious Establishment in America.* New York.
1961b. *The Precarious Vision: A Sociologist Looks at Social Fictions and Christian Faith.* New York.
1967. (and Thomas Luckmann) *The Social Construction of Reality: A Treatise in the Sociology of Knowledge.* New York.
1969. *A Rumor of Angels: Modern Society and the Rediscovery of the Supernatural.* New York.

BLOCH, ERNST

1970a. *Man on His Own: Essays in the Philosophy of Religion,* translated by E. B. Ashton. New York.

1970b. *A Philosophy of the Future,* translated by John Cumming. New York.

BLOCK, HASKELL

1966. "Cultural Anthropology and Contemporary Literary Criticism" in *Myth and Literature: Contemporary Theory and Practice,* edited by John Vickery. Lincoln, Neb.

BLOTNER, JOSEPH

1966. "Mythic Patterns in *To the Lighthouse*" in *Myth and Literature: Contemporary Theory and Practice,* edited by John Vickery. Lincoln, Neb.

BODKIN, MAUD

1934. *Archetypal Patterns in Poetry: Psychological Studies of Imagination.* London.

1951. *Studies of Type: Images in Poetry, Religion, and Philosophy.* London.

BONHOEFFER, DIETRICH

1967. *Letters and Papers from Prison,* translated by Reginald Fuller. 2nd ed. New York.

BOOTH, WAYNE

1961. The Rhetoric of Fiction. Chicago.

BORGMANN, ALBERT

1968. "The Transformation of Heidegger's Thought" in *Philosophy Today #1,* edited by Jerry Gill. New York.

BRADBURY, JOHN

1965. *The Fugitives.* New Haven, Conn.

BRÉE, GERMAINE

1972. *Camus and Sartre: Crisis and Commitment.* New York.

BROOKS, CLEANTH

1947. *The Well Wrought Urn: Studies in the Structure of Poetry.* New York.

1955. (editor) *Tragic Themes in Western Literature.* New Haven, Conn.

1959. (and Robert Penn Warren, editors) *Understanding Fiction.* New York.

1960. (and Robert Penn Warren, editors) *Understanding Poetry.* 3rd ed. New York.

1962a. "Christianity, Myth, and the Symbolism of Poetry" in *Christian Faith and the Contemporary Arts,* edited by Finley Eversole. New York.

1962b. "Literary Criticism: Poet, Poem, and Reader" in *Varieties of Literary Experience,* edited by Stanley Burnshaw. New York.

1963a. *The Hidden God: Studies in Hemingway, Faulkner, Yeats, Eliot, and Warren.* New Haven, Conn.

1963b. *William Faulkner: The Yoknapatawpha Country.* New Haven, Conn.

BROWN, NORMAN

1959, *Life against Death: The Psychoanalytical Meaning of History.* Middletown, Conn.

1966. *Love's Body.* New York.

BRUNNER, HEINRICH EMIL

1946. *Natural Theology: Comprising "Nature and Grace" by Professor Dr. Emil Brunner and the Reply "No" by Dr. Karl Barth,* translated by Peter Fraenkel. London.

BUBER, MARTIN

1955. *Legend of the Baal-Shem,* translated by Maurice Friedman. London.

1958. "Arts and the Man" in *To Hallow This Life: An Anthology,* edited by Jacob Trapp. New York.

1967. "Replies to My Critics," in *The Philosophy of Martin Buber,* edited by Paul Schilp and Maurice Friedman. LaSalle, Ill.

1968. *On the Bible: Eighteen Studies,* edited and translated by Nahum Glatzer. New York.

BUCKLEY, VINCENT

1959. *Poetry and Morality: Studies on the Criticism of Matthew Arnold, T. S. Eliot, and F. R. Leavis.* New York.

1968. *Poetry and the Sacred.* London.

BUKHARIN, NIKOLAI

1953. "Poetry and Society" in *The Problems of Aesthetics: A Book of Readings,* edited by Eliseo Vivas and Murray Krieger. New York.

BULTMANN, RUDOLPH

1951 and 1955. *Theology of the New Testament,* translated by K. Grobel. 2 vols. New York.

1957a. *History and Eschatology: The Presence of Eternity.* New York.

1957b. "Introduction" in *What Is Christianity?* by Adolf Harnack, translated by Thomas Saunders. New York.

1958. *Jesus and the Word,* translated by L. Smith and E. Lantero. New York.

1961. (et al.) *Kerygma and Myth: A Theological Debate,* edited and translated by Hans Bartsch and Reginald Fuller. New York.

BURCKHARDT, TITUS

1967. *Sacred Art in East and West: Its Principles and Methods,* translated by Lord Northbourne. London.

BURKE, KENNETH

1945. *A Grammar of Motives.* Gloucester, Md.

1950. *A Rhetoric of Motives.* Gloucester, Md.

1953. *Counter-Statement.* 3rd ed. Los Altos, Calif.

1954. "Fact, Inference, and Proof in the Analysis of Literary Symbolism" in *Symbols and Values: An Initial Study,* edited by Lyman Bryson et al. New York.

1957. *The Philosophy of Literary Form.* New York.

1961. *The Rhetoric of Religion: Studies in Logology.* Boston.

1964a. *Perspectives by Incongruity: Studies in Symbolic Action* and
1964b. *Terms for Order: Studies in Evaluation,* edited by Stanley Hyman and Barbara Karmiller. 2 vols. in 1. Bloomington, Ind.

1967. "A Theory of Terminology" in *Interpretation: The Poetry of Meaning,* edited by Stanley Hopper and David Miller. New York.

BUSH, DOUGLAS

1966. *Engaged and Disengaged.* Cambridge, Mass.

CAMPBELL, JOSEPH
1968. *The Masks of God.* 4 vols. New York.

CAMUS, ALBERT
1956. *The Rebel: An Essay on Man in Revolt,* translated by Anthony Bower. New York.
1963. *Notebooks, 1935–1942,* translated by Philip Thody. New York.
1968. *Lyrical and Critical Essays,* edited and translated by Philip Thody and Ellen Kennedy. New York.

CARNAP, RUDOLF
1959. "The Elimination of Metaphysics through Logical Analysis of Language" in *Logical Positivism,* edited by Alfred J. Ayer. New York.

CARY, NORMAN
1968. "Christian Criticism in the Twentieth-Century: A Survey of Theological Approaches to Literature." Ph.D. dissertation, Wayne State Univ. Detroit.

CASSIRER, ERNST
1955. *The Philosophy of Symbolic Forms,* translated by Ralph Manheim. 3 vols. New Haven, Conn.

CHALMERS, R. C.
1965. (and John Irving, editors) *The Meaning of Life in Five Great Religions.* Philadelphia.

CHRISTIAN, WILLIAM
1972. *Oppositions of Religious Doctrines: A Study in the Logic of Dialogue among Religions.* New York.

COBB, JOHN, JR.
1965. *A Christian Natural Theology: Based on the Thought of Alfred North Whitehead.* Philadelphia.
1967a. "From Crisis Theology to the Post-Modern World" in *Toward a New Christianity: Readings in the Death of God Theology,* edited by Thomas Altizer. New York.
1967b. *The Structure of Christian Existence.* Philadelphia.

COLIE, ROSALIE
1967. "Literature and History" in *Relations of Literary Study: Essays on Interdisciplinary Contributions,* edited by James Thorpe. New York.

COLLINGWOOD, R. G.
1960. *The Principles of Art.* New York.
1968. *Faith and Reason: Essays in the Philosophy of Religion,* edited by Lionel Rubinoff. Chicago.

CORBETT, PATRICK
1965. *Ideologies.* New York.

CORNFORD, F. M.
1957. *From Religion to Philosophy: A Study in the Origins of Western Speculation.* New York.

COX, HARVEY

1965. *The Secular City: Secularization and Urbanization in Theological Perspective.* New York.

1967. *On Not Leaving It to the Snake.* New York.

1969. *The Feast of Fools: A Theological Essay on Festivity and Fantasy.* Cambridge, Mass.

CRANE, R. S.

1952. (editor) *Critics and Criticism: Ancient and Modern.* Chicago.

1953. *The Languages of Criticism and the Structure of Poetry.* Toronto.

CREWS, FREDERICK

1967. "Literature and Psychology" in *Relations of Literary Study: Essays on Interdisciplinary Contributions,* edited by James Thorpe. New York.

1969. "A. A. Milne's Honey-Balloon-Pit-Gun-Tail-Bathtubcomplex" in *The Overwrought Urn,* edited by Charles Kaplan. Indianapolis.

1970. (editor) *Psychoanalysis and Literary Process.* Cambridge, Mass.

CROCE, BENEDETTO

1965. *Guide to Aesthetics,* translated by Patrick Romanell. New York.

CRYSTAL, DAVID

1965. *Linguistics, Language, and Religion.* New York.

DAICHES, DAVID

1938. *Literature and Society.* London.

1951. *Willa Cather: A Critical Introduction.* New York.

1952. "Theodicy, Poetry, and Tradition" in *Spiritual Problems in Contemporary Literature: A Series of Addresses and Discussions,* edited by Stanley Hopper. New York.

1956. *Critical Approaches to Literature.* Englewood Cliffs, N. J.

1957. *Milton.* London.

1963. *Virginia Woolf.* 2nd ed. Philadelphia.

1964. *A Study of Literature for Readers and Critics.* New York.

1967. *Literary Essays.* Chicago.

DAVIES, HORTON

1959. *A Mirror of the Ministry in Modern Novels.* New York.

DAY, DOUGLAS

1966. "The Background of the New Criticism," *Journal of Aesthetics and Art Criticism* 24:3 (Spring).

DEFFNER, DONALD

1965. "Theology and Modern Literature," *Concordia Theological Monthly* 36 (November).

DEMETZ, PETER

1967. *Marx, Engels, and the Poets: Origins of Marxist Literary Criticism,* translated by Jeffery Sammons. Chicago.

DENDLE, BRIAN

1968. *The Spanish Novel of Religious Thesis, 1876–1937.* Princeton, N. J.

DETWEILER, ROBERT
1964. *Four Spiritual Crises in Mid-Century American Fiction.* Gainesville, Fla.

DEWART, LESLIE
1966. *The Future of Belief.* New York.

DEWEY, JOHN
1934. *A Common Faith.* New Haven, Conn.

DILLEY, FRANK
1964. *Metaphysics and Religious Language.* New York.

DILLISTONE, FREDERICK
1960. *The Novelist and the Passion Story.* New York.

DIXON, JOHN, JR.
1963. "Is Tragedy Essential to Knowing? A Critique of Dr. Tillich's Aesthetic," *Journal of Religion* 43 (October).

DOUGLAS, WALLACE
1966. "The Meanings of 'Myth' in Modern Criticism" in *Myth and Literature: Contemporary Theory and Practice,* edited by John Vickery. Lincoln, Neb.

DRIVER, TOM
1960a. "Religion and Literature," *Union Seminary Quarterly Review* 15 (January).
1960b. *The Sense of History in Greek and Shakespearean Drama.* New York.
1968. "The Latent Image: Literary Sources of Theological Understanding," *Union Seminary Quarterly Review* 23 (Winter).

DUNHAM, JAMES
1947. *The Religion of Philosophers.* Philadelphia.

DURANT, WILL
1970. (and Ariel Durant) *Interpretations of Life: A Survey of Contemporary Literature.* New York.

EBELING, GERHARD
1964. "Word of God and Hermeneutic" in *The New Hermeneutic,* edited by James Robinson and John Cobb, Jr. New York.

EDEL, LEON
1964. (editor) *Literary History and Literary Criticism.* New York.
1966. "Hawthorne's Symbolism and Psychoanalysis" in *Hidden Patterns: Studies in Psychoanalytic Literary Criticism,* edited by Leonard and Eleanor Manheim. New York.
1967. "Literature and Biography" in *Relations of Literary Study: Essays in Interdisciplinary Contributions,* edited by James Thorpe. New York.

ELIADE, MIRCEA
1959. *The Sacred and the Profane,* translated by Willard Trask. New York.
1963. *Patterns in Comparative Religion,* translated by Rosemary Sheed. New York.

1964. *Shamanism: Archaic Techniques of Ecstasy*, translated by Willard Trask. New York.

1969. *The Quest: History and Meaning in Religion*. Chicago.

ELIOT, T. S.

1932. *Selected Essays, 1917–1932*. New York.

1933. *The Use of Poetry and the Use of Criticism*. London.

1936. *Essays Ancient and Modern*. New York.

1949. *Christianity and Culture*. New York.

1956. "The Frontiers of Criticism," *Sewanee Review* 64:4 (Autumn).

1965. *To Criticize the Critic and Other Writings*. London.

ELLMANN, RICHARD

1965. (and Charles Feidelson, editors) *The Modern Tradition: Backgrounds of Modern Literature*. New York.

EMPSON, WILLIAM

1947. *Seven Types of Ambiguity*. New York.

1950. *Some Versions of Pastoral*. Philadelphia.

1968. "How to Read a Modern Poem" in *Modern Poetry: Essays in Criticism*, edited by John Hollander. New York.

ENGLAND, MARTHA

1966. (and John Sparrow) *Hymns Unbidden: Donne, Herbert, Blake, Emily Dickinson, and the Hymnographers*. New York.

ERLICH, VICTOR

1955. *Russian Formalism: History and Doctrine*. New York.

EVANS-PRITCHARD, E. E.

1967. "The Nuer Concept of Spirit in Its Relation to the Social Order" in *Myth and Cosmos: Readings in Mythology and Symbolism*, edited by John Middleton. New York.

FAIRCHILD, HOXIE

1939–1968. *Religious Trends in English Poetry*. 6 vols. New York.

FARLEY, EDWARD

1960. *The Transcendence of God: A Study in Contemporary Philosophical Theology*. Philadelphia.

FEAVER, J. CLAYTON

1967. (and William Horosz, editors) *Religion in Philosophical and Cultural Perspective: A New Approach to the Philosophy of Religion through Cross-Disciplinary Studies*. New York.

FERGUSSON, FRANCIS

1953. *The Idea of a Theater: A Study of Ten Plays*. New York.

FERRÉ, FREDERICK

1961. *Language, Logic, and God*. New York.

1968. "Science and the Death of 'God'" in *Science and Religion: New Perspectives in the Dialogue*, edited by Ian Barbour. New York.

FEUERBACH, LUDWIG

1957. *The Essence of Christianity*, translated by George Eliot. New York.

FIEDLER, LESLIE

1960. *No! In Thunder: Essays on Myth and Literature.* Boston.

1967. *Love and Death in the American Novel.* 2nd ed. New York.

FITCH, ROBERT

1957. "Christian Criticism of Literature" and a reply by Tom Driver, *Christianity and Crisis* 17 (April 29 and July 8).

FLEW, ANTONY

1955. (et al.) "Theology and Falsification" in *New Essays in Philosophical Theology,* edited by Antony Flew and Alasdair MacIntyre. New York.

FOSTER, M. B.

1957. " 'We' in Modern Philosophy" in *Faith and Logic: Oxford Essays in Philosophical Theology,* edited by Basil Mitchell. London.

FOSTER, RICHARD

1962. *The New Romantics: A Reappraisal of the New Criticism.* Bloomington, Ind.

FOWLIE, WALLACE

1968. *The French Critic: 1549–1967.* Carbondale, Ill.

FRAIBERG, LOUIS

1960. *Psychoanalysis and American Literary Criticism.* Detroit.

FRAMPTON, MARALEE

1968. "Religion and the Modern Novel" in *The Shapeless God: Essays on Modern Fiction,* edited by Harry Mooney, Jr., and Thomas Staley. Pittsburgh.

FRAZER, SIR JAMES

1964. *The New Golden Bough,* revised by Theodor Gaster. New York.

FREUD, SIGMUND

1953. *The Future of an Illusion,* translated by W. D. Robson-Scott. New York.

1957. "The Claims of Psychoanalysis to Scientific Interest" in *Works (Standard Edition),* edited by James Strachey et al. Vol. 13. London.

1962. *Civilization and Its Discontents,* translated by James Strachey. New York.

1969. *The Interpretation of Dreams,* translated by James Strachey. New York.

1970. "The Theme of the Three Caskets," translated by C. Hubback, in *Freud, Character and Culture,* edited by Philip Rieff. New York.

FRIEDMAN, MAURICE

1963. *Problematic Rebel: An Image of Modern Man.* New York.

FRIEDMAN, MELVIN

1970. (and John Vickery, editors) *The Shaken Realist: Essays in Modern Literature in Honor of Frederick J. Hoffman.* Baton Rouge, La.

FRIEDMAN, RUDOLPH

1960. "*Struwelpeter,* a Psychoanalytical Interpretation" in *Parodies: An Anthology from Chaucer to Beerbohm,* edited by Dwight MacDonald. New York.

FROMM, ERICH
1967. *Psychoanalysis and Religion*. New York.

FRYE, NORTHROP
1962. *Fearful Symmetry: A Study of William Blake*. Boston.
1963a. *Fables of Identity: Studies in Poetic Mythology*. New York.
1963b. (editor) *Romanticism Reconsidered*. New York.
1963c. *The Well-Tempered Critic*. Bloomington, Ind.
1966. *Anatomy of Criticism: Four Essays*. Princeton, N. J.
1973. "The Search for Acceptable Words," *Daedalus* (Spring).

FRYE, ROLAND MUSHAT
1961. *Perspective on Man: Literature and the Christian Tradition*. Philadelphia.

FULLER, EDMUND
1958. *Man in Modern Fiction: Some Minority Opinions on Contemporary American Writing*. New York.

FUNK, ROBERT
1966. *Language, Hermeneutic, and Word of God: The Problem of Language in the New Testament and Contemporary Theology*. New York.
1967. (editor) *History and Hermeneutic*. New York.

GADAMER, H. G.
1960. *Wahrheit und Methode: Grundzüge einer philosophischen Hermeneutic*. Tubingen.

GALLUP, DONALD
1969. *T. S. Eliot: A Bibliography*. 2nd ed. New York.

GARAUDY, ROGER
1966. *From Anathema to Dialogue: A Marxist Challenge to the Christian Churches,* translated by Luke O'Neill. New York.

GARDNER, HELEN
1959. *The Business of Criticism*. New York.

GASTER, THEODOR
1969. *Myth, Legend, and Custom in the Old Testament: A Comparative Study with Chapters from Sir James G. Frazer's "Folklore in the Old Testament."* New York.

GEERTZ, CLIFFORD
1966. "Religion as a Cultural System" in *Anthropological Approaches to the Study of Religion,* edited by Michael Bantan. London.

GERVING, HOWARD
1969. *A Checklist of the Herbert Read Archive*. Victoria.

GILKEY, LANGDON
1969a. *Naming the Whirlwind: The Renewal of God-Language*. New York.
1969b. "New Modes of Empirical Theology" in *The Future of Empirical Theology,* edited by Bernard Meland. Chicago.
1972. "The Dimensions of Dupré," *Commonweal* 64 (October 20).

GLICKSBERG, CHARLES

1960. *Literature and Religion: A Study in Conflict.* Dallas.

1963. *The Tragic Vision in Twentieth-Century Literature.* Carbondale, Ill.

GOGARTEN, FRIEDRICH

1970. *Despair and Hope for Our Time,* translated by Thomas Wieser. Philadelphia.

GOODMAN, NELSON

1968. *Languages of Art: An Approach to a Theory of Symbols.* New York.

GOODMAN, PAUL

1947. *Kafka's Prayer.* New York.

1954. *The Structure of Literature.* Chicago.

GRAY, STANLEY

1964. "The Social Meaning of the New Novel in France" in *Literature and Society,* edited by Bernice Slote. Lincoln, Neb.

GREBSTEIN, SHELDON

1968. (editor) *Perspectives in Contemporary Criticism.* New York.

GRIFFIN, ERNEST

1968. "Bibliography of Literature and Religion," unpublished monograph. Univ. of Alberta.

GRIFFIN, WILLIAM

1966. "The Use and Abuse of Psychoanalysis in the Study of Literature" in *Hidden Patterns,* edited by L. F. and E. B. Manheim. New York.

GUARDINI, ROMANO

1937. *The Spirit of the Liturgy,* translated by Ada Lane. London.

1952. "The Legend of the Grand Inquisitor," *Cross Currents* 3 (Fall).

1955. *Sacred Signs,* translated by G. Branham and W. Cladek. St. Louis.

1956. "Dostoevsky's Idiot, A Symbol of Christ," *Cross Currents* 6 (Fall).

1961. *Rilke's Duino Elegies: An Interpretation,* translated by K. G. Knight. Chicago.

GUHA, NARESH

1968. *W. B. Yeats: An Indian Approach.* Jadavpur.

GUNN, GILES

1971. (editor) *Literature and Religion.* New York.

GUNTER, BRADLEY

1970. *The Merrill Checklist of T. S. Eliot.* Chicago.

HAMILTON, WILLIAM

1966. "Banished from the Land of Unity" in *Radical Theology and the Death of God* by Thomas Altizer and William Hamilton. New York.

HAMMER, LOUIS

1967. "The Relevance of Buber's Thought to Aesthetics" in *The Philosophy of Martin Buber,* edited by Paul Schilp and Maurice Friedman. LaSalle, Ill.

HARKNESS, BRUCE

1969. "The Secret of 'The Secret Sharer' Bared" in *The Overwrought Urn,* edited by Charles Kaplan. Indianapolis.

HARRIS, NIGEL

1968. *Beliefs in Society: The Problem of Ideology.* London.

HART, RAY

1968. *Unfinished Man and the Imagination: Toward an Ontology and a Rhetoric of Revelation.* New York.

HARTMAN, GEOFFREY

1954. *The Unmediated Vision: An Interpretation of Wordsworth, Hopkins, Rilke, and Valéry.* New Haven, Conn.

1964. *Wordsworth's Poetry, 1787–1814.* New Haven, Conn.

1970. *Beyond Formalism: Literary Essays, 1958–1970.* New Haven, Conn.

HARTSHORNE, CHARLES

1941. *Man's Vision of God and the Logic of Theism.* New York.

1963. (and William Reese, editors) *Philosophers Speak of God.* Chicago.

1967a. *A Natural Theology for Our Time.* LaSalle, Ill.

1967b. "Religion in Process Philosophy" in *Religion in Philosophical and Cultural Perspective,* edited by J. Clayton Feaver and William Horosz. New York.

HARTT, JULIAN

1963. *The Lost Image of Man.* Baton Rouge, La.

1967. *A Christian Critique of American Culture: An Essay in Practical Theology.* New York.

HARVEY, VAN

1966. *The Historian and the Believer: The Morality of Historical Knowledge and Christian Belief.* New York.

HAUGHTON, ROSEMARY

1967. *The Transformation of Man: A Study of Conversion and Community.* London.

1972. *The Theology of Experience.* Paramus, N. J.

HEIDEGGER, MARTIN

1949. *Existence and Being,* edited with introduction by Werner Brock. Chicago.

1962. *Being and Time,* translated by John Macquarrie and Edward Robinson. New York.

1971. *Poetry, Language, Thought,* translated by Albert Hofstadter. New York.

HELLER, ERICH

1957. *The Disinherited Mind: Essays in Modern German Thought and Literature.* New York.

1965. *The Artist's Journey into the Interior, and Other Essays.* New York.

HENRY, CARL

1966. *Frontiers in Modern Theology.* Chicago.

HEPBURN, RONALD

1957. "Poetry and Religious Belief" in *Metaphysical Beliefs: Three Essays* by Stephen Toulmin et al. London.

1966. *Christianity and Paradox: Critical Studies in Twentieth-Century Theology*. Indianapolis.

HESCHEL, ABRAHAM

1955. "Symbolism and Jewish Faith" in *Religious Symbolism*, edited by Frederick Johnson. New York.

HIRSCH, E. D., JR.

1967. *Validity in Interpretation*. New Haven, Conn.

HOFFMAN, FREDERICK

1957. *Freudianism and the Literary Mind*. 2nd ed. Baton Rouge, La.

1964. *The Mortal NO: Death and the Modern Imagination*. Princeton, N. J.

1967. *The Imagination's New Beginning: Theology and Modern Literature*. Notre Dame, Ind.

HOLBROOK, CLYDE

1963. *Religion: A Humanistic Field*. Englewood Cliffs, N. J.

HOLLAND, NORMAN

1959. *The First Modern Comedies: The Significance of Etherege, Wycherley, and Congreve*. Bloomington, Ind.

1964. *The Shakespearean Imagination*. New York.

1966. *Psychoanalysis and Shakespeare*. New York.

1968a. *The Dynamics of Literary Response*. New York.

1968b. "Psychological Depths and 'Dover Beach'" in *Perspectives in Contemporary Criticism*, edited by Sheldon Grebstein. New York.

HOOK, SIDNEY

1961. *Quest for Being: And Other Studies in Naturalism and Humanism*. Westport, Conn.

HOPPER, STANLEY

1952. (editor) *Spiritual Problems in Contemporary Literature: A Series of Addresses and Discussions*. New York.

1967. (and David Miller, editors) *Interpretation: The Poetry of Meaning*. New York.

HOSPERS, JOHN

1968. "Implied Truths in Literature" in *Contemporary Studies in Aesthetics*, edited by Francis Coleman. New York.

HOWE, IRVING

1952. *William Faulkner: A Critical Study*. New York.

1957. *Politics and the Novel*. New York.

1963. *A World More Attractive: A View of Modern Literature and Politics: Essays 1950–1963*. New York.

1967. *Thomas Hardy*. New York.

1970. *Decline of the New*. New York.

HUGHES, PHILIP

1966. (editor) *Creative Minds in Contemporary Theology*. Grand Rapids, Mich.

HULME, T. E.
1936. *Speculations: Essays on Humanism and the Philosophy of Art,* edited by Herbert Read. New York.

HYMAN, STANLEY
1948. *The Armed Vision: A Study in the Methods of Modern Literary Criticism.* New York.

INGARDEN, ROMAN
1967. "Aesthetic Experience and the Aesthetic Object" in *Readings in Existential Phenomenology,* edited by Nathaniel Lawrence and Daniel O'Connor. Englewood Cliffs, N. J.

ISENBERG, ARNOLD
1968. "The Problem of Belief" in *Contemporary Studies in Aesthetics,* edited by Francis Coleman. New York.

JAEGER, WERNER
1960. *The Theology of the Early Greek Philosophers.* New York.

JARRETT-KERR, MARTIN, C. R.
1954. *Studies in Literature and Belief.* New York.
1964. *The Secular Promise: Christian Presence amid Contemporary Humanism.* London.
1970. *William Faulkner.* Grand Rapids, Mich.

JASPERS, KARL
1952. *Tragedy Is Not Enough,* translated by Harold Reiche et al. Boston.
1959. *Truth and Symbol,* translated by Jean Wilde et al. New York.
1969. *Philosophy,* translated by E. B. Ashton. Chicago.

JENKINS, DAVID
1965. "Note: Literature and the Theologian" in *Theology and the University,* edited by John Coulson. London.

JUNG, CARL G.
1958. *Psyche and Symbol: A Selection from the Writings of C. G. Jung,* edited by Violet de Laszlo. New York.
1959. *The Archetypes and the Collective Unconscious,* translated by R. F. C. Hull. New York.
1965. *Answer to Job,* translated by R. F. C. Hull. London.
1966. *The Spirit in Man, Art, and Literature,* translated by R. F. C. Hull. New York.
1973. *The Portable Jung,* edited by Joseph Campbell, translated by R. F. C. Hull. New York.

KAELIN, EUGENE
1962. *An Existentialist Aesthetic: The Theories of Sartre and Merleau-Ponty.* Madison, Wisc.

KALLICH, MARTIN
1970. *The Other End of the Egg: Religious Satire in Gulliver's Travels.* Bridgeport, Mich.

KARANIKAS, ALEXANDER
1966. *Tillers of a Myth: Southern Agrarians as Social and Literary Critics.* Madison, Wisc.

KEEN, SAM
1969. *Apology for Wonder*. New York.
1970. *To a Dancing God*. New York.

KENNICK, W. E.
1964. (editor) *Art and Philosophy: Readings in Aesthetics*. New York.

KILLINGER, JOHN
1963. *The Failure of Theology in Modern Literature*. New York.

KIRK, G. S.
1970. *Myth: Its Meaning and Functions in Ancient and Other Cultures*. Berkeley, Calif.

KITAGAWA, JOSEPH
1969. (and Charles Long, editors) *Myths and Symbols: Studies in Honor of Mircea Eliade*. Chicago.

KNOX, GEORGE
1957. *Kenneth Burke's Categories and Critiques*. Seattle, Wash.

KRIEGER, MURRAY
1956. *The New Apologists for Poetry*. Minneapolis.
1960. *The Tragic Vision: Variations on a Theme in Literary Interpretation*. New York.
1966. (editor) *Northrop Frye in Modern Criticism*. New York.

KRIS, ERNST
1965. *Psychoanalytic Explorations in Art*. New York.

KROEBER, A. L.
1952. (and Clyde Kluckhohn) *Culture: A Critical Review of Concepts and Definitions*. New York.

KUHN, THOMAS
1970. *The Structure of Scientific Revolutions*. 2nd ed. Chicago.

KUSHNER, EVA
1963. "The Critical Method of Gaston Bachelard" in *Myth and Symbol: Critical Approaches and Applications*, edited by Bernice Slote. Lincoln, Neb.

LANGER, SUSANNE
1953. *Feeling and Form*. New York.
1957. *Philosophy in a New Key: A Study in the Symbolism of Reason, Rite, and Art*. Cambridge, Mass.
1958. (editor) *Reflections on Art: A Source Book of Writings by Artists, Critics, and Philosophers*. Baltimore.
1967. *An Introduction to Symbolic Logic*. 3rd ed. New York.

LAWRENCE, D. H.
1922. *Fantasia of the Unconscious*. London.

LAWRENCE, NATHANIEL
1967. (and Daniel O'Connor, editors) *Readings in Existential Phenomenology*. Englewood Cliffs, N.J.

LEACH, EDMUND

1967. "Genesis as Myth" in *Myth and Cosmos: Readings in Mythology and Symbolism*, edited by John Middleton. New York.

LEAVIS, F. R.

1953a. *The Common Tradition*. New York.

1953b. "The Responsible Critic: Or the Function of Criticism at Any Time," *Scrutiny* 19 (Spring).

LEMON, LEE

1965. (and Marion Reis, editors and translators) *Russian Formalist Criticism: Four Essays*. Lincoln, Neb.

LEÓN-PORTILLA, MIGUEL

1963. *Aztec Thought and Culture: A Study of the Ancient Nahuatlo Mind*, translated by Jack Davis. Norman, Okla.

LE SAGE, LAURENT

1967. *The French New Criticism: An Introduction and a Sampler*. University Park, Penn.

LESSER, SIMON

1957. *Fiction and the Unconscious*. Boston.

LESSING, ARTHUR

1968. "Marxist Existentialism" in *Philosophy Today #1*, edited by Jerry Gill. New York.

LEVIN, HARRY

1952. *The Overreacher: A Study of Christopher Marlowe*. Cambridge, Mass.

1957. *Contexts of Criticism*. Cambridge, Mass.

1960. *James Joyce: A Critical Introduction*. 2nd ed. New York.

1963. *The Gates of Horn: A Study of Five French Realists*. New York.

1966. *Refractions: Essays in Comparative Literature*. New York.

LEVI-STRAUSS, CLAUDE

1963. *Structural Anthropology*, translated by Claire Jacobson and B. G. Scholpf. New York.

1966. *The Savage Mind*. Chicago.

LEWIS, C. S.

1936. *The Allegory of Love: A Study in Medieval Tradition*. New York.

1942. *A Preface to Paradise Lost*. New York.

1961. *An Experiment in Criticism*. New York.

1967. *Of Other Worlds: Essays and Stories*, edited by Walter Hooper. New York.

1969a. *A Mind Awake: An Anthology of C. S. Lewis*, edited by Clyde Kilby. New York.

1969b. *Selected Literary Essays*, edited by Walter Hooper. New York.

1970. *God in the Dock: Essays on Theology and Ethics*, edited by Walter Hooper. Grand Rapids, Mich.

LEWIS, R. W. B.

1955. *The American Adam: Innocence, Tragedy, and Tradition in the Nineteenth Century*. Chicago.

1959. *The Picaresque Saint: Representative Figures in Contemporary Fiction.* Philadelphia.
1965. *Trials of the Word: Essays in American Literature and the Humanistic Tradition.* New Haven, Conn.
1967. *The Poetry of Hart Crane: A Critical Study.* Princeton, N. J.

LOMMEL, ANDREAS
1967. *Shamanism: The Beginnings of Art,* translated by Michael Bullock. New York.

LONERGAN, BERNARD, S. J.
1972. *Method in Theology.* New York.

LOVEJOY, ARTHUR
1960. *Essays in the History of Ideas.* Santa Barbara, Calif.
1961. *The Great Chain of Being: A Study of the History of an Idea.* Cambridge, Mass.

LOWENTHAL, LEO
1957. *Literature and the Image of Man: Sociological Studies of the European Drama and Novel, 1600–1900.* Boston.
1967. "Literature and Society" in *Relations of Literary Study: Essays on Interdisciplinary Contributions,* edited by James Thorpe. New York.

LUBAC, HENRI DE, S. J.
1967. *The Mystery of the Supernatural,* translated by Rosemary Sheed. New York.

LUKÁCS, GEORG
1962. *Realism in Our Time: Literature and the Class Struggle,* translated by John and Necke Mander. New York.
1964. *Studies in European Realism,* translated by Edith Bone. New York.

LYNCH, WILLIAM, S. J.
1960. *Christ and Apollo: The Dimensions of the Literary Imagination.* New York.
1970. *Christ and Prometheus: A New Image of the Secular.* Notre Dame, Ind.

MACDONALD, DWIGHT
1957. *Memoirs of a Revolutionist: Essays in Political Criticism.* New York.
1962. *Against the American Grain.* New York.
1969. *Dwight MacDonald on Movies.* Englewood Cliffs, N. J.

MCKEAN, KEITH
1961. *The Moral Measure of Literature.* Chicago.

MCKINNON, EDWARD
1971. *Truth and Expression.* Paramus, N. J.

MCLEAN, MILTON
1967. (editor) *Religious Studies in Public Universities.* Carbondale, Ill.

MCLUHAN, MARSHALL
1969. *The Interior Landscape: The Literary Criticism of Marshall McLuhan, 1934–1962,* edited by Eugene McNamara. New York.

MACQUARRIE, JOHN
1966. *Principles of Christian Theology*. New York.
1967. *God-Talk: An Examination of the Language and Logic of Theology*. New York.

MALRAUX, ANDRÉ
1953. *The Voices of Silence,* translated by Stuart Gilbert. New York.
1960. *The Metamorphosis of the Gods,* translated by Stuart Gilbert. New York.

MANDER, JOHN
1961. *The Writer and Commitment*. London.

MANHEIM, LEONARD
1966. (and Eleanor Manheim, editors) *Hidden Patterns: Studies in Psychoanalytic Criticism*. New York.

MANUEL, FRANK
1965. *Shapes of Philosophical History*. Stanford, Calif.

MARCEL, GABRIEL
1951. *Homo Viator: Introduction to a Metaphysic of Hope,* translated by Emma Craufurd. Chicago.
1967. *Searchings*. Paramus, N.J.

MARCUSE, HERBERT
1955. *Eros and Civilization: A Philosophical Inquiry into Freud*. Boston.

MARÍAS, JULIÁN
1967. "Philosophic Truth and the Metaphoric System" in *Interpretation: The Poetry of Meaning,* edited by Stanley Hopper and David Miller. New York.

MARITAIN, JACQUES
1943. *Art and Scholasticism with Other Essays,* translated by J. F. Scanlan. 2nd ed. New York.
1953. *Creative Intuition in Art and Poetry*. New York.
1960. *The Responsibility of the Artist*. New York.

MARSHALL, KENNETH
1963. "Wieman's Philosophy of Art" in *The Empirical Theology of Henry Nelson Wieman,* edited by Robert Bretall. New York.

MARTIN, JAMES, JR.
1966. *The New Dialogue between Philosophy and Theology*. New York.
1970. *Empirical Philosophies of Religion*. Freeport, N.Y.

MARTY, MARTIN
1964–1973. (and Dean Peerman, editors) *New Theology*. 10 vols. New York.
1966. *Varieties of Unbelief*. New York.

MARTZ, LOUIS
1954. *The Poetry of Meditation: A Study in English Religious Literature of the Seventeenth Century*. New Haven, Conn.
1969. *The Poem of the Mind: Essays on Poetry, English and American*. New York.

MARX, KARL
1947. (and Frederick Engels) *Literature and Art: Selections from Their Writings.* New York.

MASLOW, ABRAHAM
1964. *Religions, Values, and Peak Experiences.* Columbus, Ohio.

MASTERS, R. E. L.
1966. (and Jean Houston) *The Varieties of Psychedelic Experience.* New York.

MATTHIESSEN, F. O.
1941. *American Renaissance: Art and Expression in the Age of Emerson and Whitman.* New York.

MAY, ROLLO
1961. (editor) *Symbolism in Religion and Literature.* New York.

MEHTA, VED
1965. *The New Theologian.* New York.

MELAND, BERNARD
1934. *Modern Man's Worship.* New York.
1969. (editor) *The Future of Empirical Theology.* Chicago.

MERLEAU-PONTY, MAURICE
1964a. *Sense and Non-Sense,* translated by Hubert and Patricia Dreyfus. Evanston, Ill.
1964b. *Signs,* translated by Richard McCleary. Evanston, Ill.

METZ, JOHANNES
1969. *Theology of the World,* translated by William Glen-Doepel. New York.

MICHAELSEN, ROBERT
1965. *The Study of Religion in American Universities: Ten Case Studies with Special Reference to State Universities.* New Haven, Conn.

MIDDLETON, JOHN
1967. (editor) *Myth and Cosmos: Readings in Mythology and Symbolism.* New York.

MILLER, DAVID
1969. *Gods and Games: Toward a Theology of Play.* New York.

MILLER, J. HILLIS
1957. "Franz Kafka and the Metaphysics of Alienation" in *The Tragic Vision and the Christian Faith,* edited by Nathan Scott, Jr. New York.
1963. *The Disappearance of God: Five Nineteenth-Century Writers.* Cambridge, Mass.
1965. *Poets of Reality: Six Twentieth-Century Writers.* New York.
1967. "Literature and Religion" in *Relations of Literary Study: Essays on Interdisciplinary Contributions,* edited by James Thorpe. New York.
1970. *Thomas Hardy: Distance and Desire.* Cambridge, Mass.

MILLER, PERRY
1956. *Errand into the Wilderness.* New York
1967. *Nature's Nation.* Cambridge, Mass.

MITCHELL, BASIL
1957. (editor) *Faith and Logic: Oxford Essays in Philosophical Theology.* London.
1969. "The Justification of Religious Belief" in *New Essays on Religious Language,* edited by Dallas High. New York.

MOELLER, CHARLES
1962. *Littérature du XXe siècle et christianisme.* 4 vols., 9th ed. Paris.
1970. *Man and Salvation in Literature,* translated by Charles Quinn. Notre Dame, Ind.

MÖLTMANN, JURGEN
1967. *Theology of Hope: On the Ground and the Implications of a Christian Eschatology,* translated by James Leich. London.
1969. *Religion, Revolution, and the Future,* translated by Douglas Meeks, New York.

MORAN, GABRIEL, F.S.C.
1966. *Theology of Revelation.* New York.

MOREAU, JULES
1961. *Language and Religious Language: A Study in the Dynamics of Translation.* Philadelphia.

MORRISON, CLAUDIA
1968. *Freud and the Critic: The Early Use of Depth Psychology in Literary Criticism.* Chapel Hill, N.C.

MOSELEY, EDWIN
1962. *Pseudonyms of Christ in the Modern Novel: Motifs and Methods.* Pittsburgh.

MUELLER, WILLIAM
1959. *The Prophetic Voice in Modern Fiction.* New York.

MUIR, EDWIN
1965. *Essays on Literature and Society.* 2nd ed. Cambridge, Mass.

MURRAY, HENRY
1960. (editor) *Myth and Mythmaking.* New York.

MUSURILLO, HERBERT, S.J.
1962. *Symbolism and the Christian Imagination.* Baltimore.

NATANSON, MAURICE
1962. *Literature, Philosophy, and the Social Sciences: Essays in Existentialism and Phenomenology.* The Hague.

NICOLSON, MARJORIE
1962. *Science and Imagination.* Ithaca, N.Y.
1963. *Mountain Gloom and Mountain Glory: The Development of the Aesthetics of the Infinite.* New York.

NIEBUHR, H. RICHARD
1956. *Christ and Culture.* New York.

NIEBUHR, REINHOLD
1944. *The Children of Light and Children of Darkness: A Vindication of Democracy and a Critique of Its Traditional Defense.* New York.

NOON, WILLIAM, S.J.
1957. *Joyce and Aquinas.* New Haven, Conn.

NORTON, ALOYSIUS
1961. (and Joan Nourse, editors) *A Christian Approach to Western Literature: An Anthology.* Paramus, N.J.

NOTT, KATHLEEN
1953. *The Emperor's Clothes.* New York.

NOVACK, GEORGE
1966. *Existentialism versus Marxism: Conflicting Views on Humanism.* New York.

NOVAK, MICHAEL
1969. "Philosophy and Fiction" in *Philosophy Today #2,* edited by Jerry Gill. New York.
1970. *The Experience of Nothingness.* New York.
1971. *Ascent of the Mountain, Flight of the Dove: An Invitation to Religious Studies.* New York.

NYGREN, ANDERS
1948. "The Role of the Self-Evident in History," *Journal of Religion* 28 (October).

OGDEN, SCHUBERT
1966. *The Reality of God and Other Essays.* New York.

OLSHEWSKY, THOMAS
1969. (editor) *Problems in the Philosophy of Language.* New York.

ONG, WALTER, S.J.
1962. *The Barbarian Within and Other Fugitive Essays and Studies.* New York.
1967a. *In the Human Grain, Further Explorations of Contemporary Culture.* New York.
1967b. *The Presence of the Word: Some Prolegomena for Cultural and Religious History.* New Haven, Conn.

ORTEGA Y GASSET, JOSE
1968. *The Dehumanization of Art: and Other Essays on Art, Culture, and Literature,* translated by Helene Weyl et al. Princeton, N.J.

OTT, HEINRICH
1967. "Language and Understanding" in *New Theology #4,* edited by Martin Marty and Dean Peerman. New York.

OXENHANDLER, NEAL
1960. "Ontological Criticism in America and France," *Modern Language Review* 55.

PAGE, ROBERT

1965. *New Directions in Anglican Theology: A Survey from Temple to Robinson.* New York.

PALMER, RICHARD

1969. *Hermeneutic: Interpretative Theory in Schleiermacher, Dilthey, Heidegger, and Gadamer.* Evanston, Ill.

PANICHAS, GEORGE

1967. (editor) *Mansions of the Spirit: Essays in Literature and Religion.* New York.

PANNENBERG, WOLFHART

1967. "Hermeneutics and Universal History" in *History and Hermeneutic,* edited by Robert Funk. New York.

PANOFSKY, ERWIN

1939. *Studes in Iconology: Humanistic Themes in the Art of the Renaissance.* New York.

1948. *Albrecht Dürer.* 2 vols. Princeton, N.J.

1955. *Meaning in the Visual Arts: Papers in and on Art History.* New York.

PEGIS, ANTON

1955. *Christian Philosophy and Intellectual Freedom.* St. Paul, Minn.

PEPPER, STEPHEN

1949. *The Basis of Criticism in the Arts.* Cambridge, Mass.

1965. *Aesthetic Quality: A Contextualistic Theory of Beauty.* Westport, Conn.

1966. *World Hypotheses: A Study in Evidence.* Berkeley, Calif.

PETERSSON, ROBERT

1970. *The Art of Ecstasy: Teresa, Bernini, and Crashaw.* New York.

PHILIPSON, MORRIS

1963. *Outline of Jungian Aesthetics.* Evanston, Ill.

PHILLIPS, WILLIAM

1957. (editor) *Art and Psychoanalysis.* New York.

POULET, GEORGES

1956. *Studies in Human Time,* translated by Elliott Coleman. Baltimore.

1959. *The Interior Distance,* translated by Elliott Coleman. Baltimore.

PRAZ, MARIO

1958. *The Flaming Heart: Essays on Crashaw, Machiavelli, and Other Studies in the Relations between Italian and English Literature from Chaucer to T. S. Eliot.* New York.

PRICE, KINGSLEY

1968. "Is There Artistic Truth?" in *Contemporary Studies in Aesthetics,* edited by Francis Coleman. New York.

QUINE, WILLARD

1969. "Two Dogmas of Empiricism" in *Problems in the Philosophy of Language,* edited by Thomas Olshewsky. New York.

RABIL, ALBERT, JR.
1967. *Merleau-Ponty: Existentialist of the Social World.* New York.

RADER, MELVIN
1962. (editor) *A Modern Book of Esthetics: An Anthology.* 3rd ed. New York.

RAHNER, KARL, S.J.
1963. "Christianity and Non-Christian Religions" in *The Church: Readings in Theology,* translated and edited by Canisianum students. New York.
1966. *Theological Investigations.* Vol. 4, translated by Kevin Smyth. Baltimore.
1967. *Theological Investigations.* Vol. 3, translated by Karl-H. and Boniface Kruger. Baltimore.
1968. "Demythologization and the Sermon" in *The Renewal of Preaching, Theory and Practice,* edited by Karl Rahner, S.J. Paramus, N.J.
1969. *Theological Investigations.* Vol. 6, translated by Karl-H. and Boniface Kruger. Baltimore.

RAHV, PHILIP
1949. *Image and Idea: Fourteen Essays on Literary Themes.* New York.
1965. *The Myth and the Powerhouse.* New York.
1969. *Literature and the Sixth Sense.* Boston.

RAMSEY, IAN
1967. *Religious Language: An Empirical Placing of Theological Phrases.* New York.

READ, HERBERT
1945. *A Coat of Many Colors: Occasional Essays.* London.
1949. *Wordsworth.* New York.
1956. *The Nature of Literature.* New York.
1960. *The Forms of Things Unknown: Essays toward an Aesthetic Philosophy.* New York.
1963. *The Contrary Experience: Autobiographies.* New York.
1967. *Poetry and Experience.* New York.
1968. *The Cult of Sincerity.* London.

RICHARDS, I. A.
1925. (and C. K. Ogden and James Wood, editors) *The Foundations of Aesthetics.* London.
1926. *Principles of Literary Criticism.* 2nd ed. London.
1929. *Practical Criticism: A Study of Literary Judgment.* New York.
1935. *Coleridge on Imagination.* New York.
1936. *The Philosophy of Rhetoric.* New York.

RICHARDSON, HERBERT
1967. *Toward an American Theology.* New York.

RICOEUR, PAUL
1965. *Fallible Man: Philosophy of the Will,* translated by Charles Kelbley. Chicago.
1967. *The Symbolism of Evil,* translated by Emerson Buchanan. New York.

ROBERTS, JAMES
1964. "The Role of Society in the Theater of the Absurd" in *Literature and Society,* edited by Bernice Slote. Lincoln, Neb.

ROBINSON, JAMES M.
1959. *A New Quest of the Historical Jesus.* Naperville, Ill.
1963. (and John Cobb, Jr., editors) *The Later Heidegger and Theology.* New York.
1964. (and John Cobb, Jr., editors) *The New Hermeneutic.* New York.
1968. (editor) *The Beginnings of Dialectic Theology,* translated by Keith Crim and Louis de Grazia. Richmond, Va.

ROBINSON, JOHN A. T.
1967. *Exploration into God.* Stanford, Calif.

ROGERS, ROBERT
1970. *A Psychoanalytic Study of the Double in Literature.* Detroit.

ROSENTHAL, RAYMOND
1968. (editor) *McLuhan: Pro and Con.* New York.

ROSS, MALCOLM
1954. *Poetry and Dogma: The Transfiguration of Eucharistic Symbols in Seventeenth Century English Poetry.* New Brunswick, N. J.

ROUGEMONT, DENIS DE
1952. "Religion and the Mission of the Artist" in *Spiritual Problems in Contemporary Literature: A Series of Addresses and Discussions,* edited by Stanley Hopper. New York.
1956. *Love in the Western World,* translated by Montgomery Belgion. 2nd ed. New York.
1963a. *The Christian Opportunity,* translated by Donald Lehmkuhl. New York.
1963b. *Love Declared: Essays on the Myth of Love,* translated by Richard Howard. New York.

RUECHERT, WILLIAM
1963. *Kenneth Burke and the Drama of Human Relations.* Minneapolis.
1969. (editor) *Critical Responses to Kenneth Burke, 1924–1966.* Minneapolis.

RUITENBEEK, HENDRIK
1964. (editor) *Psychoanalysis and Literature.* New York.

RULAND, RICHARD
1967. *The Rediscovery of American Literature: Premises of Critical Taste, 1900–1940.* Cambridge, Mass.

SACKS, SHELDON
1966. *Fiction and the Shape of Belief: A Study of Henry Fielding, with Glances at Swift, Johnson, and Richardson.* Berkeley, Calif.

SARTRE, JEAN-PAUL

1949. *What Is Literature?* translated by Bernard Frechtman. New York.

1955. *Literary and Philosophical Essays,* translated by Annette Michelson. New York.

1963. *Saint Genet, Actor and Martyr,* translated by Bernard Frechtman. New York.

SAYERS, DOROTHY

1956. *The Mind of the Maker.* New York.

1963. *The Poetry of Search and the Poetry of Statement: and Other Posthumous Essays on Literature, Religion, and Language.* London.

SCHILLEBEECKX, EDWARD, O.P.

1968. *The Concept of Truth and Theological Renewal,* translated by N. D. Smith. New York.

SCHILLER, JEROME

1969. *I. A. Richards' Theory of Literature.* New Haven, Conn.

SCHILP, PAUL

1941. (editor) *The Philosophy of Alfred North Whitehead.* Evanston, Ill.

SCHLOVSKY, V.

1965. "Sterne's Tristram Shandy: Stylistic Commentary" in *Russian Formalist Criticism: Four Essays,* edited and translated by Lee Lemon and Marion Reis. Lincoln, Neb.

SCHOLES, ROBERT

1966a. (editor) *Approaches to the Novel: Materials for a Poetics.* 2nd ed. San Francisco.

1966b. (and Robert Kellogg) *The Nature of Narrative.* New York.

SCHORER, MARK

1965. "The Burdens of Biography" in *To the Young Writer,* edited by A. L. Bader. Ann Arbor, Mich.

SCOTT, NATHAN, JR.

1964. (editor) *The New Orpheus: Essays toward a Christian Poetics.* New York.

1966. *The Broken Center: Studies in the Theological Horizon of Modern Literature.* New Haven, Conn.

1968. (editor) *Adversity and Grace: Studies in Recent American Literature.* Chicago.

1969. *Negative Capability: Studies in the New Literature and the Religious Situation.* New Haven, Conn.

1971. *The Wild Prayer of Longing: Poetry and the Sacred.* New Haven, Conn.

SHINN, ROGER

1968. *Man: The New Humanism.* New Directions in Theology Today, edited by William Hordern, vol. 6. Philadelphia.

SHORT, ROBERT

1965. *The Gospel According to Peanuts.* Richmond, Va.

SHUMAKER, WAYNE
1960. *Literature and the Irrational: A Study in Anthropological Backgrounds.* Englewood Cliffs, N. J.

SIMMEL, GEORG
1955. "A Contribution to the Sociology of Religion," translated by W. W. Elwang, *American Journal of Sociology* 60 (May).

SIRJAMAKI, JOHN
1948. "Culture Configurations in the American Family," *American Journal of Sociology* 53 (May).

SLOTE, BERNICE
1963. (editor) *Myth and Symbol: Critical Approaches and Applications.* Lincoln, Neb.

SMART, JAMES
1967. *The Divided Mind of Modern Theology: Karl Barth and Rudolf Bultmann, 1908–1933.* Philadelphia.

SMIDT, KRISTIAN
1961. *Poetry and Belief in the Work of T. S. Eliot.* 2nd ed. London.

SMITH, JONATHAN
1969. "Earth and Gods," *Journal of Religion* 49 (April).

SMITH, RONALD GREGOR
1966. *Secular Christianity.* New York.

SMITH, WILFRED CANTWELL
1969. "Secularity and the History of Religions" in *The Spirit and Power of Christian Secularity,* edited by Albert Schlitzer, C.S.C. Notre Dame, Ind.

SMITHLINE, ARNOLD
1966. *Natural Religion in American Literature.* New Haven, Conn.

SONTAG, SUSAN
1967. *Against Interpretation and Other Essays.* New York.
1969. *Styles of Radical Will.* New York.

SPENCER, THEODORE
1969. "How to Criticize a Poem" in *The Overwrought Urn,* edited by Charles Kaplan. Indianapolis.

SPENDER, STEPHEN
1936. *The Destructive Element: A Study of Modern Writers and Beliefs.* Boston.
1954. *The Creative Element.* London.

SPITZER, LEO
1963. *Classical and Christian Ideas of World Harmony: Prolegomena to an Interpretation of the Word 'Stimmung,'* edited by Anna Hatcher. Baltimore.

STALLMAN, ROBERT
1949. (editor) *Critiques and Essays in Criticism, 1920–1948.* New York.
1950. (editor) *The Critic's Notebook.* Minneapolis.

STEINER, GEORGE

1959. *Tolstoy or Dostoevsky: An Essay in the Old Criticism.* New York.

1967. *Language and Silence: Essays on Language, Literature, and the Inhuman.* New York.

STENSON, STEN

1969. *Sense and Nonsense in Religion: An Essay on the Language and Phenomenology of Religion.* Nashville.

STEVENSON, C. L.

1959. "The Emotive Meaning of Ethical Terms" in *Logical Positivism,* edited by Alfred J. Ayer. New York.

STEWART, JOHN

1965. *The Burden of Time: The Fugitives and Agrarians.* Princeton, N. J.

SUTTON, WALTER

1963. *Modern American Criticism.* Englewood Cliffs, N. J.

TATE, ALLEN

1953. *The Forlorn Demon: Didactic and Critical Essays.* Chicago.

TEILHARD DE CHARDIN, PIERRE, S. J.

1958. *Building the Earth,* translated by Noel Lindsay. Paris.

1961. *The Phenomenon of Man,* translated by Bernard Wall. New York.

1965a. *The Divine Milieu: An Essay on the Interior Life,* translated by Bernard Wall. New York.

1965b. *Hymn of the Universe.* New York.

1967. *Writings in Time of War,* translated by René Hague. New York.

TE SELLE, SALLIE

1966. *Literature and the Christian Life.* New Haven, Conn.

1968. "What Is 'Religion' in Literature?" *America* (December 14).

THOMAS, O. C.

1972. "Where Are We in Theology?" in *New Theology #9,* edited by Martin Marty and Dean Peerman. New York.

THORPE, JAMES

1967. (editor) *Relations of Literary Study: Essays on Interdisciplinary Contributions.* New York.

TILLICH, PAUL

1932. *The Religious Situation,* translated by H. Richard Niebuhr. New York.

1955. "Religion and the Visual Arts," unpublished paper for the Theological Discussion Group. Washington.

1956. "Existentialist Aspects of Modern Art" in *Christianity and the Existentialists,* edited by Carl Michalson. New York.

1965. *Dynamics of Faith.* New York.

1966. *On the Boundary: An Autobiographical Sketch.* New York.

1967. *Systematic Theology.* 3 vols. in 1. Chicago.

TOULMIN, STEPHEN

1957. (and Ronald Hepburn and Alasdair MacIntyre) *Metaphysical Beliefs: Three Essays.* London.

1968. *An Examination of the Place of Reason in Ethics.* London.

TOYNBEE, ARNOLD
1969. *Experiences.* New York.

TRILLING, LIONEL
1939. *Matthew Arnold.* New York.
1943. *E. M. Forster.* New York.
1950. *The Liberal Imagination: Essays on Literature and Society.* New York.
1955. *The Opposing Self: Nine Essays in Criticism.* New York.
1956. *A Gathering of Fugitives: Essays.* Boston.
1965. *Beyond Culture: Essays on Literature and Learning.* New York.

TROTSKY, LEON
1924. *Literature and Revolution,* translated by Rose Strunsky. New York.

TURNELL, MARTIN
1938. *Poetry and Crisis.* London.
1961. *Modern Literature and the Christian Faith.* London.

UNAMUNO, MIGUEL DE
1925. *Essays and Soliloquies,* translated by J. E. C. Flitch. New York.
1945. *Perplexities and Paradoxes,* translated by Stuart Gross. New York.
1967. *Our Lord Don Quixote: The Life of Don Quixote and Sancho with Related Essays,* translated by Anthony Kerrigan. Princeton, N. J.

VAHANIAN, GABRIEL
1964. *Wait without Idols.* New York.
1967. *The Death of God: The Culture of Our Post-Christian Era.* New York.

VAN BUREN, PAUL
1972. *The Edges of Language: An Essay in the Logic of a Religion.* New York.

VAN DER LEEUW, GERARDUS
1963a. *Religion in Essence and Manifestation,* translated by J. E. Turner. 2 vols. New York.
1963b. *Sacred and Profane Beauty: The Holy in Art,* translated by David Green. New York.

VIA, DANIEL, JR.
1967. *The Parables: Their Literary and Existential Dimension.* Philadelphia.

VICKERY, JOHN
1963. "The Golden Bough: Impact and Archetype" in *Myth and Symbol: Critical Approaches and Applications,* edited by Bernice Slote. Lincoln, Neb.
1966. (editor) *Myth and Literature: Contemporary Theory and Practice.* Lincoln, Neb.

VIVAS, ELISEO
1950. *The Moral Life and the Ethical Life.* Chicago.
1953. (and Murray Kireger, editors) *The Problems of Aesthetics: A Book of Readings.* New York.
1955. *Creation and Discovery: Essays in Criticism and Aesthetics.* New York.
1960. *D. H. Lawrence: The Failure and the Triumph of Art.* Evanston, Ill.

1963. *The Artistic Transaction and Essays on Theory of Literature.* Columbus, Ohio.

WACH, JOACHIM

1961. *The Comparative Study of Religions,* edited by Joseph Kitagawa. New York.

WAGGONER, HYATT

1959. "The Current Revolt against the New Criticism," *Criticism* 1 (Summer).

1967. " 'Point of View' in American Literary Scholarship and Criticism" in *Mansions of the Spirit: Essays in Literature and Religion,* edited by George Panichas. New York.

WAISMANN, FRIEDRICH

1959. "How I See Philosophy" in *Logical Positivism,* edited by Alfred J. Ayer. New York.

WALTER, ERICH

1958. (editor) *Religion and the State University.* Ann Arbor, Mich.

WASIOLEK, EDWARD

1967–71. (editor) *The Dostoevsky Notebooks.* 5 vols. Chicago.

1971. *Dostoevsky: The Major Fiction.* Boston.

WATTS, ALAN

1947. *Behold the Spirit: A Study in the Necessity of Mystical Religion.* New York.

1950. *The Supreme Identity: An Essay on Oriental Metaphysic and the Christian Religion.* New York.

1968. *Myth and Ritual in Christianity.* Boston.

WEILAND, J. SPERNA

1968. *New Ways in Theology,* translated by N. D. Smith. New York.

WEINTRAUB, KARL

1966. *Visions of Culture.* Chicago.

WEISINGER, HERBERT

1953. *Tragedy and the Paradox of the Fortunate Fall.* London.

1964. *The Agony and the Triumph: Papers on the Use and Abuse of Myth.* East Lansing, Mich.

WELLEK, RENE

1949. (and Austin Warren) *Theory of Literature.* New York.

1956. "The Criticism of T. S. Eliot," *Sewanee Review* 64 (Summer).

1963. *Concepts of Criticism,* edited by Stephen Nichols. New Haven, Conn.

1970. *Discriminations: Further Concepts of Criticism.* New Haven, Conn.

WHEELWRIGHT, PHILIP

1954. *The Burning Fountain: A Study in the Language of Symbolism.* Bloomington, Ind.

WHITE, HELEN

1936. *The Metaphysical Poets: A Study in Religious Experience.* New York.

WHITEHEAD, ALFRED N.
1926. *Science and the Modern World.* New York.
1961. *Adventures of Ideas.* Riverside, Calif.

WIEMAN, HENRY
1936. (and Bernard Meland) *American Philosophies of Religion.* New York.

WILD, JOHN
1959. "Man and His Life-World" in *For Roman Ingarden: Nine Essays in Phenomenology.* The Hague.

WILDER, AMOS
1952a. *Modern Poetry and the Christian Tradition: A Study in the Relation of Christianity to Culture.* New York.
1952b. "Protestant Orientation in Contemporary Poetry" in *Spiritual Problems in Contemporary Literature,* edited by Stanley Hopper. New York.
1958. *Theology and Modern Literature.* Cambridge, Mass.
1964. *The Language of the Gospel: Early Christian Rhetoric.* New York.
1969. *The New Voice: Religion, Literature, Hermeneutics.* New York.
1971. "The Uses of a Theological Criticism" in *Literature and Religion,* edited by Giles Gunn. New York.

WILLEY, BASIL
1934. *The Seventeenth Century Background: Studies in the Thought of the Age in Relation to Poetry and Religion.* London.
1949. *Nineteenth Century Studies: Coleridge to Matthew Arnold.* New York.
1958. "Christianity and Literature," *London Quarterly and Holborn Review* 183 (July).

WILLIAMS, CHARLES
1943. *The Figure of Beatrice: A Study in Dante.* London.
1950. *He Came Down from Heaven* and *The Forgiveness of Sins.* London.

WILLIAMS, DANIEL DAY
1961. "Tradition and Experience in American Theology" in *The Shaping of American Religion,* edited by James Smith and Albert Jamison. Princeton, N. J.
1967. *What Present-Day Theologians Are Thinking.* 3rd ed. New York.
1968. *The Spirit and the Forms of Love.* New York.

WILSON, EDMUND
1934. *Axel's Castle: A Study in the Imaginative Literature of 1870–1930.* New York.
1947. *Wound and the Bow: Seven Studies in Literature.* New York.
1950. *Classics and Commercials: A Literary Chronicle of the Forties.* New York.
1952a. *The Shores of Light: A Literary Chronicle of the Twenties and Thirties.* New York.
1952b. *The Triple Thinkers: Twelve Essays on Literary Subjects.* London.
1956. *A Piece of My Mind: Reflections at Sixty.* New York.
1969. *Dead Sea Scrolls, 1947–1969.* New York.

WIMSATT, WILLIAM K., JR.

1946. (and Monroe Beardsley) "The Intentional Fallacy," *Sewanee Review* 54 (July).

1949. (and Monroe Beardsley) "The Affective Fallacy," *Sewanee Review* 57 (January).

1957. (and Cleanth Brooks) *Literary Criticism: A Short History*. New York.

1967. "The Domain of Criticism" in *Aesthetic Inquiry: Essays on Art Criticism and the Philosophy of Art,* edited by Monroe Beardsley and Herbert Schueller. Encino, Calif.

1968. "What to Say about a Poem" in *Perspectives in Contemporary Criticism,* edited by Sheldon Grebstein. New York.

WINTERS, IVOR

1957. *The Function of Criticism: Problems and Exercises*. Chicago.

AUTHOR INDEX